# Critical feminism
## Argument in the disciplines

# Ideas and Production

Over recent years the study of the humanities has changed beyond all recognition for many of us. The increasing attention given to theories of interpretation and writing has altered the intellectual circumstances and perspectives of the various disciplines which compose the group. The studies of literature, history, society, politics, gender and philosophy are increasingly finding common ground in shared assumptions about intellectual procedure and method. **Ideas and Production** addresses this common ground.

We are interested in the investigation of the particular historical circumstances which produce the culture of a period or group, and the exploration of conventionally unregarded or understudied work. We are also interested in the relationship of intellectual movements to institutions, and the technological and economic means of their production. It is through the study of the circumstances and conditions in which ideas are realised that the humanities can develop fresh approaches in a period of rapid and exciting social and intellectual change.

As thought and learning become increasingly international and older political and intellectual structures give way, **Ideas and Production** is concerned to investigate new intellectual horizons from the perspective of competing theories and methods, and through the rethinking of old or settled definitions.

**Ideas and Production** welcomes the potential of debate and intervention, as well as the careful study of materials. The series is aimed at the student, teacher and general reader and encourages clarity and directness in argument, language and method.

*Edward J. Esche, Penelope Kenrick,*
*Rick Rylance, Nigel Wheale*

# Critical feminism

## Argument in the disciplines

*Edited by Kate Campbell*

Open University Press
*Buckingham* · *Philadelphia*

ıs published by
ess in collaboration with
ıc

.sity Press
.rt, 22 Ballmoor
ɔnam MK18 1XW

.900 Frost Road, Suite 101
Bristol, PA 19007, USA

First published 1992
Reprinted 1994

*A catalogue record of this book is available from the British Library*

*Library of Congress Cataloging-in-Publication Data*

Critical feminism: argument in the disciplines/edited by
  Kate Campbell.
      p.    cm. — (Ideas and production)
  Includes bibliographical references and index.
  ISBN 0-335-09757-X (pbk)
  1. Feminist criticism.   2. Feminist theory.   I. Campbell, Kate,
  1952–    . II. Series.
  H01190.C75   1992
  305.42'01 — dc20                              91–443093 CIP

Typeset by Type Study, Scarborough
Printed in Great Britain by St Edmundsbury Press Ltd,
Bury St Edmunds, Suffolk

# Contents

# Contributors

*Carolyn Burdett* is currently researching the work of Olive Schreiner for her D.Phil. thesis at the University of Sussex. She has held a Tutorial Fellowship in the School of Cultural and Community Studies at Sussex, teaching feminism and women's writing.

*Kate Campbell* has degrees in English and History, and has taught adults and in schools. Her PhD thesis at the University of East Anglia was on the inter-relationship of Henry James, literature and journalism.

*Lena Dominelli* is Professor of Social Administration at Sheffield University. She studied English Literature and Sociology as an undergraduate and subsequently qualified as a social worker. Her books include: *Love and Wages* (1986); *Anti-Racist Social Work* (1988); *Feminist Social Work* (with E. McLeod) (1989); *Women and Community Action* (1990); *Women Across Continents: Feminist Comparative Social Policy* (1991); *Gender, Sex Offenders and Probation Practice* (1991).

*John Goode* lectured in English at the University of Reading 1964-1974, was Reader at Warwick 1974–1989 and was Professor of English at Keele University from 1989 until his death in 1994. His books include *George Gissing: Ideology and Fiction* (1978), and *Thomas Hardy. The Offensive Truth* (1988). His articles relevant to feminist criticism include 'Woman and the literary text', in *The Rights and Wrongs of Women*, J. Mitchell and A. Oakley (eds.) (1976), and 'Sue Bridehead and the New Woman', in *Women Writing and Writing about Women*, Mary Jacobus (ed.).

*Margaret Iversen* lectures in art theory and history at Essex University. Her writing on contemporary art practices includes a discussion of Mary Kelly's work, 'Difference: on representation and sexuality', in *m/f* (1986) 11, 12.

*Mary Kelly* is an artist and lives in New York. Her two major projects which have been exhibited in England and America are *Post-Partum Document* and *Interim*. Her writing on contemporary art issues includes 'Reviewing modernist criticism', in *Screen* (1981) 2, and she has curated exhibitions of contemporary art such as *Beyond the Purloined Image* (1983), Riverside Studios. She has also taught on a number of educational programmes.

*Paula Nicolson* is a Lecturer in Psychology at the University of Sheffield Medical School. She is a founder member of the British Psychological Society's Psychology of Women Section, and her research interests are post-natal depression, female sexuality, and gender and age discrimination. She is currently researching the ideology of psychosexual counselling; barriers to women's career progression in obstetrics and gynaecology; and ageism and sex discrimination in the workplace.

*Griselda Pollock* is Professor of Art History at Leeds University. She has been a leading contributor to discussion of feminist issues in art history. Her publications include *Old Mistresses: Women, Art and Ideology* (Routledge 1981), *Framing Feminism: Art and the Women's Movement, 1970–1985* (Pandora 1987), both with Roszika Parker; and *Vision and Difference: Femininity, Feminism and the Histories of Art* (Routledge 1988).

*Rick Rylance* is Senior Lecturer and Field Leader in English at Anglia Polytechnic. He has published widely on nineteenth and twentieth-century topics including *Debating Texts: A Reader in Twentieth-Century Literary Theory and Method* (Open University Press 1987) and *Roland Barthes* (Harvester forthcoming).

*Deborah Thom* teaches in the History and Social and Political Sciences Faculties in the University of Cambridge, and is a fellow of Robinson College. She has worked on women's employment and education and is currently researching into the history of child psychology in Britain.

Cover illustration by Charlie Ann Turner, cover design by Will Hill.

Text illustrations

Art Editor: Will Hill

# Acknowledgements

The editors acknowledge the help of the following individuals and organizations who have assisted in the production of *Critical Feminism: Argument in the Disciplines*: Mike Salmon, Tom Allcock, Steve Marshall of Anglia Polytechnic, and John Skelton and Sue Hadden of the Open University Press for their material support in establishing Ideas and Production as a Series; Ian Gordon, Head of the Department of Arts and Letters, Anglia Polytechnic, for his consistent support for the project; Nicky Morland and Chris Coward of Computer Services, Anglia Polytechnic, Cambridge, and Clive Bray and Ian Hornsey of the Department of Arts and Letters for invaluable help in the production process; the BTEC HND Illustration students and course administrators, Department of Arts and Letters, for their enthusiastic participation in production of the volume. We would also like to thank Rick Allen, Nora Crook, Felicia Gordon, and Michelle Stanworth for their help in refereeing contributions. Thanks also to Judith Mastai of Vancouver Art Gallery for permission to publish her transcription of Mary Kelly's and Griselda Pollock's conversation which she organized in Vancouver Art Gallery, June 1989.

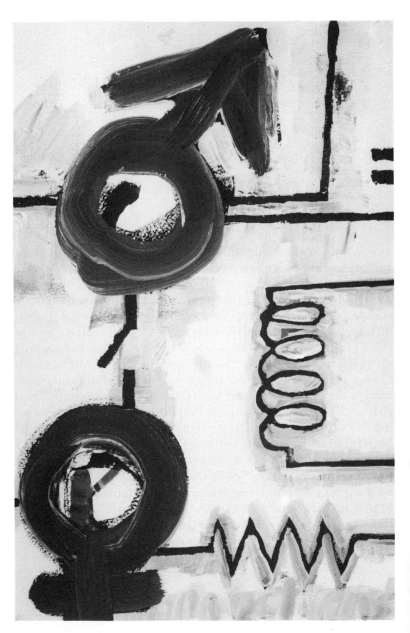

*Andrew Coleman*

# 1

## Introduction: matters of theory and practice – *or*, we'll be coming out the harbour

### Kate Campbell

If we are not for ourselves, who are we? if we are only for ourselves, what are we?[1]

Many of the chapters of *Critical Feminism* aspire to more than the current half-life of feminism's presence in the academy. Ideally this book will be read by those who preside over or work in or near it, including those who think that women's interests have been adequately accommodated there. In the last twenty years or so feminism has been institutionalized to the extent of being imported and housed in interdisciplinary 'women's studies', women's journals, conferences and associations, and increasing across-the-boards thematic attention to women, gender and sexuality – with concomitant adjustments in the literary and artistic canons and historical understanding. All in all, men's ears are now often deferentially turned to women's 'voices'. It would be mistaken to belittle the significance of these developments, and the broader feminist movement of which they are a part, not least in bringing about a situation in which academic women can now, alongside other women, much more readily 'assert themselves with pride'.[2]

But this change in attitudes, and the many institutional developments, seem in some respects to have barely impinged on the academy, in that they have often made little radical difference to long established ways of proceeding, from the gender composition of who customarily teaches whom to the ongoing vitality of the assumption that knowledge is not socially and politically produced and productive. Accordingly some of the chapters of this book tell of feminist interventions in, and departures from, mainstream practices more than of their thorough-going reconstruction.[3] In this introduction I offer a slant on why this is so, a slant which turns on the metaphor of the academy harbouring feminism: building it up and replenishing it in some ways, yes; but at the same time given to running it dry, keeping it within walls, seeing to its overall containment.

In exploring this harbouring I use literary criticism as a focus, as the area most familiar to me, and in view of the fact that many of the issues and attitudes seen in it are evident in other disciplines. In particular the relationship between feminism and the theoretical 'penumbra' of deconstruction is significant in all fields of study. The fairly strong association of literary criticism and feminism makes it especially apt as a focus although, as I point out, the relationship between the two is somewhat anomalous, for its proficiency in addressing women's 'oppression' seems in some respects to buttress their inequality. Here, and more generally, I argue the importance of attending to immediate political considerations and not discarding the veteran liberal goal of equality – of not slighting the material facts and practices of power for the more sophisticated dispensations of consciousness which the intellect is usually keen to take for its home and the academy to nurture. Hence out of a range of important issues of concern to feminists in the academy I will consider especially the imbalance between the sexes teaching in it. For convenience, and in accord with the representation of disciplines in the book as a whole, I disregard the 'hard' sciences, where the imbalance is most striking. In general, feminist analyses significantly undermine the distinction between 'hard' and 'soft' sciences.

## I

Feminists are of course divided precisely on the issue of whether the transformation of existing academic practices is possible and desirable, or whether men's ways of doing things are so inimical to women as to require that their academic pursuits have separate existence. For example, in the field of literary criticism Ellen Messer-Davidow maintains that feminist literary criticism is incompatible with literary study as such. Whereas the strategy of earlier critics – since the late 1960s – was mostly reformatory, adjusting the literary canon to include women, and focusing on those women who appear in texts where men had hitherto monopolized attention – Ophelia rather than Hamlet, say – she enumerates a much wider front on which traditional practices are now under attack:

> the literary constructs of canon, history, curriculum, authorship, reading, and scholarship/criticism; the developmental goal of autonomy and the intrapsychic assumption of individualism; the concept that female is to male as nature is to culture; the distinction of public and private and the qualification for political participation; models of language competence and the notion of a masculine generic; the stance of objectivity, the evolutionary concepts of scarcity and competition, and the dichotomy of physiology and environment. Finally, feminists in all fields criticise traditional methodologies for radical disjunction, objectification, dichotomization, hierarchical arrangement, faulty universalization, and effacement of important qualities.[4]

When the dust settles it may appear questionable if there is anything left for the assertion of so much falsity to rest on. But the the critique is an immanent one to the point of seeming at times almost to parody the methods it attacks. While the rhetorical force of such a list is to impress the absolute divergence between feminist and traditional practice – a case of dichotomization if ever there was one – as *Critical Feminism* suggests, the reality is that the individual items of this agenda are being raised piecemeal within existing disciplines – and not only by feminists – albeit with little sign of profound restructuring so far. Though Messer-Davidow invokes the reform-or-revolution axis according to which feminists have customarily been divided, the volume of work which is currently being undertaken on the specific points she enumerates tends to point rather to the possibility of eventual fundamental reconstructions through the processes of reform. This is supported by the immediate circumstances of her text's production – an edition of *New Literary History* rather than a feminist journal; and an edition at that which specifically set up her piece as an invitation for argument, among such stalwarts of the profession of literary criticism as Gerald Graff.

As *Critical Feminism's* contributors indicate, the point on which most academic feminists are agreed – beyond a common unease with things as they are (remarked by Deborah Thom), and a sense that changes are necessary in their disciplines – is the political character of feminism; and, as a necessary adjunct to the goal of ending women's oppression, the imperative of 'giving women a voice'. But though feminism is by common definition political – in that it is about nothing if not ending women's inequality, oppression and subordination – the political consciousness of feminists varies widely, and there is little obvious agreement otherwise, scarcely any consensus as to the shape feminism's successful academic implementation might take. The very presence of feminism in the academy is criss-crossed with the paradoxes of women asserting their interests in an institution which has never shaken off its founding character of commitment to men's studies – primarily men researching and writing and thinking and producing 'knowledge' in men's ways for men about men (if now offering feminist chairs to the ladies).[5] The problem of *Men in Feminism* seems pale in comparison with the sometimes dimly perceived dimensions of this problem in the first place of women in men's place.[6] By identifying as she does the many specific areas in which feminists are already busy challenging the practices of different academic disciplines, Messer-Davidow does at least convey the profound implications of feminist critiques.

One of the places where a fundamental sense of anomaly as to women's place in the academy at all does often surface (beyond the visible discrepancies between the men and women on the platform at degree ceremonies and so on) is in an ongoing strand of resistance to theory.[7] Or, more accurately, more often than critical theory in itself, it is the menace of its hegemony in the academy, and in particular of theories which seem to discount reality for its discursive projection, together with the political implications of this, that are currently arousing protest. Here it is instructive to set Messer-Davidow's essay beside Barbara Christian's recent chapter on 'The Race for Theory'. This traverses the grounds of the case against it, from repudiation of white abstract logic as normative and so perniciously co-opting black radicalism, to a more general sense of its injustice and intellectual imperialism. So for instance Christian notes how present critical language surfaced 'just when the literature of peoples of color . . . began to move to "the center"': 'the literature of blacks, women of South America and Africa, etc., as overtly 'political' literature, was being pre-empted by a new Western concept which pro-claimed that reality does not exist.'[8] It is not so much theory itself that is here under attack, as a particular current configuration of it that comes across as 'prescriptive, exclusive, elitist', scandalously nonchalant as to its political repercussions. The irony is that, as Christian recognizes, the textualist theories she sees as now reigning initially constituted an uprising, in which dispossessed groups shared, against certain peremptory white patriarchal assumptions.

The problem in general, however, is that, whatever its content, theory tends to appear 'prescriptive, exclusive, elitist' to those far away from it. The very activity of specification can appear to threaten the diversity of women's positions by the prescriptivism that seems built into it. Moreover specification seems to fly in the face of the historicist and materialist awareness that study of women habitually induces – the sense that we are historically, geographically, economically and psychically fluctuating identities. Insistence on historicity and materiality has in fact become the common strong plank – the somewhat paradoxical sign – of many a 'feminist' practice.[9]

So when Toril Moi pronounces that feminism is a 'theoretical and political practice committed to the struggle against patriarchy and sexism', she is somewhat at odds with a recurrent strand of thinking according to which incongruity attaches to the very undertaking of theory by women.[10] The fact that this attitude cannot withstand much scrutiny seems in many ways less noteworthy than its recurrence. It has been fuelled academically by *l'écriture féminine's* sense that the abstraction of theory epitomizes man-made language, against which women's interests demand writing based in the body. In that the academy harbours theory, so the thinking goes, it is inimical to feminism. For because theory has traditionally been monopolized by men in an academy which excludes women, it remains a strong temptation to essentialize this – 'men theorize, women experience' – and for women to disclaim against and renounce it, as Elaine Showalter seemed to do in 1983 when she urged that feminism should give up communicating with 'the white fathers, even at the price of translating its findings into the warp of their obscure critical languages'.[11] The reference to the 'white fathers' inserts a necessary race and class specificity into the phenomenon of antagonism. The all too evident loss of immediate purchase on the world outside academia that can attend 'obscure' language further encourages the conclusion that theory is harmful to feminism.

Against this, in her collection of essays on *Gender and Theory*, Linda Kauffman rightly points to the interactions between feminism and critical theory.[12] The extent of this interaction has been, and is, such that it would seem to make any attempt by feminism to do without theory self-destructive. (By this token, men are so much 'in' feminism already it would be impossible to extricate them.) Whatever the exact reasons why 'the sex/gender system' has become visible only now – i.e. in the last twenty years or so – the critique of objectivity and more general awareness of the politics of knowledge that have been crucial in feminist analyses are symptomatic of an intellectual climate in which marxist, Foucauldian and deconstructionist analyses have in particular figured prominently.[13] Thus exposures of the gender basis of the literary and artistic canons in some senses ran in tandem with marxist and materialist critiques which had deployed similar strategies in unveiling their ideological construction. In this general respect feminists can be seen as the beneficiaries as well as the promoters of a distinctively modern inflection of academic inquiry, a political inflection encapsulated in Edward Said's insistence, 'Who writes? and for whom?'

Beyond the more straightforward intellectual significance of theoretical positions in feminism lies the fact that they have often served to sanction and encourage individual women to become feminists. I am thinking for instance of Clifford Geertz' noticeable presence in the literary critic Annette Kolodny's account of her development as a feminist – not only in frequently serving as an authority for the ideas she is putting across, but more basically through his arguing for the relocation of meaning and significance in the perceptions and consciousnesses of subjects previously objectified and discounted. It seems to me that this shift away from the clarity of traditional modes of apprehending alien cultures towards thicker descriptions which try to do justice to their alterity, producing more complicated, quite different understandings, could not but be inspiriting for women uneasy in conventional man-made systems. Accordingly, when Kolodny writes that 'what had once been "felt individually as personal insecurity" came at last to be "viewed collectively as structural inconsistency" (Geertz 1973: 204)', Geertz seems to be not so much providing the language for an emboldened selfhood of feminism as one of its instigators.[14] In its much-quoted challenges to official representations of the world the work of Mikhail Bakhtin seems to have a similar appeal and heuristic value for feminists.

It is not my purpose to dwell on women's debts to men – heaven forbid! – but rather to stress the value of theory to women, a value tied to the institution of the academy which usually shelters it. The problem with theory and the abstraction on which it depends – and the academy in general – for many feminists centres rather on the purposes they serve and the uses to which they are put. For feminist theory shares with Marxist theory an insistence that its point is to change the world. In this it must divest itself of the detachment traditionally tied to it, a detachment registered in popular perjorative use of the word 'theoretical', and which was instrumental in making theory, and philosophy, the university's crown. Here it is worth pursuing the essay by Toril Moi, 'Men against Patriarchy', from which I have already quoted. For in the course of that essay she expresses impatience with the 'theoretical' tenor of some 'feminist' academic discourse that is shared by many other women. Though she argues for theory, it is for theory which doesn't lose sight of political realities, and which is strengthened by engagement in movements committed to overcoming oppression.

The remarkable fact that the distinction between 'feminist' and 'feminist literary critical' writing was lost sight of in the volume *Men in Feminism* is to her indicative of the frequently too theoretical – or 'academic' – character of American academic feminism. As she writes of the chapters of *Men in Feminism*, 'There is in these texts a disconcerting tendency to see feminism as at once an isolated, self-sufficient enclave located firmly within academia and as the only political struggle relevant for women' (185).[15] Gayle Greene for one writes in the same spirit, criticizing writing in general which, 'obfuscating to the point of being disempowering', proceeds without a sense of dialectical relationship between theory and practice, 'where things get talked about in a never-never land of bourgeois idealism removed from the realities of people's lives or of the [literary] profession'.[16] There is a pronounced perversity in the movement dedicated to all women appearing thus stranded within the walls of academia; and in particular in its dehydration in those practices which more than any other seem at first sight to proffer access to immediate experience, literature and its criticism.

With three of the chapters of this book coming from academics engaged in literary criticism, it's worth considering briefly the place of it in feminism that Moi remarks. Still writing of *Men in Feminism*, she continues:

> There is in these texts a deplorable absence of non-academic, or even non-literary critical settings. It is as if the political horizon of these feminists, male and female, stretches no further than to the MLA. But the question of men in feminism is not *identical* with the question of men in feminist literary criticism. (186)

Moi tends to discount the in-house aspect of the identification – thus that political theorists and historians for instance may entirely disagree with it – and is writing of the situation in America. But it seems fair to say that in England too literary criticism appears at the forefront of academic feminism – which is not to confuse the presence of feminist literary critics at feminist conferences, and its cradling of 'feminist' readers, say, with the question of its 'success'.

In part literary criticism's feminist profile has something to do with the traditional receptivity of 'literature' (noted by Rick Rylance) to areas of experience for which, albeit mediated as they have been through men's perceptions, there was otherwise no academic place (and in this respect Moi's complaint asks to be turned around). This and other factors have meant that the discipline, together with its variants in 'comparative literature', has demonstrated pronounced assimilative capacities whereby we have habitually encountered in it that which has academic life outside it. Hence to say that the political horizon of literary criticism stretches no further than a particular professional association is in actual fact to acknowledge that it stretches wide intellectually, in a pan-European concourse from Vološinov to Wollstonecraft to Veblen to Kristeva to many current feminist historians among numerous others.[17] In this limited sense lit. crit. has been supra-national and an inter-disciplinary study – a typical feminist academic practice – of sorts. Amongst such intellectual riches, it is perhaps not surprising that its politics do not seem to surmount petty professional rivalries.

The climate of such an inter-textual universe favours an attention to textuality which is hardly conducive to political action. In this it tends to perpetuate the detachment which academic practices have traditionally enjoined and promoted in the self-referential orientation of scholarship. Against the not uncommon assumption that English, as a 'soft' discipline, is somewhat quite separate from demands for detachment and objectivity,[18] Messer-Davidow outlines how its subject matter and methods are implicated in them:

> Implicitly, the epistemology of traditional literary study indicates the entities that exist in that domain – authors, works, audiences, representations, and media – and the methods used to investigate them – differential, integral, principled, causal, inferential, and analogical thinking. Boundaries are an important feature of these entities; maintaining them is what the methods do. . . . The knowers can vanish into anonymous objectivity, or stand aside as disinterested critics and impartial spectators. . . . As knowers recede behind their methodologies, existence and knowledge loom large and autonomous. (67)

Indeed from early attempts to link it to philology the history of academic English involves a succession of attempts to ground the 'discipline' in the scientific paradigm that came to the fore in the reform of the ancient universities from around the mid-nineteenth century.[19] One of the signs of a 'discipline' was a hard scientific edge, the resolution with regard to its subject matter and its boundaries that Messer-Davidow emphasizes. The fact that the institutionalization of English was accompanied by the professionalization of literary criticism intensified the need to set it on a scientific footing. Only relatively recently has attention turned to the construction of the professions; and the academy, and the institutions of authorship and literary criticism in particular, begun to be examined in this light – as bodies representing the vested interests of those who belong to them, so that the demystification of objectivity and authorship is related to that of professionalism.[20]

But the scientific methodology and epistemology that underpin English are at odds with its frequent tendency to discount material realities. If the university has appeared to embrace science, it has traditionally been on this condition, that empirical data are kept in proper places. In that the present facts and statistics of gender inequalities are the provenance of sociology and the social sciences those in other disciplines are discouraged from raising and dwelling on them. The exasperation of many women with the 'never-never land' tenor of much feminist literary discussion which we have seen voiced by Moi and Greene signals anger that the lives of many women are being short-changed by a wanton disregard of what is happening, as the 'immediate needs and demands of feminism' remain dissociated from the projects of academic feminism.[21]

Here it is helpful to consider further literary criticism's characteristic concern with women's 'oppression' rather than their inequality. As Anne Phillips points out in her introduction to *Feminism and Equality*, the choice of words which feminists use in their construction of women's problems signals considerable difference among them. Those referring to women's 'inequality' stress how women are denied what has been granted to men; allusions to women's 'oppression' impress the weight which bears down on them to keep them in certain places; and references to their 'subordination' imply a more active and deliberate keeping them down by the holders of power.[22] But where Phillips focuses on the broad shifts in the use of these key terms over time, the present collection indicates how disciplinary specialization is also a significant factor in their use. For instance, the concept of equality seems to lend itself to the quantative methods of social science and psychology, and the contributors from these disciplines draw attention to the gender inequalities in the present distribution of power within them; whereas in literary criticism the relatively nebulous notion of women's 'oppression' is much more in evidence. It seems to me that a certain obliviousness of present material facts and a related disdain of the notion of 'equality' as vulgar have served feminism poorly in literary criticism.[23]

In particular the recent critical motif of women's 'voices' seems symptomatic of its frequent tendency to glamourize and de-materialize women's existence. Of course our voices need to be heard, and feminism depends on women learning to give their own accounts and to speak on their own behalf, breaking silence. But 'voices' can easily *be* plaintive as silence, the two together the recto and the verso of a mythologizing and incapacitating literary book: we have to reckon with the fact that as 'voices' we're at our most incorporeal, and apt to be locked into victim scenarios. Where, after all, would we be most likely to encounter men as 'voices' (as distinct from the singular authoritative 'voice' of an individual man) if not in the clamour of victims – such as the voices of protest and sadness in black American spirituals?

The immediate political danger of apprehending women as voices, or even a collective voice, seems twofold: firstly, that the means may be confused for the end – a real problem, as Moi insists:

> Feminism, then, is something *more* than the effort to express women's experience: it is at once a relatively comprehensive analysis of power relations between the sexes, and the effort to change or undo any power system that authorises and condones male power over women. [my emphasis] (183)

Secondly, that because voices lend themselves to impersonation, the illusion can be maintained that men can speak for women. But when a man speaks on behalf of women, he necessarily comes from a different position, without experience of the grosser injustices and the pilulous rubs of sexism which together teach that it is primarily women and not men that patriarchy oppresses.[24] If, as Greene writes, 'Being a feminist begins in outrage at injustice (which we think we know from justice) and requires an energy which is often best fuelled by anger' (80), men are ultimately ignorant of our particular stories and their politics are lacking by so much at least.

It's easy to not even realize there is a problem in what's going on in English, and the academy in general, if its substance is not brought to notice. In this regard editing this journal has brought home one specific meaning of what has become an orthodoxy of feminist analysis – that 'the separation of academic disciplines only mirrors and reinforces the separation of most spheres of social life, and it is through this separation that gender differences and inequalities are maintained.'[25] For the direct attention that Paula Nicolson and Lena Dominelli give to the gender imbalances at the higher levels of their professions (with an informing conceptual allegiance to 'equality') is something that English criticism has barely considered up to now: for all that we ask 'Who writes? and for whom?', the question of 'Who teaches whom?' has been overwhelmingly ignored in terms of gender. Notwithstanding recent emphasis on self-reflexivity in literary criticism and attention to men's construction of a canon, the gender profile of the teaching of English in Higher Education, and its character as a part of public life and as an exercise of power, have been scarcely addressed. As a prominent American, Nannerl Keohane, writes of a not dissimilar blindness in political science:

> Why should this radical assymetry by sexes not itself have been a research problem of the first magnitude for the

discipline throughout the years? Why, that is, was it taken for granted that men and not women should populate the public sphere, and why did so few observers stop to meditate upon this fascinating fact?[26]

Terry Lovell's book, *Consuming Fictions*, is exceptional in high-lighting the paradox whereby the subject in which female students noticeably outnumber men is overwhelmingly domi-nated by men at higher teaching levels.[27] As mostly female students sit in rows before mostly male teachers who enlighten them even on such subjects as the medical construction of woman as hysteric around the turn of the century, I suggest that a critical practice might as properly contemplate more immediate manifestations of male power. The academic practice apparently most sympathetic to feminism appears curiously academic in its feminism when it comes to this point.

At Anglia Polytechnic in Cambridge, the teaching institution behind this book, as Rick Rylance rightly notices the ratio of men to women teaching full-time on the English degrees is six to one. The disparity in power evident here in English is compounded by the fact that there is not one woman among the twelve depart-mental heads at the college. Since these heads manage the budgets for their respective departments, this represents a fairly spectacular exclusion of women from power. It constitutes an irrefutably 'academic' dimension to 'feminism' in the academy which is echoed nationally in the relatively recent statistic that women comprise only fifteen per cent of academic staff in the country.[28]

If all the different academic divisions at Anglia in Cambridge – and wherever there are large imbalances in other academic institutions – quite literally made the weighting towards men visible, by displaying the photographs of those teaching in them on public noticeboards, it could be used to help produce pressure at a grass-roots level for shifting the imbalance, especially in disciplines like English given to harbouring feminism. (As I write, as a result of this introduction's raising the matter, the English division will be asked to decide whether to adopt the practice.) Given the organization of pressure by feminist men and women alike, it should appear more important to fill vacant posts with women: to make doing so without contravening the law an overriding factor in drawing up shortlists; and to give priority to other dispossessed groups. Filling posts with women requires recognition that their lives are often 'punctuated' differently from men's, and – following from this – the removal of some of the criteria of selection which effectually exclude many of them.[29] Serious attention to these obstacles is necessary, rather than devices such as the current coded recruitment of women in English on the basis of 'interest in feminist studies'. This recruitment tends to contain the challenge that women present by circumventing substantial structural alterations.

Admittedly there is, as Deborah Thom maintains (see p. 27) no necessary correlation between gender and political attitude, no guarantee that women teachers will be feminist (i.e. themselves concerned to redress the inequalities of the present situation, and to further women's interests). But we should allow for the possibility that the absence among them of any necessary commitment to feminism – rather the reverse, the tendency of many women in power at present who are not 'professional feminists' to be *not* noticeably feminist – may be partly a function of their isolation from their own sex, an adaptive phenomenon that could be shed in an altered environment of power, where women need not be so ashamed of – and passed over for – being different and being for each other in a way that most men have failed to be for them. Against the fairly prevalent assumption usefully outlined by Keohane, that for aspirants to powerful positions the 'holding of office imposes certain attitudes and behaviours that will prove more important than any differences based on sex', there lies the other argument that she puts forward: 'as women become more numerous in public office, they will bring a distinctive set of traits and concerns that will begin to alter the character of public life' (90). Can anyone seriously *not* see that having men and women about in more equal numbers in public life might at the least make 'certain attitudes and behaviours' uncertain?

It's worth noting in passing how many are given to citing Mrs Thatcher as some sort of proof of the utopianism of such a view, when what her case seems rather to illustrate is a capacity to propitiate a collective unconscious resistant to change. So for instance we see the usually more reasonable Michael Ignatieff sounding off like Colonel Blimp – as if the vehemence of his language establishes a case in default of his logic:

> Surely the one unequivocally good thing about having Mrs.
> Thatcher as Prime Minister was that the event reduced the

question of the sex of those who hold power and display competitive aggression to its proper insignificance. She did nothing except prove that she could play the game as rough as any man. What this reveals in turn is that women's right to equal opportunity is a strong enough claim not to require the spurious defence that if women were in power, they would run the world in a softer, gentler way than men. They wouldn't.[30]

Oh the relief! but what the case of Mrs Thatcher reveals rather here is a lapse of logic commensurate with a need to demystify women. The discernment of lack of difference in this instance is effactually elevated into a grand principle of identity. What is lacking is any awareness of the self-perpetuating dynamics of the present system, according to which Mrs Thatcher proves next to nothing.

It is in fact debatable how much a fairly crude behavioural approach to remedying existing inequalities would produce enough women for the jobs going in the academy and obviate deeper structural analyses of, and redress of, the reasons for inequality. In that it has been dedicated to depth investigations of problems it would seem that such a bald quasi-behavioural approach to redressing its imbalances – whereby you don't for the time being so much worry about the reasons why things are unequal as do something to rectify them – would be antipathetic to the academy, though the move to teaching in modalities and an emphasis on breadth over depth may somewhat counter this. As it stands, the mention of some of the immediate facts of inequality surrounding this book jars with the detachment that academia and professionalism inculcate. But professionalism, after all, if not a cloak for self-serving and closing ranks, needs to accept criticism for what it is worth in line with an ethos of serving truth and the common good.

The consequence of attention to the world – of a properly critical feminism – Moi suggests, is the realization that feminism is not the only political struggle relevant for women: 'in the global context today, oppressive sexual power relations are not always the most important (in the sense of the most painful) form of exploitation' (185). And yet the very radical prioritization of 'the most painful' as 'the most important', and the consequent apparent relegation of feminism besides other movements for social change, seems testimony to an originating source of value that may be called feminist not least for want of any better name to cover such an ability to mandate movements other than itself and to work alongside them, to abandon the monolithic. A truly critical feminism (one most given to making critical differences) will include, she is here proposing, a capacity to be self-critical and defer to other forms of oppression, so cutting itself down in size where appropriate in a way that no other political movement has yet undertaken, in a working-together that moves away from the gender identification that brought it into being.

Admittedly this gravitation is risky, from its ring of maternalism to the danger that feminism will become ineffectual through dilution. As it is there are too many men and women about whose realization that the oppression of women is only one among many forms of it leads, either outright or in effect, to feminism's deprecation. But if we are desirous of others' support, it behoves us to attend to them as they to us; as John Goode notes, 'nothing could be more convenient for the ecology of selective practices than that such [oppressed] groups should experience such oppressions in radically different and exclusive forms' (p. 132).

The pronounced gravitation of feminist analyses to analyses of other forms of oppression is indeed a distinctive feature of the movement, and, it seems to me, not something to want to disown: both morality and utility require it. Those who resist the identification of women with caring and distinctively 'feminine' attributes, as replicating 'too closely for comfort the very stereotypes feminists once tried to avoid' (Phillips, 4), have nonetheless to reckon with the evidence that many feminists *are* turning to other forms of inequality and oppression. In discussing one feminist's position, Phillips presents what seems to me a legitimately historico-biological, and constructive – if patently hazardous – perspective on the phenomenon:

> Largely because of their role as mothers, women have become the guarantors of a deeper humanity, carrying a sense of community, of belonging, of selflessness and care. Feminism should be building on this, not capitulating to a narrower self-interest. (17)

If on the one hand feminism looms to many women as a menacing prioritization of the aspect of their existence that has systematically oppressed them, the other sides of the case, which we have just seen Moi leaning to, were impressively noted by Foucault:

> the real strength of the women's liberation movement is not that of having laid claim to the specificity of their sexuality and the rights pertaining to it, but that they have actually departed from the discourse conducted within the apparatuses of sexuality . . . a veritable movement of de-sexualisation, a displacement effected in relation to the sexual centering of the problem, formulating the demand for forms of culture, discourse, language, and so on, which are no longer part of that rigid assignation and pinning-down to their sex which they had initially in some sense been politically obliged to accept in order to make themselves heard.[31]

## II

In the last twenty-five years especially women academics have brought to light more and more of the distortions perpetrated in traditional 'objective' studies that misrepresent the world and women particularly. The next three chapters broach this deficiency. To begin with, examining the interrelationship of feminism and history, Deborah Thom offers a historical perspective on the former, drawing attention to the great variety of understandings of their identity that women have manifested over the years. She also considers some of the major questions currently confronting feminists in history, which are echoed in other disciplines.

Following this, after initial attention to the gender imbalances in her discipline, Paula Nicolson's study of feminism and academic psychology focuses on its treatment of women's biological functions – functions which are widely taken as 'given', and on which much of the belief in female difference is based. She outlines a persistent refusal among the discipline's mostly male professionals to come to terms with the economic, social, academic and political circumstances that might obviate or mitigate their ascriptions of inadequacy, inferiority, abnormality and difference to women. In this chapter the lay reader can quickly get a broad sense of quite how much academic feminism is up against, and its reverberations in popular culture. Though intentionally not a comprehensive piece, it is in the spirit of the significantly titled volume which Dale Spender edited (and which covers some of the same ground as *Critical Feminism*), *Men's Studies Modified* (1985). This provided a litany of the ommission of women in the codification of knowledge and its methods of proceeding in discipline after discipline. As Spender summarized: 'Fundamental to feminism is the premise that women have been 'left out' of codified knowledge; where men have formulated explanations in relation to themselves, they have generally either rendered women invisible or classified them as deviant.'[32]

Even today it seems that the main areas where women are encouraged to be different are in the ghettoes of 'women's studies' and Feminist practices, the enclaves of academically licensed sex which many women are, not surprisingly, reluctant to join since – especially after the education they have had – they may well experience the suggestion that they do so as a put-down, as invidiously not taking them seriously and tagging them as different (try suggesting seriously to men that they embark on 'men's studies'). It seems that, for many women, electing to pay attention academically to their identity as women paradoxically requires either considerable sophistication or a not-minding that (especially to those brought up before the lessening of more overt sexual discrimination) seems to verge on mindlessness (or, somewhere in between perhaps, a certain opportunism). Deborah Thom encapsulates the related, more general paradox, that

> to prioritize the simple, single divide of gender is to make visible the one feature of life that may systematically oppress women or, if celebrated as an alternative view of the hierarchy of power, disempower women in a world of common humanity. To talk of woman is to hide the individual woman or to reduce her to what is the lowest common denominator in her life and that of others. (p. 48)

The artist Mary Kelly pursues the last point in discussing the application of the term 'feminist' to any particular practice, since it sets a false trail inasmuch as it supresses the multivariety of ways in which women set about asserting their presences. Exhibiting a salutary rivalry, (let us not forgo our envy, our anger, until the feminism it serves inaugurates a different order!) she fastens on the term's potentially inimical bearing, as a generaliz-ation,· on the individual woman. Thus in so far as the term 'feminist' may properly be applied 'it would be more a matter of

. . . the 'specificity' of all these practices [contributing in some way to the ongoing debate in the women's movement] rather than any generalization you could make about feminism, and I think that this is also a very important point because, after all, what the boys always do is deny, adamantly, any kind of covering term or tendency for their *unique* production (p. 201).

Lena Dominelli's panoramic chapter on feminism and social work emphasizes the interrelationship between theory and practice and the radical dimensions of feminism. In its way her categorical mode of writing seems as representative of current feminist utterance as quite different sorts of writing – such as Rachel Blau du Plessis' – which announce feminist credentials. No other chapter exhibits quite such a rooted sense that to be caught up in feminism is to be caught up practically in changing the way things are done, in a close reading of reality that runs from the most minute details to our 'loftiest intellectual formulation'; and that the initiative in this belongs with women, whose interests are best served in co-operation with each other.

Carolyn Burdett's chapter on Olive Schreiner is the most narrowly focused. But in presenting a close study of the writer and one of her short stories she turns over many issues important to academic feminists. So for example she questions notions of creativity and the norms by which Schreiner has been judged and discusses Schreiner's approach to Wollstonecraft. She also examines the significance and problems of the act of writing for Schreiner, related to her conflicting pulls towards equality with, and difference from, men. She ends by opening up the question of the racism which has recently preoccupied literary critics as the problematic corollary of Schreiner's feminism.

This tension for modern readers between the different ideological stances of a writer is one of the matters which John Goode raises in the course of a wide-ranging discussion which involves sustained attention to the interrelationship of socialism and feminism, an interpretation of the place of men in feminism, and an endeavour to come to terms with deconstruction's challenge to the notion of representation. These matters, along with much else in a relatively informal piece which centres on a reading of *Middlemarch*, are conducive to and symptomatic of arguments extending beyond the discipline of literary criticism. His stance of standing back from feminism seems somewhat belied by an insistence on the specificity of the class mechanisms of women's oppression that is wholly in their interests. Rick Rylance examines the question of the position of a male literary critic sympathetic to feminism at length, discussing what he sees as its successful impact in literary studies. He contrasts the present currency of feminist values with the oppression of thirty and forty years ago as seen in the poetry and fiction of the period. He concludes by considering the vexed questions of the terms in which different kinds of feminism can best be apprehended, where he asserts distance from post-structuralist readings.

Lastly, the conversation – if that isn't too decorous a word for an exchange that grows heated – between Mary Kelly and Griselda Pollock nearly three years ago is reprinted here as a significant historical document of the issues now being raised in feminist art practices, as presented by two of their major exponents – one an artist, the other a leading figure in art history. Margaret Iversen's introduction makes the conversation more accessible than it might otherwise be. The nature of a demystified artistic process; the character of interventions in art which can be called feminist, and in particular the problems associated with the choice of paint as a medium; the relationship of academic feminism to feminism elsewhere; the appropriateness of interpretations of modernism; and the opportunism that attends the presence of women – both literal and figuratively – in the academy: these are some of a sweep of issues that make this exchange an appropriate concluding chapter. The academic context in which Pollock operates appears in some respects interestingly non-prescriptive compared with Kelly's practice, although some of the tension between the two centres on the art historian's academic attempt to pin feminism down, looking for 'threads of feminism that cross all these diverse practices'.

The agreement of the contributors to write in an inter-disciplinary volume signals a readiness to engage with those outside their own ways of thinking that I hope will be followed by its readers deciding to read in as inter-disciplinary a fashion as possible: the character of a book, as the literary critics remind us, is largely a function of the way in which it is read, so that an 'inter-disciplinary' volume is so largely by courtesy of its readers. As an editor I echo Griselda Pollock when she says that 'I don't accept that by listening to what is actually being said in a range of practices that one is necessarily saying "anything goes"'. Part of the point of *Critical Feminism* is to enable those who are already feminist to hone their understanding of it in encountering the unfamiliar. In this sense, by inviting its readers to take issue with what is being presented and to try to clarify in their own minds the implications of feminism, the book can be seen as a variation of the dialogue form. The two chapters written by men seem to have particular polemical and perhaps admonitory use. My introduction has been concerned to open things up and induce effective criticism.

Direct address of the impact of feminism is important. But the inclusion of more specific analyses from literary critics and the final conversation – demonstrating the multiplicity of issues arising in and from it in practice – has increased the feminist texture of the book as a whole. In that address of 'the impact' of feminism invites certain sorts of historical and logical-positivist approaches, having many of them might have tended to mean having too many, a succession of the same perhaps as much as a succession of different stories.

The main point of *Critical Feminism* is to increase awareness of feminism's critical implications. As some major injustices in society have been overcome, feminist or women's studies are firmly established in the academy, and the prevailing straitened economic climate seems hostile to all but narrowly economic considerations, it seems especially important to maintain momentum and prevent feminism becoming stalled at this point; and specifically to try to convey to those born in the last twenty-five years or so why feminism is not simply a defunct cause. Where feminists are absorbed in and by predominantly self-referential discussions in particular disciplines or *l'écriture féminine* they are open to the danger of cheating women by augmenting discursive and fragmented figurings of the world. While in their work they are crucial in pulsing out agendas for their more lay sisters, they can easily obscure feminism's identity as a 'movement' at all – that is, its identity as a 'combined endeavour' (*OED*) of women to redress the injustices that are done to them. An interdisciplinary collection counteracts this by asserting the existence of a movement accessible not only to those 'in the know'. An irony of thus opening things up here, however, is that we seem to be at a juncture when what are in some respects the epiphenomena of the 'success' of feminism make more arduous philosophical and methodological analyses, together with substantial structural changes, imperative.

The book has been compiled partly against the grain of an initial projection which, true to an academic outlook, assumed that feminism was just an issue to tackle and let run its course like any other. In such circumstances a feminist editor may have to challenge the assumptions and practices of her predominantly male editorial colleagues used to doing things their way, for whom, however well disposed and feminist, feminism hasn't the same priority. Even so, I am grateful for the assistance, support and hard work that they – Nigel Wheale, Rick Rylance, Ed Esche, and Will Hill, together with Penelope Kenrick – have given in seeing this book through; and to all besides who have variously contributed towards its production – Rick Allen, Nora Crook, Duncan Double, Felicia Gordon, Michelle Stanworth, and Deborah Thom – as well as the others who have written in and illustrated it. Especial thanks to Judith Mastai of the Vancouver Art Gallery for allowing me to include the conversation between Griselda Pollock and Mary Kelly which she transcribed.

Having indicated a need for academic disciplines to broaden their parameters of inquiry, I want lastly to point, somewhat contrarily, to the importance of continuing 'esoteric' academic inquiry; and to suggest that a particular problem at present for feminist academics, and academics representing other dispossessed groups – as well (if somewhat paradoxically in the present context) as for all those properly committed to 'truths' – is how to admit political awareness without collapsing the moral and intellectual dimensions of life: how to incorporate knowledge of the vested interests served in learning without voiding the enterprise; how to prevent particular reductive functional analyses passing as whole stories. These uneasy tasks are encapsulated in the idea of our dancing – or at least edging our way – through minefields. Somewhere along the line they involve commitment to the idea, currently heretical to many, and the idea of the language of, a common humanity.

The irony of feminism in academic institutions is that as a rule their practices are not noticeably more enlightened than those of institutions without special claims to knowledge and truth. As long as knowledge is routinely dissociated from politics things are unlikely to change, but their public cohabitation runs the risk, like marriage, of collapsing them into one. If neutral knowledge has been the dominant and official partner in a secret relationship with politics – brushing the latter out of sight – their public association should not portend its total eclipse. The desire to insist on a 'neutral' component of knowledge seems to me as significant as its imputed fallaciousness, and to be inseparable from the urge to make feminism prevail – having as much to do with ethics as epistemic fallacy.[33] Though 'neutral' knowledge is no longer free-standing and so high on a hill this is not necessarily a change for the worse, nor a foolish aim; but to more than cast these post-modern shadows now is to go beyond the scope of this introduction to critical, and self-critical, feminism.[34]

## References

1. This is a plural adaptation of a variation of a Talmudic saying encountered twenty-odd years ago. The nearest I can get to it for now is Eric Fromm's epigraph to *The Fear of Freedom* (1942):

    > If I am not for myself, who will be for me?
    > If I am for myself only, what am I?
    > If not now – when?

    Talmudic Saying, *Mishnah*, Abot.
2. See Phillips, Ann (1987). *Feminism and Equality*. Oxford, Blackwell, p 4. Phillips, it seems to me rightly, notes the profound sea change whereby women's aspirations for equality are no longer so likely to be expressed androgynously, in the longing to be a 'person' instead of a woman.
3. For a study which made this point nearly ten years ago see Langland, Elizabeth, and Gove, W. (eds.) (1983). *A Feminist Perspective in the Academy: The Difference it Makes*. London, University of Chicago Press. The editors concluded that 'women's studies has yet to have a substantial influence on the traditional curriculum, principally because such analyses challenge fundamental assumptions in each discipline' (p. 1).
4. Messer-Davidow, Ellen (1987). 'The philosophical bases of feminist literary criticism' (hereafter cited in text), *New Literary History*, Autumn 1987, p. 91. The listing which we see in this deserves consideration as a device common to feminist analyses. For review of the early development of American feminist literary criticism – which has greatly influenced English – see Kolodny, A. (1980). 'Dancing through the minefield: some observations on the theory, practice and politics of a feminist literary criticism', *Feminist Studies*, 6, 1 (Spring).
5. For analysis of traditional studies as men's studies see Spender, Dale (ed.) 1981. *Men's Studies Modified*. Oxford, Pergamon, especially pp. 23–28. For generally useful discussion of the fundamental problem of the sense in which women can be seen to be announcing 'new' forms of rationality at all, and of the positioning of their criticisms in relation to men's, see Louise Marcil-Lacoste, 'The trivialization of the notion of equality', in Harding, Sandra, and

Hentikka, Merril B. (eds.) (1983). *Discovering Reality: Feminist Perspectives on Epistemology, Metaphysics, Methodology, and Philosophy of Science*. London, D. Reidel.

6. For address of this issue, see especially Jardine, Alice, and Smith, P. (eds.) (1987). *Men in Feminism*. London, Methuen.

7. See also Wolff, Janet (1990). 'The problem of theory and the problem of women', *Feminine Sentences*. Cambridge, Polity, p. 7ff.

8. Christian, Barbara. 'The race for theory', in L. Kauffman (ed.) (1989) *Feminism and Institutions: Dialogues on Feminist Theory*. Oxford, Blackwell, p. 229, p. 231.

9. For a study which negotiates the conflicting pulls in history towards specific identity and its refusal see Riley, Denise (1988). *Am I That Name? Feminism and the Category of 'Women' in History*. Basingstoke, Macmillan.

10. Moi, Toril, 'Men against patriarchy' (hereafter cited in text), in Kauffman, L. (ed.) (1989) *Gender and Theory: Dialogues on Feminist Criticism*. Oxford, Blackwell, p. 182.

11. Quoted in *Gender and Theory*, p. 3.

12. Ibid., p. 2.

13. The question as to why we were all so blind seems much better addressed on this broad front than in terms of individual culpability. See especially Sandra Harding on 'Why has the sex/gender system become visible now?' in *Discovering Reality*.

14. Kolodny, (see note 3), reprinted in *Men's Studies Modified*, p. 24.

15. Against Moi's view, it should be pointed out that Terry Eagleton's rather odd contribution *does*, albeit implicitly, connect working-class and women's oppression.

16. Greene, Gayle, 'The uses of quarelling' (hereafter cited in text), in *Feminism and Institutions*, p. 80.

17. Note here John Goode's use of the work of feminist historians like Catherine Hall and Leonore Davidoff (p. 143).

18. See Terry Lovell (1987) *Consuming Fictions*, London, Verso, p. 139 ff.

19. See for instance Heyck, T.W., (1982). *The Transformation of Intellectual Life in Victorian England*. London, Croom Helm, especially Chapter Five, 'The impact of science'.

20. With regard to authorship and the construction of the canon in particular, several literary critics have taken up sociological analyses of the professions, most frequently that of Bledstein, B. (1976), *The Culture of Professionalism*, New York, W.W. Norton. See, for instance, Richard Brodhead (1986), *The School of Hawthorne*, Oxford, Oxford University Press, on Henry James (a key figure in this context) p. 112 ff.; and note 14, p. 235, for a list of other important sociological writings on the profession as a social form.

21. See here also Wolff's call for the integration of the approaches of textual critique and sociological analysis, *Feminine Sentences* p. 103 ff.

22. Phillips, *Feminism and Equality* pp. 1–2 (hereafter cited in text).

23. For an impressive plea for the continuing importance of the goal of 'equality' that nonetheless acknowledges its limitations, see Juliet Mitchell, 'Women and equality', in *Feminism and Equality*; for Phillips's summary formulation of the question of its desirability and the different constructions of it, see pp. 2–3.

24. The point is made by Moi also, p. 183, in her chapter which is a response to another in *Gender and Theory*, 'Me(n) and feminism'.

25. Woolf, p. 105.

26. Keohane, Nannerl O. (President of Wellesley College), 'Speaking from silence: women and the science of politics' (hereafter cited in text), in *A Feminist Perspective in the Academy*, p. 87.

27. *Consuming Fictions*, see especially Chapter Seven.

28. Figures (for 1985) taken from 'Forty Years On: The CUWAG Report on the Numbers and Status of Academic Women in the University of Cambridge', September 1988, p. 18. The study emphasizes that this university, like most others, is a 'chilly' place for women.

29. For instance, insistence on youth when drawing up shortlists can impede women particularly. The CUWAG report provides a useful summary of obstacles to women's advancement, ranging from 'homosocial reproduction' (p. 6) to the operation of 'informal networking' (p. 7). Though focused on Cambridge University the report draws on research concerning academic institutions in general, and most of its observations are relevant to many of them.

30. *The Observer*, 23 June 1991.

31. Michel Foucault, quoted in a note in *Gender and Theory*, p. 7. For general discussion of the relationship between the thinker and the movement see Irene Diamond and Lee Quinby (eds) (1988) *Feminism and Foucault: Reflections on Resistance* Boston, Northeastern University Press.

32. Dale Spender in 'Introduction', p. 2.

33. For specific consideration of feminist rejection of continued allegiance to a 'neutral' component of knowledge see Marcil-Lacoste (note 5). But that the notion of neutrality is as indispensable as the notion of truth seems evident on reflection on Marcil-Lacoste's dictum that 'it is necessary to unfold the theoretical and practical conditions and implications of a sexually neutral notion of validity, if only to determine when and how neutrality becomes pseudo-neutrality.' (132)

34. On post-modernism's challenge to truth, especially at the 'cutting edge' of science, see for instance Lawson, Hilary, and Appignanesi, Lisa (eds.) (1989). *Dismantling Truth: Reality in the Post-Modern World*. London, Weidenfeld and Nicolson.

# 2

# A lop-sided view: feminist history or the history of women?

## Deborah Thom

There is is an irony in discussing feminism in a series called *Ideas and Production* because the relationship between women, ideas and production has been so overdetermined by women's role in reproduction. Feminism is, especially, but not only, about women, but it is primarily the activity of giving them a voice, an access to power hitherto denied. It therefore includes many different sorts of political argument; it encompasses Mary Wollstonecraft's feminism, her 'wild wish' that women should no longer be subordinated to their bodies and the passions which their bodies encouraged in them;[1] the existential determinism of de Beauvoir's 'second sex';[2] Christabel Pankhurst's radical feminism which placed women's interests against heterosexual sex,[3] and the contemporary argument of suffragists, that women's sex or sexuality was an irrelevance compared to their lack of citizenship.[4] Hence the ambiguity in my title and in the project of juxtapozing feminism and history. The place to find the value in that juxtaposition is in an understanding of the differences in feminism as expressed throughout its history rather than in tracing similarities, or assuming homogeneity.

Both feminism and history are social products themselves and participants in both activities produce ideas in a way which is in part determined by their circumstances. Changes in the sets of ideas are common to intellectual and political life – in other words they need to be perceived historically themselves. There are a hundred years at least of the regular production of feminist ideas, many more of women's reflection upon their social position and

*Colin Wilkin*

its determinants. Most people who have reflected on such matters have been women (as is generally the case in histories of the experience of being oppressed, those most interested in the analysis are those most partisan in the politics). Beyond that there are very few things that feminists have in common apart from an unease with things as they are, and therefore a common problem of the construction placed on things as they were. They share also a sense of critique, of making that unease which is fundamental to their activity general among practitioners of history. But they are divided about the importance of differences and the political significance of difference. From this division follows the division between those who study women and those who study woman-hood.

### The 'fair' sex *or* the argument has two sides

There is a simple divide between historical theorists on the position of women. On the one side are those who argue that women are simply citizens (or not), differentiated as men are by race, class, region, religion and occupation, so that there is no more a subject 'women's history' than there is a subject 'men's history'. History is always a particular history, with a hierarchy of significance headed by visible structures of power which are described as such by contemporaries – monarchs and parliaments – and any other set of interests is secondary. Typical of such historians is Lord Elton, who has dismissed women's history as part of his general attack on social history. Such an attack is founded on a real theoretical position, which is that to prioritize gender as a division in society is a mistake.[5] Allied to this position – although politically opposed to it – is one which also gives precedence in the discussion to the dominant attitudes of the day. It similarly takes the conceptual structures of an epoch and emphasizes gender within them. What it shares then with the traditional historians like Elton is a central concern with power – but to discourse is given the dominant role in inscribing power relations in a society, among which *for women* their gender plays a leading part. Joan Scott is perhaps the major exponent of this in general accounts of gender and history.[6]

On the other side (which unites two very disparate tendencies) are those who argue that for women the most important thing is their gender, the *common* experiences deriving from the rhetorical construction of womanhood, and the legal, social and economic disadvantages of womanhood. In particular, they see sex and motherhood as the proper subjects of history. This approach unites the social historian of women and the feminist who may not share a politics as a result but who do share a focus on the structures of gender which prioritizes the body, lived experience and the commonality of women's lives. To say then that this divide is simple is not to say that it is meaningless, but it is no more useful a description of the historical enterprise than to say that all history is or is not about the divisions caused by ethnicity. It is interesting precisely in its variability. Gender, like ethnicity, does derive from the subject's innate corporeal qualities – however subsequently determined by social agencies – but the meaning of gender, like the meaning of ethnicity, can only be located historically. In raising questions about history I am not doing the synthetic task of summarizing the many works on history that have already been produced. Jane Lewis did this excellently in her contribution to Dale Spender's *Mens' Studies Modified* (1981) at a time when the volume of work was more manageable than it is now a decade later, so although this is a historicist account it is a very sketchy one which has the intention of demonstrating the persistence of certain fundamental questions involved in the project of thinking politically about women. Specialist journals, academic appointees, courses and fields of study all indicate that the question of studying women historically is not whether it should be done but how.

Feminism has made a major contribution to history, but feminists have not always gained from history the political advances they hoped to make. Crudely, that feminists want emancipation is undeniable – but whether they get it by writing about women or womanhood is not always clear. I am going to take examples from work written mostly by British historians about Britain to describe the influence of a political movement that is also a discourse – feminism – on a discourse that has political implications – history. Nowhere has it been more widely recognized than in feminist contributions to history that the history the historian writes is the history of her own times. Since women's participation in public life is of comparatively recent date it is not surprising that in accounts of the history of history women hardly appear until the nineteenth century. The writing of history demands certain material conditions which effectively excluded all but a handful of women in Britain until then. Theorists of women's position did exist and often wrote with reference to the past, but none of them explicitly wrote history. That is to say that the production of history is a luxury to those who are subordinated and most women, however powerful in the domestic sphere or as political figures by birth, were subordinated both socially and legally – much less likely to have an education or even functional literacy than their brothers. The art of writing history was in some ways thought of as inappropriate for those few women who lived by their pens, and those fewer still who wrote on the situation of women. As Mary Astell, the conservative political theorist and advocate of the improvement of women's lives and education, observed with some irony,

> They allow us plays, poetry and romances, to divert us and themselves, and when they would express a particular esteem for a woman's sense, they recommend history; tho' with submission History can only serve us for amusement and a subject of discourse. For tho' it may be of use to the men who govern affairs, to know how their fore-fathers acted, yet what is this to us, who have nothing to do with such business?[7]

It was no part of Astell's enterprise to propose any new way in which History might be written. Even so she was critical of those rare accounts of the 'great and good actions of women' dealt with by the remark, 'That such women acted above their sex. By which one must suppose they wou'd have their readers understand, that they were not women who did those great actions, but that they were men in petticoats.'[8] Her acuteness of observation and her wit give Astell a high place in the annals of thinkers about the position of women, but she was not part of a movement for change, so that, although her work inspired some contemporary enthusiasm and her writings and life were recorded, she left no followers or school. Her understanding was critical and thus valuable as understanding of the social order of her day. It did not inspire much history, except in the late twentieth century when she has become another subject of study herself.

This account will deal, then, with feminist writing arising from feminist movements, and try to place it in the material construction of the day in order to trace the varying ways in which history has been altered by feminists and by feminism. I start with the simplest pair of positions which represent feminism, around which two poles the rest must revolve, here ignoring chronology. The second section makes a quick chronological survey of the relationship between feminism and history. The third looks at some recent writings to demonstrate the extent and the limits of the mutual interdependence of history and feminism.

## Male oppressor, woman victim

One feminism argues that gender is not a historical construction but an essential – the feminism of radical feminists such as Andrea Dworkin. For her, gender relations are always structured by one simple central ahistorical fact – men oppress women. The agency of that oppression is heterosexual sexual intercourse.[9] This position has been newly inflected by Catherine Mckinnon in an analysis of women and the state.[10] Hers is a bracing and rigorous account of the reason why women continue to be subordinated in the USA despite a materially rich society and a quite complex legislative programme of equal opportunity. A forerunner of this position is Christabel Pankhurst, a leader of suffragette agitation with her mother, Mrs Emmeline Pankhurst, in the years 1900–1914. She argued in 'The Great Scourge and How to End it'[11] that the solution to sexually transmitted disease – which she saw as one of the main weaknesses of the society of her day, in itself an oppressor of women – was 'Votes for Women and Chastity for Men'. Implicit in this position is the same location of oppression in the difference between male and female desire, which is read off from a biological difference – of internal and external genital organs – as a representation of power relations. An edifice of verbal and visual rhetoric was created by the activities of Pankhurst's followers in the Women's Social and Political Union which sold postcards of Saint Christabel, emphasizing the martyrdom of the female activist, particularly the hunger-striker; used the image of Joan of Arc, virginal soldier-martyr; and maintained that all women were oppressed by the existence of female prostitution which began with the deflowering by rape of a child sold into 'white slavery'. Chastity for men would of course ultimately mean chastity for women – and in many ways the account is one which argues for celibacy. The rhetoric of this debate downplays sex between women since the arguments are essentially heterosexual in structure, in Dworkin's version of the 1980s and Pankhurst's of the 1910s, as they assume that power in sex is between the two genders, not individual participants irrespective of gender.[12]

The history that comes from this viewpoint shares several

features with the work of the French theorist Michel Foucault.[13] It foregrounds the discourses of a society rather than some democratic notion of the practices of the majority; it removes some historical questions entirely. History is inescapably general, individual agents are merely creatures of the discourse of their times. It turns the historian's attention to sex and sexuality, where gender is most closely inscribed on to individuals. This radical feminist tradition has generated much work which contends that the project of historical explanation must include domains previously excluded as private, in particular arguing that discourse about sex constitutes an important domain of power. This feminism has been influential in two ways: firstly in recognizing the way in which women are particularly constrained by the law as heterosexual sexuality is controlled through the regulation of the deviant female rather than through men; secondly in maintaining that women themselves prioritize the life they lead as sexed beings.[14]

Women's concern with sexuality led to one great and successful campaign to change a law, the campaign against the Contagious Diseases Acts in the 1870s. This was organized by a woman, Josephine Butler, who used to great effect the horrifying demonstration of the impact on women of sexual morality's double standard. In the course of her campaign she spoke in public about the effects of sexually transmitted disease on women's bodies. This was not so unusual in the discourse of evangelists who fulminated against sex; what was unusual was the way in which she waved the speculum that doctors used on prostitutes during their compulsory vaginal examination under the Acts. This was, as she pointed out, instrumental rape. The example is interesting because it raises the issue of the way in which discourse about sex and the double standard offers ambiguous support for a feminist project; and also the way in which religion is yoked to constructions of the social in the nineteenth century, making its concept of social explanation different from ours.

Butler herself was interested in the historical roots of women's position, but not in doing history. That as an activity was inspired by the suffrage activists of the United States who were looking for examples of women's sense, civic virtue and strength of mind and character. In newspapers, pamphlets and books great women were described and rescued from obscurity, so too were the exemplary lives of the suffering. The genre was not new, it is characteristic of the evangelist tracts of the period 1820 to 1860. Popular history of the turn of the century followed a life-and-achievements model both in structure and narrative, and of course much of the popular fiction was about young women because so much of it was for young women. What feminism contributed was the sense that these achievements were representative of a sex and not of those who were unlike the rest of their sex. Such writings were always caught between the exemplary and celebratory nature of the genre and the need to explain the continuing subordination of all women, partly on the basis of the wrongs done to women, partly on the basis of the achievements of a few women who tried to right the wrongs.

**Feminism as critique**

One of the problems for the historian motivated by feminism is the contradiction between how women are and how they might be. Perhaps the earliest feminist discourse that confronted this issue over history was that of Mary Wollstonecraft, not just in her *A Vindication of the Rights of Women* but in her published accounts of the French Revolution and her educational manuals as well as her novels. She attacked the societies of her own day for avoiding real historical understanding in favour of essentialism, which she summed up in the attitude that 'Woman ought always to be subjected because she has always been so' (*A Vindication*, p. 69). However she pointed out too that women were not, in the society of her day, equipped to achieve all the things of which they could be capable, for the mind will ever be unstable that has only prejudices to rest on, and the female virtue of obedience needed to be replaced by intransigence – 'when forebearance confounds right and wrong it ceases to be a virtue'. Wollstonecraft's argument against women's subordination was that it was based upon the effect of passion which disturbed the order of society. She wanted to demonstrate that it was the superior ordering of society that an educated womanhood would achieve: an individual woman would acquire 'the dignity of conscious virtue' and in so doing would become a 'better wife and mother'. In this way she made a set of political arguments about women as a wasted resource, as misused potential, that rested on the tension between what was and what could be, but also recognized and prioritized difference. She was arguing that women should escape the tyranny of the emotional life because it weakened them and thus society. Bitterly she pointed out that often a 'neglected wife was the best mother'. There is thus a double tension between the interests of men and women, and between the interests of women's particular social role and their universal humanity.

In her texts Wollstonecraft constantly exploited the notion that the personal is the political but she also sought to undermine it, because she saw that as a part of women's burden. Denise Riley has pointed to these tensions at the heart of Wollstonecraft's writing and her political project as a whole, in *Am I That Name?* (1988). She has also argued that this paradox is an essential component of any speaking on the subject 'woman'. It is and remains the central question in any discussion of the analysis embodied in any feminist writing or discourse. But it is not the only subject that feminism has brought to history, since history as wrought by feminism has not been just about how women are spoken of but how they act or how they speak of themselves – which may well be at variance with their ascribed behaviour. Wollstonecraft could say that women had always been subjected – but she felt no need to describe that subjection historically as differentiated. Her problem was to overcome the Rousseauan belief in a state of nature at all, to claim that gender relations were culturally determined, and to predict that only women's own activity could overcome this determination. Hence the impact of Enlightenment thought was to emphasize activity and activism, to look to the successes who escaped from subjection as an inspiration for all.

### Stories we tell ourselves

Heroism was the dominant mode of historical explanation in the period in which women were challenging for power in Parliament. Hence the historic figures of interest to suffrage activists were usually those whose heroism had been of an unusual kind. The archtype for suffragettes was Joan of Arc. She was virginal, militant and embodied suffering for a cause. Christabel Pankhurst called her forces 'the women's army', and demanded the sacrifice of 'normal' expectations, either of marriage and children, or of a career in those occupations opening to women (something perhaps forgotten by later commentators). Joan of Arc had been a soldier and a martyr, whose cause had been challenged but who had not ultimately wavered. She represented the discipline that was needed to maintain an illegal set of activities in a small organization operating in secrecy. She also represented some of the more dubious pleasures of self-sacrifice. There were other exemplars of women who were seen as early activists for a cause they had construed in other ways. The search for the exemplary was a task requiring historical skills but more often than not these skills were not used. History was the maintenance of a collective narrative, a skein in which new brightly coloured threads could be woven, in which the history of women joined that of the nation, democracy and the English common law as a slow glorious unfolding towards an improving present. What was distinctive about this feminist version of Whig history was the way in which these accounts, these empowering stories, celebrated new values. Biography of Joan of Arc was joined by biography of Elizabeth Fry (the Quaker prison reformer), accounts of Florence Nightingale's contribution to nursing, descriptions of the female monarchs who had held power and exercised it – Elizabeth I and Boadicea. However the implications of these popular studies were ambiguous. The suffragettes could argue that these histories demonstrated women's strength, civic virtue and abandonment of self in the interests of the greater good.

Opponents could argue these were the qualities which made them exceptional and the lack of these qualities was more evident in women in general than in men. They could also argue that the separation of public from private was unassailed by these few women in public life. If women's real claim to be participants in the public sphere was based on their mothering experience or capacities, most women would always wish to make that a priority in their lives so that these exceptions only proved the rule. History was always a minority interest among the feminists of the period 1900–1914, partly perhaps because of the necessary emphasis on political action rather than reflection or study, partly because writing history, finding out sources, learning the investigative skills required, understanding a period – all require time and money to sustain. Woolf's plea for a new history of women in *A Room of One's Own* specifically requested this new history from some student of Girton or Newnham, the few women who had access to the resources needed to write new history rather than re-write the old. 'What we want', she wrote,

> is a mass of information; at what age did she marry; how many children had she as a rule; what was her house like; had she a

room to herself; did she do the cooking; would she be likely to have a servant? All these facts lie somewhere, presumably, in parish registers and account books; the life of the average Elizabethan woman must be scattered about somewhere, could one collect it and make a book of it. It would be ambitious beyond my daring, I thought, looking about the shelves for books that were not there, to suggest to students of those famous colleges that they should rewrite history, though I own it often seems a little queer as it is, unreal, lop-sided; but why should they not add a supplement to history? calling it of course, by some inconspicuous name so that women might figure there without impropriety?[15]

Woolf's writing of social commentary was rediscovered by feminists of the 1970s, and her plea has been frequently cited. I will address the question of whether it has been answered – as Joan Scott says that it has – later; what I want to address for now is the nature of the plea itself. Woolf was a sponsor of the organization for working-class women who worked in the home, the Women's Cooperative Guild. This organization was set up in 1894 by Mrs Lawrenson, the wife of a Woolwich vicar, to stop women – who controlled domestic expenditure – from undermining their husbands' cooperative movement by buying goods more cheaply elsewhere. Very quickly these maternalist intentions were themselves undermined by the new organization's members who turned it into a campaigning movement which addressed matters of concern to themselves far beyond the shop door – maternity, education, the vote and, most contentiously of all, birth control and divorce. Divorce was a subject of such delicacy that their support for divorce law reform cost them the financial support of the Cooperative Union, the umbrella movement for all local co-ops. In short this organization, which was the women's political body with which Woolf most associated herself (while recognizing the profound differences that lay between herself and these women), was one which advocated the writing of a new politics in women's interest – particularly that of the working-class woman who worked in her own home.

They also argued for the use of new evidence in furtherance of their political demands. Their two most influential books, which were collectively written – *Maternity: Letters from Working Women* and *Life As We Have Known It* – argued that their experience of life was an unheeded source of information which should be given greater political influence. The unedited words of these women were therefore seen as more truthful and more powerful than the careful, artistic productions of those professional authors – such as Woolf – who supported them. In these books were raw details of everyday life that were in a sense being spoken aloud for the first time. Women described their confinements, the need to work immediately after them, the resort to abortifacients when pregnancy was intolerable and the physical details of childbirth in overcrowded homes without adequate hot water. All of this added up to make an extremely powerful case for maternity benefit payable to the mother; but it also added up to a new claim for reportage, for the authenticity of experience which Woolf longed for. This experience provided a powerful argument about women, who were thus located in the domestic by their own defenders. The novelty of this reporting is that it is introduced by writers but not mediated very much through the construction of a narrative which they put on the material. This is their own work, albeit less innocent of literary technique than the presentation implied, since the soliciting of reports had set the terms of the narrative. This makes all the more remarkable their assured handling of concepts previously used to place women in public discourse as victims.

Feminists contributed another technique which prioritized experience in the period of suffrage agitation, the social survey work best represented by the Fabian Women's Group. Sally Alexander has described their work in the introduction to a set of papers edited from the pamphlets they produced. They looked at the lives of women and portrayed their findings statistically with a range of empirical data and often novel methodology. In writing *Round About a Pound a Week* Mrs Pember Reeves described the daily struggle to maintain respectability in working-class Lambeth. She demonstrated how women coped with inadequate income, large families and poor housing. The conclusion of the study was that political commentary which deplored the inadequacies of the working-class mother was misconceived; it was only due to her competence that these families kept going at all.

These writers were not historians, they were polemicists. But they were developing a newly politicized sense of narrative which, in describing the lives of women, constituted evidence to indicate that in many ways Woolf's plea was neither so novel nor so long in being met as historians of the history of women have argued. It was no accident that Virago's reclamation of works of the past as history should have started with many of these texts, themselves now primary sources for historians. They too are subject to the paradox of the history based on experience – which is the nature of the project. Much of this description is exemplary. It shows the efforts women make and the difficulties they contend with, but there always remains the centrality of their experience as potential or actual mothers to their political claims. The account is always based on the experience of the majority of British women – heterosexual, white, working-class.

## Difference celebrated

The First World War and the ten years after it saw a burgeoning of books about the position of women and the development of women's history by both professionals and amateurs. This distinction is worth attending to because publishers distinguish between the popular and the academic, with the idea of who the reader is affecting the marketing. Much history of this period was written as biography. The notion that this was an appropriate form for women's accounts of their lives was already well established. What this period showed was that Mary Astell's rueful recognition of the exclusion of women from the public concerns of history was being seen not as a disadvantage but an alternative. War itself emphasized this with what both historians and some of their contemporaries saw as a profound divide between the military and the Home Front. Separate spheres were here being written into history, and proving fruitful as a means of exploring new areas of historical investigation. Biography is often an opportunity to explore the insight of feminism and anti-feminism alike that for women the domestic, the gender-related world of love, children and the home seems more important than Parliament and court. The narrative is shaped by the genre and inherently foregrounds the personal. It is also inherently celebratory and exemplary. At the same time many of these histories can be woven together to form one history, a history of an entire gender recorded in a series of anecdotes or vignettes. Many women who worked as professional writers found this a lucrative way of maintaining an interest in the affairs of women, many feminist activists turned to instant history as a way of earning a living.[16]

Feminist authors increasingly turned to history as they constructed an explanation of the subjection of women which could be inserted into the discourses of the day. From 1913 to 1930 there was indeed a very large number of books published with titles including the word 'woman' or, more likely, if by feminists, 'women'. Most of them were not of the 'men in petticoats' variety at all. But they were most assuredly of the great deeds and actions type. In the post-war years feminist activists of the suffrage agitation still had to fight for the vote because it had only been granted to women over thirty in 1918. Many of their actions have been described as decline, as the failure of feminism – although Jane Lewis for some time has been arguing that there is no failure here, only the reordering of feminist movements.[17] The splits observed by historians of suffrage, looking for one continuous 'movement', can easily be seen as an expansion of political activism – specialization not retrenchment. While some individuals were exhausted by the struggle for the vote and the exigencies of life in wartime many others took the skills they had learned fighting for the vote into new fields – pacifism, sex reform, education, trade unionism. Those commentators who wrote about women tended to shift their attention towards the lives of the poor, the mute, mothers and workers who most suffered from the over-determination involved in describing them by the name of woman. The classic figure of the period is not Joan of Arc as before the war, it is Gorky's *Mother*. The feminist culture which had been most radically critical of the gender divisions of its day had been the suffragette movement; in the post-war period, it became the socialist feminists who looked to the infant Bolshevik state for their model of utopianism. History was thus very much engaged with questions of class and production, and feminism with the lives of working-class women and reproduction. The slogan of the campaigners who fought against the spectre of maternal mortality (which had not yet declined nearly as fast as that other great indicator of social health, infant mortality) used to argue that it was 'four times more dangerous to bear a child than to go down a coal mine'. Political activism for feminists moved away from Parliament and into everyday life. The Workers Birth Control Group included writers like Naomi Mitchison and Dora Russell, both of whom 'used' history to demonstrate the contingency which altered women's lives – in other words to make arguments for recognizing the variability of human lives, human potential for change and the creative relationship possible between human beings and nature.

## Women in production

Only a few women writers began to seek to do a new sort of
history. Ivy Pinchbeck published *Women Workers and the Industrial
Revolution* in 1930, which was the best work of its kind. Her work
fitted into a tradition in English socialism – of analysis of the
'English people' – dating back to the 1880s. In this, change rather
than stability was the subject of investigation: assessing its effect
on the poor was a way of making more important the social rather
than the national idea of the people. There was a radical claim
(not stated very emphatically) which argued that the female part
of the people was as important as the male. In other words this is
critical history in a way that much of the earlier, more celebratory
accounts of the particularity and gender-determined nature of
women in society had not been. History should, she argued, be
revised. The importance of women's entry into political life and
production was as great in assessing the impact of new forms of
society as that of men. Although Josephine Butler had written
about women's work in 1869, and Barbara Drake had produced
some excellent analysis in 1919 for the report of the War Cabinet
Committee on Women in Industry[18] on the historical explanations of women's subordination in the workplace, neither had
done any historical investigation and the history and research in
their work were profoundly utilitarian. Pinchbeck did not know
what she would find in historical investigations, while earlier
polemicists went to history with the intention to prove a case.
Hence her work represents a new development in methodology –
an implicit assumption that women have made a contribution to
civil society and that it should be investigated, rather than that
they should be described as they are described by their contemporaries. History, then, should be about the lives of women as
they were rather than the concepts of gender as used about them:
women not Woman or womanhood were the subject of history.
The sources of the account were not new, and like contemporaries who developed labour history she found much material in
the publicly available domain of official records. She was not
interested in private data or life inside the home. The assumption
was that women had been participants in the world of production
and that this was worthy of analysis and record – as it had been to
contemporary commentators.

But the further assumption was that women had entered the
important area of life through industrialization – had, as it were,

entered history properly for the first time. The argument owed a great deal to Russia, and in particular to propaganda of the early days of the Bolshevik state when, as Lenin had argued, the 'woman question' would be answered by the entry of women into productive labour. That is, if women did what men did the historic division between the sexes would no longer be of any economic or social consequence. Other Bolshevik theorists in the 1920s, especially Alexandra Kollontai, had recognized the need for that model to be modified by addressing the question of whether it was not also necessary for men to do what women do – although the way it worked in practice was to suggest that all tasks should be socialized, removed from the home. These suggestions met with less enthusiasm and the organized attack on feminism, the economic crisis and the retreat from some of the early programmes ensured that such experiments as had been (like communal kitchens, public laundries, creches) were soon abandoned.[19]

In the 1970s, in the USA, Joan Scott and Louise Tilly did the same sort of synthetic collation of social history in their account of the transition to modern industrial society. Their book's title – *Women, Work and Family* – precisely delineates the concerns of this group of professional women's historians. They had worked in academic life for some time and under pressure from the forces for change in their own lives had begun to rethink professional practice. Joan Kelly summed up such a personal history in her posthumously published essay: 'The change I went through was kaleidoscopic. I had not read a new book. I did not stumble upon a new archive. No new piece of information was added to anything I knew. . . .' But the history she had been doing was 'partial, distorted, limited, and deeply flawed by these limitations.'[20]

These women worked as academics in the United States, and the change in their focus of concern, seen in the new woman-centred history they began to write, partly evolved from the demands of their students, as well as their own re-reading of the sources they had been using. They were all thus involved in a dual professional innovation. They prioritized women but in so doing they prioritized the social as well. Much of their work indeed has been subsumed in accounts of the new social history being created in this period. Socialism or Marxism had inspired a similar emphasis on social change and many of the historians of the 1970s were socialists who began to criticize the sex-blind nature of the movements in which they operated politically, and to experience women's politics through consciousness-raising groups both in the USA and the UK. Sheila Rowbotham, who worked outside conventional academic teaching in adult education, wrote *Hidden from History*, published in 1974, partly to contribute to debates already underway within socialist feminism about the nature of women's contribution to past struggles, partly to explain her dissatisfaction with the role afforded them in struggles in the present.

History, which had been obscured by ignorance and negligence among historians, also demonstrated that both the processes of record and the selection of issues obscured women. They were hidden by those who wrote down the information which became the sources, and then buried even deeper by the disinclination of historians to ask about their contribution. Rowbotham was interested in sources not widely available, many of them in the public domain but not seen as of central importance. She wrote about women who contributed to Radical Dissenting groups – socialist suffragists, pacifists, birth-controllers, communitarians. All these women had attempted to attack the structures which oppressed women and had generated new politics themselves in so doing. She revealed new heroines, traditions within which the women's movement could place itself, heartening stories to inspire future political and historical work. She also revealed the persistent repetition of such discovery and forgetting of women's radical movements.

Rowbotham's work thus related to – while not fully supporting – the other conceptual framework which inspired much history in the 1970s, patriarchy. How far, women historians wanted to ask, was such neglect a piece of deliberate – if not either articulated or conscious – behaviour by men? As Jane Lewis wrote of this history – in *Men's Studies Modified* – a focus on women was a reordering of the priorities of history, an essentially radical act. As the book's title indicated, history along with all the other disciplines discussed would be altered simply by thinking more about women. However the structures of the account would not necessarily alter if neither sources nor questions modified the general social picture. Discussing the nature of the institutional framework by which, despite individual achievements or the effectiveness of groups of women, women in general remained subordinated, was thus involved in moving to new questions raised by trying to put women into history. This meant not centring the discussion on women themselves, not celebrating women but deploring men or more abstractly theorizing patriarchy. Thus, as Joan Kelly argued, new subjects of interest would be investigated. 'Patriarchy', she wrote in 1976, 'is at home at home. The private family is its proper domain.' Woolf's hope for an understanding of women was thus reinforced by those who wished as she did to know more about the experience of womanhood in the past in order to attack the institution of patriarchy.

Intellectual work in the late 1970s became much more separate from political struggles than it had been in the early 1970s (or alternatively, political struggle was more likely to be academic work). Women's studies courses began to appear in British universities, new journals based in the academy came to join polemical and other feminist journals. As *m/f* started publication in the late 1970s and attacked the concept of patriarchy, writers elsewhere were attempting to elaborate their descriptions of patriarchy and explain its persistence despite feminism and formal legal equality in equal pay and equal opportunities legislation of 1975 and 1976. Feminism was even less a unity than it had been in the 1910s when the division was about tactics, not about structures. However such a division was productive of much debate on domestic labour, legal status, motherhood, education and work outside the home. Most of this described the lives of working-class women. Very little of this writing was innovative in method or material, much of it was written not by historians but by economists and sociologists. This meant that it was conceptually rigorous and sophisticated but it was often based on public documents such as parliamentary commissions of enquiry – as if these were themselves not in need of critical attention. For example, to assume that the account of women's labour in mining given in the parliamentary commissions is neutral, gender-blind in the way it portrays women in mining is, as Angela John has argued, to ignore one of the fundamental revisions that feminist history should have created in the use of official texts by any historian.[21] Much of the historical work produced by writers grappling with the questions of domestic labour, of unionization and socio-legal constraints on women's success thus slotted into a debate which inspired investigative research projects – which take time to complete.

## Gender and deconstruction

But in what sense did this change in academic history bring change in methodology or a change in sources consulted? Much of the work published in the 1980s was secondary in type – rather than being devoted to new archives or styles of historical writing it reordered the old. (New techniques concentrating on experience – oral history, collective biography – were characteristic of feminist history but not peculiar to it.) There was thus a profound interrogation, deconstruction and critique of influential historical works, particularly in social history. This process has continued up until the present with illuminating results especially in Joan Scott's *Gender and the Politics of History* (1988). She criticized some historians who have claimed support for feminist ideals, especially the group who produce *History Workshop*, for simply failing to see the implications of some of the things they are saying. Does this represent a rupture between feminist historians or a fruitful development which should stimulate new work? In many ways the concentration on discourse by most contemporary feminists writing history is a blind alley in the practice of history because it is so self-referential within history itself. To undertake an historical account of the state of feminism which would do justice to this shift would be difficult, but several main factors would seem to be: the development of interdisciplinary and other courses in women's studies in the UK, which necessarily involves a lot of overview work preparing lectures for students and introducing them to the field; greatly diminished time for original research; and the stage of academic life that many eminent women have reached – wanting to take stock, look backwards and sum up the experiences of their working lives. Secondly, less material considerations lead to the elaboration of theory that is based not on new historical studies but critiques of men's work – mainly the development in social and political theory of the work of the French theorists Michel Foucault, Jacques Derrida and Jacques Lacan.

Why have feminists been so much more deferential to these theorists – who all write mostly about male lives, desires and speech – than to their feminist, or female heirs? The theoretical contribution of deconstruction to the study of texts has been profound, and historians study texts, and lives described as texts.

However the nature of the historical project is to use a variety of sources to create a text in the history they write. Hence the mediations of any one point of view in the time that has elapsed, the nature of the social context in which the view was produced, and the fate which the view-point endured through the accidents of survival into the present are an essential part of the historical assessment. There are historians who write about 'experience' as the authentic representation of the 'real' but most do not. Feminist accounts of the discourse of a day have to assess competing descriptions of a life or a phenomenon. But to assume that they are not different one from the other is to disempower women as historical and political agents. If accounts of women are merely ventriloquism when they are by women, the assumption that it is possible to act as a feminist appears to be discountenanced. If the path of French theoreticians is followed and their assumption that feminine writing and female language have to be developed to create a humane and womanly world then women are excluded from the language of common humanity and thus from power. Hence the conclusion that such work in effect reaches – that historical study gives us only the world of the dominant male voice, produces critical commentary on texts, but does not produce history.[22] The history that disdains the texts which are not about individual subjects – the data on maternal mortality, for example – is intrinsically denying the material. The history which recognizes that the data is produced and reproduced by men and women in different ways is only doing the basic job of questioning the sources. I return to the slogan of the 1920s, that it was 'four times more dangerous to bear a child than go down a coal mine'. The statistic is dubious but the politics are interesting. Lady Rhondda wanted women to be able to mine, maternalists wanted to protect mothers: both could exploit the slogan.

The ideas that did resonate and inform were those which directed the historian's attention to the nature of the text and the nature of the subjectivity of the woman who looked at the text. Hence Sally Alexander was able to use the central Lacanian theme of women as 'lack' to look at both absences and presences in public discourse, to articulate the shaping principles of nineteenth-century women's descriptions of their role as heart of a heartless world. But this concept of men as 'labour', women as 'love', is one that is there in the materials of historical study – it is the systematic recognition of that presence that is new.[23]

I share Linda Gordon's question as to how far the history produced by some work of textual analysis which queries the notion of historical agency is new or different, except in the nature of its subject.[24] I share her doubts too about the evidence of productivity in feminist history – looking at the volume of critique and seeing this as the production of theory. Such scepticism is not of the value of this work which focuses on texts and on discourses – it is valuable and it helps understanding – but it is a doubt as to the need for this to be all that goes on in the name of feminism. This doubt is created by the self-referential nature of the critique, as if the real force for women's oppression is the latest argument in a historical journal, when in fact the problems for most women, especially for feminists, may well lie in the field of political campaigning where history's lesson is only that women need always to defend their advances because they are rarely left alone to enjoy them undisturbed. Or, in other words, that the immediate needs and demands of feminism cannot be said to be necessarily linked to the historical project as they were until the mid 1970s. The study of women in history – which was mostly initiated by feminism – has been detached from the political project of feminism as it has developed its own structures, its own leaders and bureaucracy. In England there are now the journals *Gender and History*, and *Women's History Review*, there are several newly created professors who are pleased to call themselves specialists in women's history, several postgraduate courses in the field and numerous ones in undergraduate and adult education. Weber was quite right to see such processes as advances towards modernization – I in no way wish to suggest they are to be deplored – but they do of course lead to divergences among those pursuing the subject, feminist history.

One difference lies between those who study women's history and those who study gender. Among the latter are two of the leading names in feminist history – Leonore Davidoff and Catherine Hall – who produced in their book on the Victorian family and industrialization (*Family Fortunes*) an extremely powerful synthesis of their own researches in Birmingham and East Anglia and the secondary reading on the period which accounted for the development of the theories and practices of gender held by the Georgian and Victorian middle class. To adapt Marx, they show very clearly how women 'make their own history but not in circumstances of their own choosing.' Some of the history they relate refers in passing to women who had pronounced ideas about change in the position of women, and they hint, as other historians of the early Victorians have, that in many ways the elaboration of sexual difference was precisely the force which did most to undermine its dominance in the construction of the political order. This argues that to understand the history of feminism we need to look at what women think and do, not only at what is thought about and done to them.

What then is the sort of work being produced on the history of feminism? How feminist is it? Certainly the slow, arduous process of historical investigation is beginning to use or generate new data, and in so doing is filling in some of the absences from history of the past. The political claims of its practitioners are though less bold, more within the field of professionalism in history than politics. No longer is it necessary to write either as if all women were frustrated feminists prevented by men from realizing their 'true' natures, or as if those women who were feminists were deviant, 'women in trousers' rather than 'men in petticoats'. Feminists were very much like activists in other fields, subject to the structures and constraints of their own time, perhaps more critical of some of the dominant modes of thought, but not immune to them in a sort of 'sentimental priesthood', which was what Helena Swanwick argued in 1913 that they were seen to be becoming.

If historians of gender wished to account for the fact that most women live with men as well as other women and children, and that the negotiation of those relationships is as much a matter for the women as the men, historians of women have had to investigate the ways in which women rule other women, and reinforce oppressive attitudes and practices, particularly in societies with highly defined separate roles for classes, creeds or colours as well as genders. Hence the continuing interest in women's political organizations where womanhood is a central concern. Three recent books have looked at feminism as a movement: Sandra Stanley Holton's *Feminism and Democracy* (1986) investigates the political theory of militant and consti-tutional campaigners for the vote and concludes eloquently that they shared much in political philosophy and were mutually reinforcing in their campaigns; Philippa Levine's *Victorian Femin-ism* argues that women activists before the vote had an elaborate politics and strategy which should not be subordinated to the tracing back of suffrage agitation; Hal Smith's collection, *British Feminism in the Twentieth Century* (1990), emphasizes that this is not a single force waxing and waning but one which must be seen in its plurality. These books are all based on new sources, go beyond the public data of journals, books and official publications, and continue to make clear the error of the 1970s feminists who arrogantly lumped together this rich and varied past as 'first-wave' feminism.

Patricia Hollis looked at another sort of women's activism in her study of women who were active in local government after they won the right to vote and to stand for office in 1894. Her *Ladies Elect* looks at these energetic, successful local politicans who did so much to shape the institutions with which we all live. As in all these empirical studies the theoretical claims are not strongly stated but the reader should be able to see very clearly that they share a rejection of assumptions that women are a unitary category, that women are victims, that womanhood as a concept determines – rather than that their own activity shapes – their lives.

The debate between Linda Gordon and Joan Scott in *Signs* over the nature of the historian's enterprise has summarized the main divide on difference in stark detail. Gordon accuses Scott of neglecting material realities and divisions between women as demonstrated by looking at their experience of everyday life; Scott feels that Gordon is uncritical of the extent to which women's representation of their own experience is mediated through their habitation of the discourses of their own day. This is in part an argument about method. Does the historian look at endless minutiae of material existence, like Gordon's court proceedings, or does she look at what people write about women, or sex, or about power, like the essays collected by Higonnet and others in the collection on the Two World Wars called *Behind the Lines* (which has a foreword by Scott). This looks at the construction of discourses of gender, but very little at lives or experience. Gordon's comment that writers of history are still treating lives as texts without independent moral judgments of the status of the texts is probably correct, but equally problematic is Gordon's own use of the concept of social control which she attacks as denying her subjects historical agency – when, as Joan Scott argues, it might be better to theorize agency as itself a discursive effect. The dispute ends with Scott accusing Gordon of 'resisting' theory but concludes with the comment that

it is the nature of feminism to disturb the ground it stands on, even its own ground; the resistance to theory is a resistance to the most radical effects of feminism itself. Such resistance then is a sign not of decline or disarray but of the vitality of this critical movement.[25]

There is a strong sense in this exchange of the more-political-than-thou attitude characteristic of debates within feminism. Nevertheless the recognition of intellectual difference is a sign of strength, of firm location of feminism in the academy of history. In the United States feminist historians were to be found on both sides in the Seears case (brought under anti-discrimination legislation) in which one side used the arguments of sexual difference to justify unequal treatment; the other argued that these were rationalizations of oppression and should be contradicted, not supported, in the interests of women.

The women who write women's history or feminist history are many. Woolf's plea for a history less lop-sided has begun to be met. But do women figure there without impropriety? There is a sense in which they do not yet do so. It is only when women figure in all the courses of history that, it seems, feminism will have achieved success by becoming a part of the norms of historical investigation, and that is a long way off. There remains a para-dox at the heart of the relationship between feminism and history – that to prioritize the simple, single divide of gender is to make visible the one feature of life that may systematically oppress women or, if celebrated as an alternative view of the hierarchy of power, disempower them in a world of common humanity. To talk of woman is to hide the individual woman or to reduce her to what is the lowest common denominator in her life and that of others. Woolf's ironical plea for discretion is perhaps a double-edged reminder of how femininity and feminism can so easily be confused; how what *should be* is affected by what *is* and what *was* but not, ultimately, determined by them. Feminist writers of the past illuminate many of the options that face women writers of history in the present, but the material base of producing history is much broader than before, so is the institutional support. Still, the claim by Liz Stanley that all women produce theory is clearly true – we all have stories we tell of our own lives, our place in society and that of other names we call ourselves and others. However neither all women nor all feminists produce history. With cuts in part-time educational provision and educational re-sources like archives and libraries, that is increasingly in the UK something done by professionals – that is, in the academy.

In conclusion, are there no doubts about the validity of the whole enterprise? Would women do better just to get on with doing history competently and professionally as we know they can, and would that be enough? No, because the central concern of feminism, which is to explain and thus undermine the oppression of women, in no sense can be guaranteed by the fact that a woman is doing it. That is a problem of the assumption that there is any correlation between gender and political attitude. Of feminist history as an enterprise then there are few doubts; of its non-identical twin, women's history there are. Without an assumption of value, of political purpose, there seems little point in simply knowing more and more about women, but then that is to go, as the question of what history is *for* usually does, beyond the frame of inquiry. Feminism has given history an enormously improved understanding of one of the fundamental divides in society, the one between the sexes, and it has given an improved understanding of why it is that a divide is also a structure of dominance; and that uncomfortable truth means that the impropriety remains, the grit which continues to produce pearls. The tension remains between a history which raises the question of one fundamental difference between the two sexes and how that discourse works, and a history which looks at women and their experience of differences – but only histories which allow for both will gain from the twin insights feminism has brought to history; either alone will remain a little lop-sided.

## References

The place of publication is London unless indicated otherwise.

1. Wollstonecraft, M. (1792). *A Vindication of the Rights of Woman*. J. Johnson.
2. de Beauvoir, S. (1969). *The Second Sex*. Harmondsworth, Penguin.
3. Pankhurst, C. (1913) 'The Great Scourge and How to End It'. Published by E. Pankhurst.
4. Fawcett, M.G. (1920). *The Woman's Victory and After*. Sidgwick and Jackson.
5. Elton, G. (1984). *The History of England*. Inaugural lecture delivered 26 January 1984. Cambridge, Cambridge University Press.
6. Scott, J.W. (1988). *Gender and the Politics of History*. Columbia University Press.
7. Mary Astell, (1700) *Some Reflections upon Marriage*, (p. 88), quoted in Perry, R. (1976). *The Celebrated Mary Astell*. University of Chicago Press, p. 9.

8. Mary Astell, (1705), *The Christian Religion as Professed by a Daughter of the Church of England*, (p. 293), quoted in Perry (1976).
9. Dworkin, A. (1987). *Intercourse*. Secker and Warburg.
10. Mackinnon, C. (1989). *Towards a Feminist Theory of the State*. Harvard University Press.
11. C. Pankhurst, in Sheila Jeffreys (ed.) (1988) *The Sexuality Debates*, Routledge and Kegan Paul.
12. Tickner, L. (1987). *The Spectacle of Women: Imagery of the Suffrage Campaign*. Chatto and Windus.
13. Foucault, M. (1979). *The History of Sexuality*. Trans. R. Hurley. Allen Lane.
14. Such historians include: Sheila Jeffreys, *The Spinster and Her Enemies*, (1985) and *The Sexuality Debates* (1988); Jeffrey Weeks, *Sexuality* (1986); Lilian Faderman, *Surpassing the Love of Men* (1981). See also Jane Lewis, *Labour and Love* (1986), especially the chapter by Lucy Bland; and Judith Walkowitz, *Prostitution and Victorian Society* (1980).
15. Virginia Woolf, 'Life as We Have Known It', quoted in Joan Scott (1988), p. 15.
16. Dodd, K. *Women's Studies International Forum*, vol. 13, 1/2, 1990, has written recently on the partisan nature of Ray Strachey's *The Cause*; also in this category should come Sylvia Pankhurst's own histories of the period, *The Suffragette Movement* (1932) and *The Home Front* (1931), and Vera Brittain's *Testament of Youth* (1933) which fictionalized diary information. These represent the problem of evidence that 'experience' poses in that all texts are mediations – but this is a problem in any historical investigation.
17. Jane Lewis, 'Beyond sufferage: English feminism in the 1920s', *The Maryland Historian*, 7, Spring, 1975.
18. Josephine Butler, (1869). *Womens' Work and Woman's Culture*. Macmillan. Drake, B. Historical Survey to the Report of the War Cabinet Committee on 'Women in Industry', Parliamentary Papers, 1919, Cmd 139.
19. Stites, R. (1978). *Womens' Liberation in Russia*, Princeton University Press; Edmondson, L. (1984). *Feminism in Russia*, Heinemann.
20. Joan Kelly also came from the tradition of American Marxism, see further her account in the posthumously published essays *Women, History and Theory*, (1984), Chicago University Press.
21. John, A. (1984), *By the Sweat of their Brow*, Routledge and Kegan Paul; and reply to Jane Humphries in the long-running debate between Humphries and other socialist feminists on the question of the family wage (which here reflects a difference about sources), in *Feminist Review*, 1981, 7 and 9, Spring and Autumn.
22. Swindells, J. (1985). *Victorian Writing and Working Women*. Cambridge, Polity. In opposition to this view see, Stanley, L. 'Recovering women in history from feminist deconstructionism', *Women's Studies*

*International Forum*, 13, 1/2, 1990, p. 155: 'people not as they *really* but actually are constructed and construct themselves' is how she sums up this standpoint, or as a 'materially experientially grounded epistemology'.
23. Alexander, Sally. (1987). Unpublished paper delivered at *History Workshop* Conference.
24. Gordon, L., in T. de Lauretis (ed.) (1988) *Feminist Studies/Critical Studies*. Basingstoke, Macmillan.
25. L. Gordon and J. Scott reviewing each other's books in *Signs*, Summer 1990, pp. 848–860; the quotation is from Scott, p. 860.

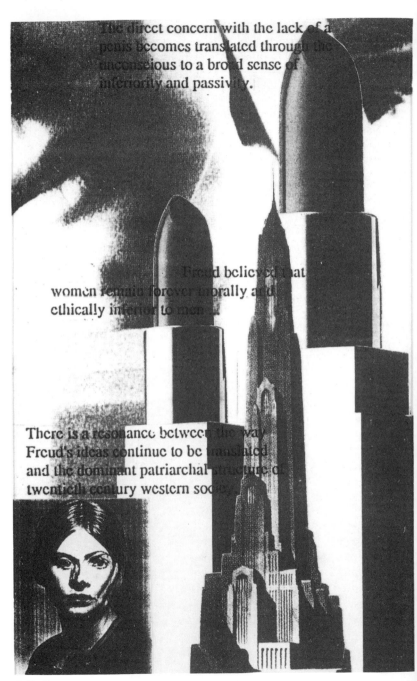

The direct concern with the lack of a
penis becomes translated through the
unconscious to a broad sense of
inferiority and passivity.

Freud believed that
women remain forever morally and
ethically inferior to men ...

There is a resonance between the way
Freud's ideas continue to be translated
and the dominant patriarchal structure of
twentieth century western society.

*Julia Groves*

academic
vards a
vomen?

## Introduction

Even when men and women are together, they elicit
different responses. A woman is not responded to by a man
in the same way that a man is responded to. This alone
makes the situation different for the man and woman being
responded to. Nor do men and women see one another in
the same way. The research literature by men (and by
women who have been trained by men) portrays women as
basically passive and dependent. This portrayal does in fact
reflect the way women tend to behave vis-à-vis men or in the
presence of men, so that the passive-dependent image
seems entirely valid from the perspective of the male world.
(Bernard 1981: 5)

This extract from Bernard conveys the essence of academic
psychology, both in terms of the way the discipline is structured
and its content. Men do not only control and organize academic
psychology but, as part of that process, they control the knowledge-claims that circumscribe the discipline. The extract also
draws attention to the complexities of the interpenetration of
'knowledge' and behaviour, which supports existing patriarchal
structures by defining the way that knowledge of women's
psychology is portrayed.

In this chapter I review the ways in which men control the
practice and knowledge-claims of psychology. It has been the
broader feminist debate that has made possible a feminist

analysis of psychology. Following feminist influences, my writing demonstrates some of the ways I have begun to think about the experience of being a female academic psychologist with a specific research and teaching interest in the pyschology of women – and, in particular, issues relating to the psychology of women's health. I first explore the gender composition of academic psychology, then consider the way that its 'knowledge' of female psychology has been constructed under men's control, and the interpenetration of this knowledge and popular ideas. The emergence of a critical feminist voice in psychology, along with examples of its key challenges to the traditional bio-medical model employed in psychology to explain women's lives, is the focus of what follows.

### Women in psychology: the emerging voice of feminism

Despite the enduring resistance of individual women to gender bias in academic psychology (Sherif 1987), it was not until the 1970s that a coherent voice of feminist scholarship began to emerge in both the USA and UK (see Chetwynd and Hartnett 1978). Attempts to establish an audience within the psychological community led to the genesis of Division 35 of the American Psychological Association (APA) for the study of the psychology of women. It took another ten years for the emergence of the British Psychological Society's (BPS) Psychology of Women Section in the UK (briefly preceded by Women in Psychology in 1985). Australia, Canada and New Zealand have now also formed coherent groups, although as yet without the weight of formal recognition. All of these organizations developed from intensive struggles which were strongly resisted by the associations concerned (see Burns 1990; Wilkinson 1990a).

These initiatives have been accompanied by the formalization of the dissemination of feminist knowledge in journals (*Psychology of Women Quarterly* and *Feminism and Psychology*), regular newsletters, a growing number of books, conferences, and symposia at broader-based psychology conferences; the opportunity for political and academic initiatives such as working parties (for example, gender representation within the BPS, see Wilkinson 1990b; courses on the psychology of women and gender relations, see Nicholson *et al.* 1990); and women occupying places on influential committees within professional organizations (see Nicolson 1992). It is only because women have been able to develop a specific feminist analysis of psychology from within – and on the margins of – psychology itself that what follows has become possible.

## Gender issues and academic psychology

The energy and enthusiasm accompanying all of this has been in stark contrast to the resistance (both overt and covert) of the academic world to the psychology of women and feminist psychology as legitimate areas of study within the psychology curriculum. This resistance is often directed towards the women who teach and research in these areas (Kagan and Lewis 1990a, 1990b). It varies in form from open verbal abuse, physical and emotional sexual harassment, to criticism of women's ability to organize their domestic/childcare arrangements to fit in with current (male-defined and structured) professional practices. It also takes a more covert form in that essential formal and informal meetings occur out of 'office' hours so that women who need to make childcare arrangements are potentially excluded. In the longer term, women's life patterns, often punctuated differently from men's, do not reflect the image of the high-flying academic in that they have not achieved prescribed 'productivity goals' by the age of thirty-five. Promotion or even academic appointments at all after that are less easily achieved (Nicolson and Phillips 1990).

This resistance is hardly surprising, as traditionally the academic community has a reactionary attitude to women's scholarship, as witnessed in Britain by the fact that only 3% of senior academic posts are held by women, and that since the changes at Oxford and Cambridge from single sex colleges men have been appointed to tenured posts in former women's colleges without the same happening in reverse (Hansard Society Commission 1990). A survey of university and polytechnic psychology departments in the UK and Eire (conducted by the BPS in 1986) showed that women comprise only 22.2% of academic staff and 15.9% of senior academic staff (see Kagan and Lewis 1990b). Fellowships (recognition of outstanding contributions to the discipline of psychology) awarded by the BPS show an overwhelming proportion of male recipients over females (by 1989 this was 513 men to 73 women over all, Morris *et al.* 1990a); similarly in the USA (in 1988) only 17.7% of the APA Fellowships had been awarded to women (APA 1988).

These severe imbalances in the gender ratios had not been considered as worthy of comment until the various psychology of women groups began to demand a review of gender representation at all levels of the profession (Wilkinson 1990b; Nicolson 1992). However, a re-defined 'gender imbalance' caused by an influx of female undergraduates has concerned the psychology establishment (at present around 79% of entrants to first year undergraduate courses in British universities are women):

> The gender imbalance amongst psychology applicants, with four fifths of first year psychologists being female, is an issue that needs addressing. Is it that psychology is particularly attractive to female applicants or are potential male applicants deterred for some reason? (Morris *et al.* 1990b: 10)

Gender is only accepted as a valid issue in psychology when men are potentially disadvantaged: the urgent question now is 'Why is psychology not attracting men?' A similar pattern may be identified in the prolonged and dramatic resistance to significant numbers of women entering clinical psychology, with the plea by Humphrey and Haward (1981) to avoid the dilution of the profession. This was echoed later:

> Almost all current trainees are female. The trend toward an increasingly female intake was first commented on in . . . [1981, see above]. The trend has indeed continued and I believe there is cause for concern. First, there is the practical problem of a nearly all-female profession providing services to men. If the situation were reversed I am sure there would be numerous letters of complaint from women and quite rightly so. However, the problems of a female dominated profession are not just the mirror image of a male dominated one. Whilst the BPS adheres to a non-sexist policy, the world at large is not necessarily so enlightened. National pay rates for women are significantly below those for men. . . . As pay and status in clinical psychology have fallen, so men are no longer being attracted into the profession. (Crawford 1989: 30)

This extract demonstrates the thinly veiled misogyny inherent in psychology: it is a cause for men's concern that women might have professional power over male clients, let alone male psychologists. Crawford's identification of discriminatory practices leads him to demand their exacerbation, rather than challenge them. Despite the limp disclaimer in this extract (line eight), most female clients of clinical psychologists have traditionally been offered a male-dominated service without any acknowledgement of the ensuing tension. Equally retrogressive ideas have currency in the USA where a marked ambivalence towards the increasing number of women with psychology PhDs is evident, as seen here: 'Although the increase in women PhD recipients is a positive development, serious questions have been raised about psychology becoming a female-dominated profession with the loss of prestige and financial remuneration usually evident in such situations' (APA 1988: 9).

The contrast here between the 'liberal' profession of psychology and the supposedly 'reactionary' legal profession, which has introduced an Equal Opportunities policy to actively encourage women undergraduates' professional advancement (Hansard Society Commission, 1990), suggests just how far patriarchy is entrenched in psychology in general and academic psychology in particular. Overt sexism has been accompanied by more subtle forms of male supremacy which have recently been documented by women psychologists who have been at the receiving end (Burman 1990).

## Knowledge, power and ideology in academic psychology

It is not only issues of equal opportunities that are at stake. There is an instrinsic relationship between the vested interests of the dominant group in relation to knowledge-claims and practices (Foucault 1973; Philp 1985) which extends beyond simply maintaining jobs for the boys. Mainstream academic psychology exists within a tradition of knowledge accumulation rather than one within which the nature and consequences of that knowledge is problematized:

> The orthodox answer to the question 'How did psychology come to be what it is?' is that psychology is a science and, as such, is guaranteed through its methods' progress towards knowledge of that part of nature that it takes as its object. This begs a supplementary question, however, a question on the terrain of philosophy of science that would probably not be thought at issue in orthodox psychology: what is the character of that knowledge and how can we know that science guarantees its truthfulness? (Hollway 1989: 87)

The ethos within academic psychology is one in which its methods and objects of study are deemed to have transcended the plane of ideas and questioning. There is an atmosphere which suggests the truth has been identified and the continuing progress towards its discovery is well under way – to question its findings and methods is contrary to the spirit of inquiry in psychology, and inimical to 'truth'. The development of critical feminist analysis, borrowing from and sharing the analytic tools of sociology, literary criticism and social psychology, has specifically enabled understanding of this process, and provided opportunities for challenge and change. Without an awareness of the structure of scientific knowledge and its relation to power, the overwhelming use of the bio-medical model in psychology to explain gender differences and women's psychology would remain unquestioned. As I demonstrate below, a naive reductionist approach to psychology via this bio-medical model has constructed a version of women's psychology which portrays them as *deficient* in relation to men, explained as a consequence of an intrinsically problematic female biology. It is a reductionist, bio-medical deficit model of women and femininity that informs not only psychological knowledge and practice, but penetrates popular knowledge, which includes women's self-image and cognitions.

Academic psychology relies largely upon a reductionist perspective towards its subject matter, and adopts a positivist approach towards its investigations (see Reason and Rowan 1981). Feminist psychology, alongside other internal critiques of the discipline (particularly from social psychology) has challenged both conceptual and methodological perspectives (see Harre and Secord 1972; Reason and Rowan 1981; Wilkinson 1986; Ussher 1992). The development of critical feminism and a feminist psychology of women has sought to be less 'ego-centric' than mainstream psychology and has elaborated alternative conceptual frameworks and appropriate methods derived from sociology, psychoanalysis and historical and literary theory (see, for example, Hollway, 1989), in particular the method of deconstruction through which the meaning of texts can be analysed in terms of ideology. As I demonstrate in the second part of this chapter, when psychological concepts are used in research literature as if they are unproblematic, it becomes possible, through deconstruction, to trace the values which underpin them. This method essentially problematizes all concepts and demands a re-evaluation of taken-for-granted ideas – such as post-natal depression and sexuality (see Weedon 1987).

The critique of the bio-medical model and the subsequent development of a feminist psychology of women and gender relations have emerged from both a deconstruction of medical and psychological texts which refer to female psychology, and an analysis of women's accounts of their own lives by women researchers (see Oakley 1980; Ussher 1989; Nicolson 1990a and b). The employment of a deficit model of female psychology is linked to the female biological capacities to become pregnant, give birth and lactate. These processes are portrayed as ensuring women's vulnerability, emotional instability and essentially passive and nurturant nature (see Bernard 1981 quoted at the start of this chapter). This approach is further supported by traditional prescriptions for female (hetero)sexuality (Jackson 1987; Jeffreys 1990; Nicolson 1990a and b).

In what follows I identify the origins of the way that psychological science constructs female psychology based upon mythological assertions about female biology. I then concentrate upon deconstructing the established model of the psychology of women as deficient in relation to men. My overall aim is to suggest how these discourses constrain explanations of female psychology; and how their deconstruction potentially provides greater diversity in conceptualization and emancipates the psychology of women.

## The psychology of women: the other side of the story

Why is a critical feminist analysis of the psychology of women apparently so threatening to academic psychologists? Psychology's claim that it is gender 'blind' or 'neutral' may be disputed on even a cursory acquaintance with the discipline's subject matter. Throughout its brief history, academic psychology has provided a clear message (implicit by default) on the psychology of women. It has:

> . . . not only omitted the consideration of women and women's activities, it has also validated the view that those activities in which men engage are the activities central to human life. It re-affirms that women are "backstage" to the "real" action. (Crawford and Maracek 1989: 149)

Women in almost all spheres of psychological concern (such as intellectual and work performance, motor skills, sexuality) seem to contrast unfavourably with men (see Ungar 1979; Ussher 1989; Nicolson 1991a and b). Indeed, even some feminist psychology has been in danger of employing a model of overall deficiency in women (Crawford and Maracek 1989), in that research by feminist psychologists over the past two decades has often attempted to describe and account for women's oppression by confirming their 'fear of success' (Horner 1970); or focused on 'exceptional women' (Lopate 1968), thereby emphasizing the incapacities of the majority. What is clear, though, is that in order to make a 'scientific' study of human psychology, it is essential to take the influence of culture and context into account. If a systematic psychology of women is to be developed, it has to attend to the value systems within which women live their lives, and to the way that women's and men's lives are related (see, for example, Hollway 1989). As one woman psychologist observed:

> Gender is inescapable. It is probably the most important determinant of any individual's life experience. For the two sexes exist in different social worlds with widely divergent pressures, rewards and expectations. In many areas of life there is no truly human experience. There is only female experience and male experience. (Rohrbaugh 1981: 3–4)

The degree to which these divergent worlds influence individual experience and position individuals in relation to the dominant value system is central to an analysis of women's psychology. The emergence of feminism as a clear (if not influential) force in academic psychology has enabled questions to be asked about women's psychology which traditionally have been avoided. Feminists in psychology recognize the centrality of questions about the characteristics of women's psychology, and how far women's and men's lives and behaviour are different, and why.

A complex picture is now being built up, within which there are debates and contrasting critiques (see Ussher 1992). Patriarchal psychology concurs with the gender difference model, but avoids the problem of causation. It borrows from and lends support to a mythology of women which is culturally pervasive, informing both popular knowledge and scientific research questions in psychology. As indicated in the following extract, it is wholly detrimental to women's emancipation and gender equality:

> Women have been seen as incarnations of both the highest good and the basest evil, of chastity and of lust, of virtue and

deceit, and the sacred and the profane. Men, and women who are co-opted by the prevalent male view, have rarely been able to perceive women simply as human beings with the same range of idiosyncrasies as themselves. Rather, they have had to make myths to explain their awesome differences and their strange powers. (Williams, 1987 :1)

This characterizes both the popular *mythology* of 'feminine nature' and a psychology of women that assumes *essential* gender differences – to the extent that some researchers were convinced they could distinguish between female and male brain structures (Sheilds 1974). The origins of this view can be traced to Darwin (see Unger 1979). The underlying assumption in this uncritical model is that women are the physically and intellectually deficient counterparts of men.

## Biological essentialism and the myth of female psychology

As I have stressed, there is a circular relationship between science and popular culture or mythology. Popular mythology to some degree informs all members of a culture, particularly if that mythology upholds their own value system. The mythology of female psychology (Williams 1987; Ussher 1989) is very much that of *women as the other*, and this view clearly forms the ideological basis of the study of the psychology of women – as men (or male-influenced women) control science. Science is influential not only within its own community, but in society as a whole via popular outlets from media reporting of knowledge to self-help books and even jokes. There is the further consideration that popular knowledge informs self-cognition and self-images, so that women evaluate themselves in the context of the popular scientific discourses (see Potter and Wetherell 1987). Thus as Bernard (1981) has indicated, it sometimes appears that the scientific version is indeed correct as the objects of scientific investigation actually behave in accordance with it in research experiments. The picture is reinforced by the exclusion of evidence that fails to correspond to the existing 'wisdom' (see Richardson, 1991a).

I now want to explore in some detail this deficit model of women's psychology and identify the mythology informing the version of women constructed in mainstream academic psychology. Although not overtly influential in it, probably the most

explanation of female psychology and femininity that
₅ to and upholds that mythology, both within it and
..y uay discourse, is that of Freud (1933), who was concerned
with the relationship between psychic development and the
gendered human body.

Freud's framework of psychological development depended
on the resolution of the Oedipal crisis at around the age of five or
six. This occurs through complex unconscious processes
whereby children become aware of the long-term implications of
their genitals gained from *identification* with the same-sex parent.
This *identification* has implications for behaviour, motivation and
the dynamics through which these are learned. There are,
however, some significant variations in the strength of these
identifications, which occur in part for girls with the discovery
that they *lack* penises. The direct concern with this lack becomes
translated, through the unconscious, into a broad sense of
inferiority and passivity; and because they hold their mothers
responsible for the lack of this highly valued object, and realize
that not only their mothers but all women lack penises, girls
begin to regard men with profound envy, and join them in
regarding women as inferior. Part of the subsequent resolution of
the Oedipal crisis is the development of the superego (con-
science) function of the psyche. Women do not identify as
strongly with authority as men, because they do not have so
much to lose. Thus they develop a weaker superego than men.
For this reason *Freud believed that women remain forever morally and
ethically inferior to men.*

The most important aspect of Freudian psychology in this
context is the way that his theories of femininity and masculinity
have *penetrated everyday understanding.* Although Freud cannot be
'blamed' for gender inequalitites, the continued employment of
literal and symbolic representations of the penis as a valued
object is present in popular mythology. Accordingly Mitchell
(1974), discussing the resolution of the Oedipal conflict, argues
that Freud's version of gender roles should be seen as symboliz-
ing the patterns of power and social order in society as represented within the family. Thus the boy identifies with his father
and all men because he acknowledges their power, and the girl is
reluctant to identify with her mother and all women because she
becomes aware of their oppression. In the 1970s there was a
'scientific revival' of the emphasis on women's reproductive roles
as setting the parameters of their psychological lives. Wilson

(1978) challenged the impact of feminism upon gender roles by arguing that change would damage the gene pool of society. His approach was 'aggressively marketed' (see Bleier 1984) so that his representations of traditional gender differences in behaviour as being 'naturally' evolved penetrated popular knowledge.

Despite challenges to these reductionist orthodoxies (Sayers 1982), re-evaluations of research on gender differences (Maccoby and Jacklin 1974), and Bem's work on psychological androgyny and gender schema theory (Bem 1974; 1981), the *models* of feminine psychology employed in practical applications of psychology reflect these reductionist explanations of gender roles and relations. They link the ability to become pregnant and give birth to nurturant and submissive qualitites in female psychology. Some feminists also see women's reproductive role as central to female psychology:

> Women's dependence on and hence exploitation by men is, they said, the direct consequence of the fact that women bear and are therefore responsible for raising children (eg. Dunbar 1970). Radical feminists thus often agree with anti-feminist biological determinists in viewing women's dependence on men as the effect of a biologically determined relation *between* childbearing and childrearing. (Sayers 1982: 187–188)

Overt recognition of the role of mythology in psychological science necessarily underlies any critical analysis, most especially since mythology 'informs' the popular consciousness of women and men, providing everyday explanations for apparent gender differences. For this reason scientists have a responsibility to problematize mythology and scrutinize the extent to which they themselves rely upon it. As I demonstrate below, critical feminist challenges within psychology are aimed at dislodging the mythological psychology of women currently active within the biomedical model.

## The construction of the female body

The mythological woman, then, embraces a variety of qualitites which are available within scientific discourse. To summarize, women's reproductive capacity circumscribes their physiological and psychological existence – and takes on specific meanings and characteristics. Women are heterosexual, passive, nurturant, envious of the male, less ethical and, because their hormones move through regular cycles, they become unpredictable, which renders them less rational than the male. They are mysterious objects in the gaze of the male scientist, for whom a woman is apt to be 'set apart as a creature not governed by the normal patterns of thought and behaviour. Given her mysterious powers, capricious moods, and feminine wiles, what baffled man can understand women? Clearly she is from a separate world' (Rohrbaugh 1981: 5).

This inacessible image is not far removed from woman as the object of romantic love. It has its origins in mythology, is manifested in the bio-medical construction of women, and has not changed substantially since the late nineteenth and early twentieth century. Contemporary clinical psychologists and medical writers do not appear to have challenged nineteenth-century notions of female psychology which predominated in medical texts where women were portrayed as illogical and weak and particularly vulnerable to their reproductive cycles (Ussher 1989). As the President of the American Gynaecological Society, Dr Englemann, graphically suggested in 1900,

> Many a young life is battered and forever crippled on the breakers of puberty; if it crosses these unharmed and is not dashed to pieces on the rock of childbirth, it may still ground on the ever-recurring shallows of menstruation, and lastly upon the final bar of the menopause ere protection is found in the unruffled waters of the harbour beyond reach of sexual storms. (Ehrenreich and English 1979: 99, quoted from Rothstein 1972: 47)

In other words, women are at the mercy of a problematic biology. Two feminist historians summarized the implications of this attitude in the past, whereby women were urged to conserve their energies for biological reproduction and men for higher, intellectual functions. It was feared that if women were too intellectual, they would damage their reproductive abilities (Ehrenreich and English 1979: 114). Women were ill-equipped for intellectual activity, and even if they should aspire in this direction, it might be inappropriate and even dangerous! Richardson (1991b) notes that engaging in any intellectual work at all was seen to jeopardize women's reproductive capacity.

This distinction between the 'natures' of women and men drawn one hundred and fifty years ago remains. It directly underlies the questions which are asked about women in current psychological and medical research in areas where their bodies are seen as vulnerable – the menstrual cycle, pregnancy, childbirth, female sexuality and the menopause. It also underlies the questions asked in other areas – are women able to perform as well as men on cognitive tasks? Are women able to be logical in their behaviour and attitudes towards others? Is it appropriate to give women responsibility and power?

Women continue to be seen as at the mercy of their raging hormones (Ussher 1989) and it is only through assessing the nature of the questions asked within psychology that it is possible to conceptualize them in a less prescriptive way. A recent study notes,

> Women and men produce ideas about menstruation, and these ideas often come into conflict . . . men have social power over women, and therefore male definitions will tend to predominate within the culture. For the same reasons, the male perspective is more accessible to the researcher than a 'female' one. (Laws 1985: 14)

### The menstrual cycle: women's intellectual deficit?

In what follows, I draw on specific examples which show the employment of the bio-medical model in psychological research as it relates directly to the oppression of women. It can be seen as more closely connected to cultural mythology than value-free inquiry.

Women experience regular endocrinological and physiological changes associated with the processes of ovulation and menstruation which occur from around the age of eleven until around the age of fifty five (Asso 1983). Images of women in relation to menstruation derived from religious, historical, cultural and scientific knowledge-claims cover the range of mythology: 'The history of attitudes towards menstruation from ancient times to the present demonstrates male fear, envy and hatred of women. The menstruating woman is called filthy, sick, unbalanced, ritually impure' (Daly 1984: 248).

Abundant evidence of this is also provided by both feminist (Laws 1983; Ussher 1989) and non-feminist writers (Shuttle and Redgrove 1980). Scientists mostly focus on negative aspects of menstruation (Shuttle and Redgrove 1980; Laws 1983; Nicolson 1991a). This focus leads to women's *exclusion* from the *normal* (that is, male) world, including the world demanding intellectual abilities. It is often assumed, for example, that women students are less likely to perform well in examinations and other assessments during the paramenstruum (just before and during the period of menstrual bleeding, see Asso 1983). These assumptions derive from the claims of scientists and teachers that,

> The periodic disturbances, to which girls and women are constitutionally subject, condemn many of them to a recurring, if temporary, diminuition of general mental efficiency. Moreover, it is during the most important years of school life that these disturbances are most intense and pervasive, and whenever one of them co-incides with some emergency, for example, an examination, girls are heavily handicapped as compared with boys. (Board of Education in Great Britain 1923: 86, quoted in Richardson 1991b: 3–4)

Dalton's (1969) similar claims continue to be widely promoted, particularly on a popular basis. However, in a series of careful comparison studies between female (pre-menstrual and mid-cycle) and male university students, and a detailed examination of the research literature, Richardson concluded that the available research evidence indicates that the process of menstruation has no effect at all upon academic performance when measured by quantitative tests or examinations, and it would appear that subjective complaints of paramenstrual dysfunction originate largely in socially mediated beliefs and expectations rather than in any objective intellectual impairment. It also appears that 'Female students seem to be at no appreciable disadvantage when they are required to take exams during the paramenstruum' (Richardson 1991b: 24). His conclusions based on his findings correspond closely to those of Sommer in the USA whose work has focused on the menstrual cycle and women's cognitive ability. After several years of study, she concludes that there is essentially no evidence to support a medical or psychological model of paramenstrual cognitive debilitation (Sommer 1983).

Sommer stresses that most scientific work on cognition during the menstrual cycle has been constrained by the prevailing mythological belief system that women's psychological capacitites are reduced during the paramenstruum. The consequence has been that the most statistically significant associations concerning the menstrual cycle are in women's self-cognitions and beliefs that their performance is impaired during the paramenstruum (Sommer 1983). In other words, both popular and scientific knowledge-claims correspond more closely to mythology than to evidence, and scientific psychologists do not pay enough attention to the philosophical and critical dimensions of their discipline (Hollway 1989).

Martin (1989) suggests that women's reports of premenstrual feelings need to be reconsidered in a social context, taking account of what women do during the rest of the cycle. If some women consider themselves less efficient premenstrually, this may be on mundane tasks. If, as appears to be the case, this is so, then perhaps the premenstrual period is a time of greater creativity which only becomes a problem if that creativity is unrecognized or thwarted. One woman in Martin's study, for example, said she felt melancholy premenstrually, but this enabled her to be reflective. Another said she wrote poetry just prior to the onset of menstrual bleeding (Martin 1989: 128–129). Perhaps scientists should be exploring why women routinely fail to resist the mundane tasks. Martin's findings are not the kind of menstrual effects which are the subject of most investigation because most researchers restrict the kinds of questions they ask.

I am not trying to argue for the existence of a 'conspiracy', that researchers have been actively and explicitly engaged in making negative attributions to femininity: such work could be easily dismissed. It is more that the research employed to 'help' women in a clinical setting – or 'justify' their failure in the context of education and employment – needs to be understood as representing an ideological rather than a value-free position. It is more appealing to attribute women's invisibility to biology than to implicate the socio-political structure since the latter calls scientific objectivity into question. A feminist perspective is no more value-free, of course, but it is only feminists who seem prepared to recognize and accept the ideology in all scholarly investigation. It has been the influence of feminism that allowed traditional concepts of women's psychology to be problematized, although in terms of publishing results, gaining research grants and other inducements to scientific progress, it is likely that proponents of the deficit model will gain more attention.

## Women, self-control and the bio-medical model: the case of PMS

Many feminists have supported the idea of PMT, and have promoted its acceptance by the medical profession, but have feared that it might be 'used against women'. I now think we have been mistaken – PMT, as constructed as a medical problem, is an idea through which women may be divided and controlled. (Laws 1983: 20)

The whole question of 'tolerance' and 'help' for women simply because they are women is so culturally pervasive that it is difficult to distinguish knowledge from mythology. Indeed, as Laws' (1983) extract here indicates, wholesale abolition of PMS/PMT is more likely to upset rather than please some women. But what is PMT/PMS?

PMT (premenstrual tension) is a relatively recent 'invention' (Frank 1931) and fits neatly into the history of bio-medical claims in relation to menstruation itself, already discussed. More recently PMT has been elevated to a PMS (premenstrual syndrome). As Ussher (1989) has demonstrated however, despite its popular acceptance, there is no agreement as to the exact hormonal configurations which precipitate this 'curse', nor as to the exact nature of the 'cure' or means of alleviation. The influence of feminist psychologist researchers on pressure groups in the USA resulted in a review of knowledge of PMS by the National Institute for Mental Health. This recognized and validated the controversy over the status of PMS or LLPDD (late luteal phase dysphoric disorder) as a diagnostic category. It was consequently not included in the main part of the official register of psychiatric disorders in the USA, but placed in an appendix with a note that it needed further investigation. However in the UK there has been no such lobby and PMS is alive and kicking in the minds of researchers, clinicians and most women. The contradictions between feminist ideas that 'help' women and those that disadvantage them by denying this 'help' remain salient.

The dramatic issue of PMS as a legal defence plea is central to the way women have been divided by the PMS discourse, and demonstrates the way that the mythology of women prevails in popular culture. In the UK, it has been used to submit a plea of 'diminished responsibility', which effactully reduces a murder charge to one of manslaughter by explicit acknowledgement that at the time of the killing the accused was mentally impaired. In three different cases in England and Wales, medical evidence of severe PMS has been accepted (see Laws 1983, Nicolson 1991a). In the USA, because of the controversy over the categorization of

PMS/LLPDD this has not occurred. There was some interest in the British cases, however, and it was used in a pre-trial hearing in New York in the case of Shirley Santos who was charged with assault on her daughter.

As Hey (1985) suggests, the idea that PMS may be used as a defence plea indicates that women are not *responsible* for themselves. Separating a female criminal from the consequences of her actions, because imblances in her hormone levels prevent her from being able to control her mind or behaviour, negates a woman's status as a human being (Hey 1985). Acknowledgement of women's violence is contrary to popular knowledge of femininity and therefore needs to be construed as *pathology* (see also Ussher 1989). Furthermore, PMS obscures the need to question the circumstances under which violence occurs. It is often as a response to persistent brutality from men. This is lost sight of in a PMS plea where the focus is upon the woman's behaviour (Nicolson 1991a for further details of these cases).

Although the *mythology of women* includes the contradictions of passivity and unpredictability, the essential component of 'femininity' is the idea of women's nurturance. Thus their violence and aggression need to be controlled – treated bio-medically and not punished. Punishment suggests that women are capable of responsibility and rationality and changing their own behaviour.

## Post-natal depression (PND): the continuing discourse of deficiency

When women do 'fulfil' their biological potential and become mothers, mythology dictates that child bearing and nurturance should come 'naturally', and the pleasures for women of this climax of their existence should be unequivocal. Why then do up to 80% of women report feeling weepy, anxious and depressed immediately after birth (Pitt 1973; Harris 1981), around 33% experience depressed moods in the following weeks (Oakley 1979), and around 24–30% report severe and prolonged depression for a year or more after the delivery of a child (Frate *et al.* 1979; Gordon *et al.* 1965)? According to the bio-medical model once again, this is because of their 'raging hormones', and these can be put right once the woman admits to the problem:

> The majority of women suffering from post-natal depression do not even realise they are ill. They believe they are bogged down by utter exhaustion and irritability . . . it is all too easy

to blame their condition on the extra work the baby brings
into her new life . . . Once the condition has been recognised
and treated the husband will be able to declare 'she's once
more the woman I married'. (Dalton 1980: 4)

Feminist psychological and sociological research in the 1970s
and early 1980s has correctly challenged this bio-medical view,
arguing that social factors are the main precipitants of PND
(Oakley 1980). It acknowledges that it is unsurprising that some
women should experience depression during the transition to
motherhood, since this is a realistic response to the stress of the
event of birth, the maternal role and other possible pressures
(Elliot 1985).

A combination of this 'social' model and the bio-medical model
has given rise to treatment initiatives (Holden 1985; Elliot 1985).
In various schemes throughout the UK, women identified as
having – or being at risk of – PND are provided with extra support
from health visitors and psychiatrists, and have opportunities for
individual and group counselling as well as advice and encouragement in baby care. The message, however, remains: *the
woman has the problem* and needs help from experts. Part of this
help is the confirmation of the woman in her role as nurturer.

What evidence has research produced to explain PND? As with
PMS, research on PND is inconclusive and characterized by its
lack of problem definition, associated poor conceptualization and
inadequate methodology (Hopkins *et al.* 1984; Nicolson 1988).
The contradictory nature of the concepts, methods and resulting
data has not escaped the attention of researchers. Steiner (1979)
argues that there is no data to support the view that the
physiology of puerperium is a cause of the symptoms of PND – at
best it might be considered a triggering factor acting on an
underlying pre-disposition. Brockington and Kumar (1982) –
psychiatrists supporting a bio-medical approach while acknowledging the existence of social factors – admit that the links
between motherhood and mental illness are tenuous. This,
however, did not prevent them editing a book focusing on this
link as well as conducting and supporting other research which
fails to problematize this connection.

During the 1980s the emphasis in the study of the psychology
of PND has moved even further from questioning the concept.
Instead, social factors and the identification of childbirth as a life
event are central to learned attention – a kind of 'factor'

reductionism. A recent conference and edited book of proceedings (Cox *et al.* 1989) provides a review of the up-to-date thinking on the subject. One example, from a discussion of the highlights from these papers, conveys the flavour:

> The outcome measure for this study was the Raskin Three Area Scale which allows for the inclusion of milder depressions and resulted in a 20% (24 scoring 7 or above) rate at 6 weeks postpartum. These were compared to the 67% (80 scoring 4 or below) who were not depressed. Depression was significantly related to the occurence of threatening events . . . Undesirable events plus other important variables (such as previous psychiatric history and marital adjustment) were entered into a multiple regression analysis. The fact that post-partum blues emerged as a significant factor only in people who had not had a life event led Paykel and his colleagues to wonder whether there were two groups – a smaller group whose depression was biological and a larger group whose depression was social. (Elliot 1990: 148–9)

The entire conference appears to have focused upon measurement and questions of whether there are different categories of depression. The aim was prediction of vulnerability and some assessment of the clinical implications. Reading Elliot's detailed review of this collection, however, the general impression is of extreme distance from the complex day-to-day experiences of women. The over-emphasis on 'intervening variables' carries with it the hidden sub-text of the bio-medical model, as can be seen in the above extract (lines 14–15). It seems as if the (mainly male) group of scientists had not actually talked to women at all; they had only needed the women to complete rating scales and check lists. Nor had they made any observations about the women's social circumstances.

There is the assumption in this 'life event' approach that childbirth itself is reduceable to a unitary biological phenomenon – removed from any individual meaning, barring intervening events or variables. It is once again women's deficiency that is being sought. There is no questioning of the social arrangements surrounding childbirth and early motherhood. The discourse on women's faulty biology is in effect translated from the predominant mythology and bolstered by knowledge-claims and popular ideas about women's 'nature'.

Other feminist research has provided evidence to challenge these knowledge-claims, but has been marginalized. The myth of femininity and mothering was called to account in one study (Breen 1975) which demonstrated that the most 'feminine' women (ie. those who claimed psychological characteristics most closely resembling stereotypical femininity) were the least well adjusted during the early weeks of motherhood. The women who scored high on 'masculine' or 'androgynous' qualities coped best, mainly because mothering requires not only 'nurturance' but independence, toughness, physical and emotional strength and determination – qualities which are polar opposites of those attributed to femininity.

The story for women, though, is further complicated by the ways in which they are positioned – and position themselves – in relation to the dominant social discourses. Once again, with PND, women expect to either 'get it' or 'avoid it' and attribute it to hormonal/biological vulnerability (Nicolson 1988). In one study I did which comprised a series of in-depth interviews across the transition from motherhood to six months after birth, it became clear that women deliberately seek out popular or serious versions of scientific knowledge for information. Their awareness of the PND discourse is so pervasive that some are even tempted to attribute non-rational motives to their rational behaviour! For instance, being upset in hospital because of the hostile or uncaring behaviour of midwives and other staff, or worry about their babies' health, becomes understood by them retrospectively as 'blues' (Nicolson 1991b). Most do not think of it this way though, and suggest that when they get anxious or weepy or depressed, it cannot be PND because they are able to provide 'rational' accounts for their emotions and behaviour. They have understood PND itself within the reductionist, bio-medical framework, and thus see it only as 'irrational' (Nicolson 1991b).

In the psychological debate on PND, there are clear indications that the knowledge-claims of the dominant group of researchers have been unshaken by contrary evidence and the calls for problematization of the concept. The theme that women's biology is 'faulty' has persisted, and the questions raised have remained within the predominant discourse and fitted into the bio-medical paradigm, despite a 'liberal disguise'. The 'life event' model has failed to take women's experiences into account, or to reconsider the starting point and problematize PND and the social/structural arrangements surrounding birth and the period of early motherhood. More women-centred critiques (eg. Breen 1975; Wearing 1984; Nicolson 1988) are not cited within this literature, although published in abstracted, refereed journals and books.

## Sexuality: passive and coy or just plain frigid?

The relationship between power and scientific knowledge-claims about female psychology is well illustrated through sexological research and related therapeutic practices. Everyday understanding of the discourse of heterosexuality as it relates to sexual intercourse acts as encouragement to women to define themselves as pathological. As with menstruation and childbirth, sexual behaviour is presented by psychologists and other scientists as a bio-medical issue. Indeed, heterosexual behaviours are more likely than any other to be attributed to biological drives with specific directions of focus (Ellis 1905; Freud 1933; see also Jeffreys 1990). But is sexuality about biological drives, or is it, once again, about gender-power relations? In order to explore the heterosexual discourse and its relationship to women's psychology, I focus upon three specific issues. The first is the way in which women are objectified by sexological science as the passive recipients of male sexual desire (eg. Snitow *et al.* 1984; Nicolson 1990b). The second is the way that knowledge-claims about normal sexuality derive from male-dominated notions, with little relation to women's practices – indeed women are discounted. The third is the way that this discounting of women's sexuality has led to self-pathologization.

## Objects of desire

At the turn of the century the science of sexology developed, and is now applauded for bringing this taboo subject into the public arena. Sigmund Freud and Havelock Ellis were foremost among these early sexologists and both lay claim to understanding and acknowledging the existence of a specific female sexuality. This sexuality is one which is essentially responsive, passive and seductive within a heterosexual framework. As Freud outlines,

> More constraint has been applied to the libido when it is pressed into the service of the feminine function . . . the accomplishment of the aim of biology has been entrusted to

the aggressiveness of men and has been, to some extent, independent of women's consent. (Freud 1933: 131–2)

Ellis, although 'recognizing' female passivity, was further concerned to explore the interaction of female and male behaviour, and show how female passivity was not to be confused with indifference. Indeed, for Ellis, it played a vital part in encouraging the male's sexual assertions:

> Except where the male fails to play his part properly, she is usually comparatively passive; in the proper playing of her part she has to appear to shun the male, flee from his approaches – even actually to repel them. Courtship resembles very closely indeed a drama or a game; and the aggressiveness of the male and the coyness of the female, are alike unconsciously assumed in order to bring about in the most effectual manner the ultimate union of the sexes. The seeming reluctance of the female is not intended to inhibit sexual activity either in the male or in herself, but to increase it in both. The passivity of the female, therefore, is not real, but only an apparent passivity, and this holds true of our own species as much as of the lower animal. (Ellis 1905: 229)

He also considered himself an advocate of women's sexual liberation by acknowledging women's sexual participation (see Jackson 1987):

> The true nature of the passivity of the female is revealed by the ease with which it is thrown off, more especially when the male refuses to accept his cue. Or if we prefer to accept the analogy of a game, we may say that in the play of courtship, the first move belongs to the male, but that, if he fails to play, it is then the female's turn to play. (Ellis 1905: 232)

Thus for both Ellis and Freud, the contrasting but compatible heterosexual roles ensured the continued existence of human sexual life. The degree to which male activity/aggression and female passivity have remained unchallenged as scientific knowledge-claims is perhaps startling. A recent study which reflected Freud's ideas about this confirmed that the main determinant of adult rates of heterosexual activity in our society is the level of male commitment (Gagnon and Simon 1973).

Such echoes underpin recent sex therapy research and case study material (eg. Haslam 1988a; 1988b; Adler 1989). Women's responsibility for men's potency through their enthusiastic acquiescence is the theme which recurs here. What about women's desires? It does not take detailed knowledge of feminist research on gender relations to suggest that female passivity in sexual behaviour and other spheres of domestic and professional life is at the root of female oppression. This is true for women who are the objects of male sexual and physical violence and sexual harassment, and for women who take on the passive, nurturant role in the family and consequently become depressed (Friedan 1979). Is a passive role in heterosexual seduction, with intercourse as its aim, women's preferred way to achieve sexual fulfillment?

### Norm-setting

Expectations of climax through sexual intercourse have become a psychological norm for women and men, employed by both therapists and patients. This is evident in research and therapeutic literature (Haslam 1988a; 1988b) and in popular everyday understanding (see for example women's magazines which consider how to get the best from your man – or men).

This norm however is problematic, with no evidence that it can withstand scientific scrutiny. Kinsey and colleagues (1953), in fact, found that more than half their sample of married women did not achieve orgasm during sexual intercourse, but could do so through masturbation. This condition was known as 'frigidity'. McVaugh (1979) estimated that twelve and a half million women in the USA were frigid, but neither Kinsey nor McVaugh saw this as a challenge to normative assumptions. However, it is Masters and Johnson (1966) who provide the details of 'normal' sexual responses. Their work, which employed physiological measures of sexual arousal and resolution, and detailed interviews, set the scene for assumptions about female sexuality that have become part of popular mythology. Relevant here are their assertions that women have clitoral rather than vaginal orgasms, and are potentially multi-orgasmic. This 'discovery' of the multi-orgasmic woman has led to the popular notion that women's frigidity may be overcome provided men know how to stimulate women's bodies appropriately. This has provided the basis for much modern sex therapy. But Masters and Johnson qualified their pronouncements in a way that has been neglected. They suggested that

Female study subjects' orgasmic inadequacy have also been primarily coitally oriented . . . female orgasmic experience usually is developed more easily and is physiologically more intense (although subjectively not necessarily satsifying), when induced by auto-manipulation as opposed to coition. (Masters and Johnson 1966: 314)

This indicates that while intercourse may be the way to achieving closeness with a partner, masturbation is the more effective means to the female orgasm. The implications of this are vital for understanding human sexuality, but female sexuality continues to be seen in relation to the image that satisfies men, rather than in relation to this finding. Norm-setting for women's sexuality remains high on the male agenda, so that women continue to seek sexual climaxes (as well as closeness) through sexual intercourse, and to see themselves as frigid if they fail. Paradoxically, it has been the liberalization of discussions on sexual behaviour, and a climate where the need for women's satisfaction has been acknowledged, that has pathologized women. This liberalization has in fact been an entrapment of women in the patriarchal, bio-medical version of events, where women's experiences and desires have not been given priority.

**Self-pathologization**

The discounting of women's experiences has led to self-evaluations according to this spurious set of norms. Both heterosexual women and their male partners, through the interpenetration of scientific knowledge-claims and popular knowledge, have been led to believe that women's 'orgasmic dysfunction' should be treated in order to maintain their couple relationship. But what of the evidence that suggests many women are in fact 'frigid'? Why is this seen as evidence of a female problem (McVaugh, 1979), rather than as a challenge to assumptions about norms? Why has women's refusal to have intercourse or the 'new' problem ISD (inhibited sexual desire: Lieff 1977) been taken as evidence of female pathology, rather than evidence of a problem with the way sexuality is understood and practised? It has to be because it is men who set the agenda and the norms, and control the knowledge-claims through which we all gain our everyday understanding of our own and others' behaviour.

Women are the objects of male desire, and if they reject this role, they need treatment! McVaugh graphically illustrates the way women are ignored in the equation: 'The great incapacitator afflicting the vagina, as well as her total personality, disables the woman, making it impossible for her to perform a normal function in an otherwise totally normal body, physiologically' (McVaugh 1979: 2). On what basis does he use the words 'incapacitator', 'afflicting', 'disables' and so on? There is no evidence that vaginal penetration should bring about orgasm or that failure to achieve orgasm is problematic other than that it has been designated so. He goes on: 'I have circumnavigated the world seven times and I have lived in many different cultures for long periods of time therefore I can definitely aver, that frigidity exists in thousands of women throughout the world. Today it is totally out of control' (McVaugh 1979: 3).

The message here is clear – frigid women are out of men's control. As Sheila Jeffreys (1990) points out, sexology has been aimed almost exclusively at ensuring that women do not resist male advances. Thus we have to assume that sexology and knowledge-claims about sexuality relate entirely to male sexuality, with women placed as the object of their desires.

## Conclusions

Women in academic psychology are excluded from power and discouraged from achieving unless they manifestly reject claims to feminism. Male psychologists argue that feminism is political not scientific, and psychology is a science, therefore the two are incompatible (see Wilkinson 1990a). However, as I have argued, the picture is more complex, and there is no evidence to suggest that the knowledge-claims of psychological science are anything but political themselves. Men dominate the discipline numerically, in their positions of power, in terms of recognition and awards for 'good' psychology. Feminist women's work is marginalized and not referred to in the mainstream, and because men with their patriarchal values control academic psychology, feminism is devalued and ignored.

Science is a powerful mediator of popular knowledge and culture: it both reflects and informs everyday understanding. This means that women and men, scientists and non-scientists have most frequent access to patriarchal values in relation to women's psychology. The influence of critical feminism in psychology has enabled a feminist debate within the discipline, although when compared with similar disciplines, it has taken longer to gain some ground. This is because psychology – more than sociology, biology or literary criticism – has had much to lose by failing to maintain the hard-science value-free illusion.

In this chapter I have attempted to develop some ideas on the way critical feminism has influenced modern psychological knowledge. It does not represent the full extent of this influence or feminist knowledge in psychology – it reflects a personal involvement.

## References

Adler, E. (1989). 'Vaginismus – Its presentation and treatment', *British Journal of Sexual Medicine*, 16, 420–424.

American Psychological Association (1988). *Women in the APA*. Washington DC, APA.

Asso, D. (1983). *The Real Menstrual Cycle*. Chichester, Wiley.

Bem, S.L. (1974). 'The measurement of psychological androgyny', *Journal of Consulting and Clinical Psychology*, 42, 155–162.

—— (1981). 'Gender schema theory', *Psychological Review*, 88, 354–364.

Bernard, J. (1981). *The Female World*. New York, The Free Press.

Bleier, R. (1984). *Science and Gender*. Oxford, Pergamon.

Board of Education (1923). *Report of the Consultative Committee on Differentiation of the Curriculum for Boys and Girls Respectively in Secondary Schools*. London, HMSO.

Breen, D. (1975). *The Birth of a First Child*. London, Tavistock.

Brockington, I.F. and Kumar, R. (1982). *Motherhood and Mental Illness*. London, Academic Press.

Burman, E. (1990). *Feminists and Psychological Practice*. London, Sage.

Burns, J. (1990). 'Women organising within psychology', in E. Burman (ed.) *Feminists in Psychological Practice*. London, Sage.

Chetwynd, J. and Hartnett, O. (1978). *The Sex Role System*. London, Routledge and Kegan Paul.

Cox, J.L., *et al.* (1989). *Childbirth as a Life Event*. Southampton, Duphar Medical Relations.

Crawford, D. (1989). 'The future of clinical psychology: whither or wither?', *Clinical Psychology Forum*, 20, 29–31.

Crawford, M. and Maracek, J. (1989). 'Psychology reconstructs the female: 1968–1988', *Psychology of Women Quarterly*, 13, 147–166.

Dalton, K. (1969). *The Menstrual Cycle*. Pelican. Harmondsworth.

—— (1980). *Depression After Childbirth*. Oxford, Oxford University Press.

Daly, M. (1984). *Gyn/Ecology*. London, The Women's Press.

Dunbar, R. (1970). 'Female Liberation as the basis for social revolution', in R. Morgan (ed.) *Sisterhood is Powerful*. New York, Random House.

Ehrenreich, B. and English, D. (1979). *For Her Own Good*. New York, Pluto Press.

Elliot, S.A. (1985). *A Rationale for Psychosocial Intervention in the Prevention of Post Natal Depression*. Paper presented at the Women in Psychology Conference, Cardiff.

—— (1990). 'Commentary on "Childbirth as a Life Event"', *Journal of Reproductive and Infant Psychology*, 8, 147–159.

Ellis, H. (1905). *Studies in the Psychology of Sex: Volume I*. New York, Random House.

Foucault, M. (1973). *The Archaeology of Knowledge*. London, Tavistock.

Frank, R.T. (1931). 'The hormonal causes of premenstrual tension', *Archives of Neurology and Psychiatry*, 26, 1053–1057.

Frate, A.D., *et al.* (1979). 'Behavioural reactions during the postpartum period: experiences of 198 women', *Women and Health*, 4, 355–371.

Freud, S. (1933/1965). J. Strachey (ed. and trans.) *New Introductory Lectures in Psychoanalysis*. New York, Norton.

—— (1977). 'Female Sexuality', in J. Strachey (ed. and trans.) *Three Essays on the Theory of Sexuality*. Vol 7, Standard Edition, 372–388. New York, Norton.

Friedan, B. (1979). *The Feminine Mystique*. Harmondsworth, Pelican.

Frieze, I.H., Parson, J.E., Johnson, P.B., Ruble, D.N. and Zellman, G.L. (1978). *Women and Sex Roles*. London, Norton.

Gagnon, J.H. and Simon, W. (1973). *Sexual Conduct: The Social Sources of Human Sexuality*. Chicago, Aldine.

Gordon, R.E., *et al.* (1965). 'Factors in postpartum emotional adjustment', *Obstetrics and Gynaecology*, 25, 158–166.

Report of the Hansard Society Commission (1990). *Women at the Top*. London, The Hansard Society for Parliamentary Government.

Harre, R. and Secord, P.F. (1972). *The Explanation of Social Behaviour*. Oxford, Blackwell.

Harris, B. (1981). 'Maternity blues in East African clinic attenders', *Archives of General Psychiatry*, 38, 1293–1295.

Haslam, M.T. (1988a). 'The assessment of sexual dysfunction: Part One', *British Journal of Sexual Medicine*, 15, 46–48.

—— (1988b). 'The assessment of sexual dysfunction: Part Two', *British Journal of Sexual Medicine*, 15, 94–99.

Hey, V. (1985). 'Getting away with murder: pre-menstrual tension and the press', in S. Laws, V. Hey and A. Eagen (eds.) *Seeing Red*. London, Hutchinson.

Holden, J. (1985). 'Postnatal depression: talking it out', *Community Outlook*, 1, 10.

Hollway, W. (1989). *Subjectivity and Method in Psychology*. London, Sage.

Hopkins, J., *et al.* (1984). 'Postpartum depression: a critical review', *Psychological Bulletin*, 82, 498–515.

Horner, M.S. (1970). 'Femininity and successful achievement: a basic inconsistency', in M.F. Horner and D. Gutman (eds.) *Feminine Personality and Conflict*. 45–74, Belmont, Brooks Cole.

Humphrey, M. and Haward, L. (1981). 'Sex differences in clinical psychology recruitment', *Bulletin of the British Psychological Society*, 34, 413–414.

Jackson, M. (1987). 'Facts of life or the eroticisation of women's oppression? Sexology and the social construction of heterosexuality', in P. Caplan (ed.) *The Social Construction of Sexuality*. 52–81 London, Tavistock.

Jeffreys, S. (1990). *Anticlimax*. London, The Women's Press.

Kagan C. and Lewis, S. (1990a). 'Where's your sense of humour? Swimming against the tide in higher education', in E. Burman (ed.) *Feminists in Psychological Practice*. London, Sage.

—— (1990b). 'Transforming psychological practice', *Australian Psychologist*, 25, 270–281.

Kinsey, A., Pomeroy, W.B., Martin, C.E. (1953). *Sexual Behaviour in the Human Female*. Philadelphia, W.B. Saunders and Co.

Laws, S. (1983). 'The sexual politics of premenstrual tension', *Women's Studies International Forum*, 6, 19–31.

—— (1985). 'Who needs PMT?' in S. Laws, V. Hey, and A. Eagen (eds.) *Seeing Red*. London, Hutchinson.

Lief, H. (1977). 'What's new in sex research? Inhibited sexual desire', *Medical Aspects of Human Sex*, 11, 94–95.

Lopate, H. (1968). *Women in Medicine*. Baltimore, John Hopkins University Press.

McVaugh, G.S. (1979). *Frigidity*. Oxford, Pergamon.

Maccoby, E.E. and Jacklin, C.N. (1974). *The Psychology of Sex Differences*. Stanford, Stanford University Press.

Martin, E. (1989). *The Woman in the Body*. Milton Keynes, Open University Press.

Masters, W.H. and Johnson, V.E. (1966). *Human Sexual Response*. London, J. and A. Churchill Ltd.

Mitchell, J. (1974). *Psychoanalysis and Feminism*. Harmondsworth, Penguin.

Morris, P., *et al.* (1990a). 'Gender representation within the BPS', *The Psychologist*, 9, 408–411.

—— (1990b). 'How and why applicants choose psychology at university', *Report to the Association of Heads of Psychology Departments*.

Nicolson, P. (1988). *The Social Psychology of 'Post-Natal Depression'*. Unpublished PhD Thesis, University of London.

—— (1990a). *Post-Natal Sexuality*. Paper presented at the Tenth Annual Merseyside Conference on Clinical Psychology, Chester College.

—— (1990b). *The Psychology and Biology of Women's Sexual Desire: Sexual Intercourse, Sexual Problems and Women's Self-Cognition*. Paper presented at the BPS London Conference, City University.

—— (1991a). 'Menstrual cycle research and the construction of female psychology', in J.T.E. Richardson (ed.) *Cognition and the Menstrual Cycle: Research Theory and Culture.* London, Springer Verlag.

—— (1991b). 'Explanations of post-natal depression: structuring knowledge of female psychology', *Research on Language and Social Interaction*, Dec, (in press).

—— (1992). 'Gender issues in the organisation of clinical psychology', in J.M. Ussher and P. Nicolson (eds.) *Gender Issues in Clinical Psychology.* London, Routledge (in press).

—— Burns, J. and Wilkinson, S. (1990). *Courses on the Psychology of Women and Gender Relations.* Paper presented at the first Annual Psychology of Women Section Conference of the BPS, University of Birmingham.

—— and Phillips, E.M. (1990). 'Ageism and academic psychology', *The Psychologist*, 3, 393–394.

Oakley, A. (1979). 'The Baby Blues', *New Society*, 4, 11–12.

—— (1980). *Women Confined.* Oxford, Oxford University Press.

Philp, M. (1985). 'Madness, truth and critique: Foucault and anti-psychiatry', *PsychCritique*, 1, 155–170.

Pitt, B. (1973). 'Maternity blues', *British Journal of Psychiatry*, 122, 431–433.

Potter, J. and Wetherell, M. (1987). *Discourse and Social Psychology: Beyond Attitudes and Behaviour.* London, Sage.

Reason, P. and Rowan, J. (1981). *Human Inquiry: A Source Book of New Paradigm Research.* Chichester, Wiley.

Richardson, J.T.E. (1991a). *Cognition and the Menstrual Cycle: Research, Theory and Culture.* London, Springer Verlag.

—— (1991b). 'The menstrual cycle and student learning', *Journal of Higher Education* (in press).

Rohrbaugh, J.B. (1981). *Women: Psychology's Puzzle.* Reading, Abacus.

Rothstein, W.G. (1972). *American Physicians in the Nineteenth Century.* Baltimore, John Hopkins University.

Sayers, J. (1982). *Biological Politics.* London, Tavistock.

Sherif, C. (1987). 'Bias in psychology', in S. Harding (ed.) *Feminism and Methodology.* Milton Keynes, Open University Press.

Shields, S.A. (1974). *The Psychology of Women: An Historical Analysis.* Paper presented at the APA Conference, New Orleans (In Unger, 1979, see below).

Shuttle, P. and Redgrove, P. (1980). *The Wise Wound.* Harmondsworth, Penguin.

Snitow, A., *et al.* (1984). *Desire and the Politics of Sexuality.* London, Virago.

Sommer, B. (1983). 'How does menstruation affect cognition, competence and psychophysiological response?', *Women and Health*, 8, 53–90.

Steiner, M. (1979). 'The psychobiology of mental disorders associated with childbearing', *Acta Psychiatrica Scandinavica*, 60, 449–464.

Unger, R.K. (1979). *Female and Male: Psychological Perspectives*. London, Harper and Row.

Ussher, J.M. (1989). *The Psychology of the Female Body*. London, Routledge.

—— (1992). 'Gender issues in clinical research', in J.M. Ussher and P. Nicolson (eds.) *Gender Issues in Clinical Psychology*. London, Routledge (in press).

Wearing, B. (1984). *The Ideology of Motherhood*. Sydney, George Allen and Unwin.

Weedon, C. (1987). *Feminist Practice and Poststructuralist Theory*. Oxford, Blackwell.

Whitelegg, E., *et al.* (1982). *The Changing Experience of Women*. Milton Keynes, Open University Press.

Wilkinson, S. (ed.) (1986). *Feminist Social Psychology: Theory and Method*. Milton Keynes, Open University Press.

—— (1990a). 'Women organising in psychology', in E. Burman (ed.) *Feminists in Psychological Practice*. London, Sage.

—— (1990b). 'Gender issues: broadening the context', *The Psychologist*, 9, 412–414.

Williams, J. (1987). *The Psychology of Women* (3rd edition). London, Norton.

Wilson, E.O. (1978). *On Human Nature*. Cambridge, Harvard University Press.

# 5

## Thrown together: Olive Schreiner, writing and politics

### Carolyn Burdett

My starting place for this reading of a short story by Olive Schreiner situates her firmly within a tradition of feminist argument, for that place is Schreiner's attempt to write an introduction to the text which is most frequently cited as the first great statement of English feminism: Mary Wollstonecraft's *A Vindication of the Rights of Woman*. But I also hope to show – although I will have time only to gesture towards it here – how the questions of sexual equality and of femininity were never absolutely discrete for Schreiner from the questions of colonial politics. Her investments and engagement in a politics of feminism led back to the most difficult and rooted problems of her position as a white woman in South Africa.

In 1886 Schreiner agreed to provide a new introduction to *A Vindication* for the Camelot Classics Series, promising that 'it will hold the substance of all my thoughts on the man and woman question'.[1] To Karl Pearson she admitted to never having read Wollstonecraft's text: 'the great point of interest in her to me is her life; I mean to treat her as a woman'.[2] That assertion recalls an earlier moment when, in a letter to Havelock Ellis, sent a short time after the publication of *The Story of an African Farm*, Schreiner writes that 'The question of woman's having the vote, and independence and education, is only part of the question, there lies something deeper'.[3]

Schreiner's concern, from the beginning, does not address itself to the key political demands of Wollstonecraft's text – those demands for equality which were so clearly still the agenda for

*Kerry Vaughan*

feminists of the 1880s – but rather it reveals her fascination to be more with Wollstonecraft's life than her text.

This fascination is not unique. Some of the most interesting readings of Wollstonecraft today confront the seeming contradiction between a text which bases its claim for sexual equality on a condemnation of femininity and a life which reads all too like the kind of melodramatic novel castigated as so unhealthy for the imagination of young women in *A Vindication*.[4] Margaret Walters' response to this contradiction is to look to Wollstonecraft's *fictional* writing: her novel *The Wrongs of Woman, or Maria* articulates 'something deeper' than the oppressive quality of conventional feminine stereotypes which is the target of *A Vindication*. There is, in Walters' phrase 'a gap between the theory and the lived experience'[5] which the (fictional) language of wrongs translates by returning us to Wollstonecraft's life.

What seems to emerge as 'deeper' than the appeal for sexual equality is femininity itself. Reinstating Wollstonecraft's fictional writing has been crucial for feminist criticism, but demonstrates a problematic tendency to repeat the divisions between didactic text, fiction and life, and to make the fictional text a privileged site for explorations of female sexuality excluded from the text of *A Vindication* through the severity of Wollstonecraft's condemnation of sensibility. The fictional text then functions as a truer articulation of the 'real' life and the 'gap between the theory and the lived experience' becomes a hierarchized relation with 'lived experience' as the absolute, privileged referent.

The question which remains to be asked is precisely what kind of femininity emerges from this passage back, via the fictional text, to the life of the woman. One problematic move is a repetition of Wollstonecraft's own position in the introduction to *A Vindication*. There, literary language is contaminatory just as femininity is through the body of the text: 'pretty superlatives' create a 'kind of sickly delicacy' which stifles truth and natural emotions.[6] The response of some feminist critics has been to analyse this passage as Wollstonecraft's placing of linguistic pleasure or literary language on the side of the feminine, and attempting to cast them both out. But in this scenario, it is again the *fictional* writing which becomes the place where the prison of sensibility is both located and subverted, which offers a 'radical challenge to patriarchy'.[7] So Wollstonecraft's placing of 'literary language' on the side of the feminine is repeated, but privileged rather than denigrated. What is needed, though, is a more adequate understanding of the relationship between writing, genre and femininity, rather than seeing fiction as the privileged site for creativity, femininity and desire as if they were simply not present in the other, didactic text.

To return then, to Schreiner. What can be made of her fascination with Wollstonecraft's life, her determination to 'treat her as a woman'? *A Vindication* might be seen to enact a narrative of the impermissibility of woman's pleasure if she is to attain rationality and full citizenship, while at the same time constructing a femininity to justify that injunction. Feminist critics then read the text of Wollstonecraft's life as a refusal of that overt narrative precisely on the grounds of the reinsertion of (another) femininity. Schreiner's response, however, shows that that process is not to be understood as 'real' femininity triumphing over the 'ideological fiction'[8] of the femininity of *A Vindication*; rather it reveals a complex set of difficulties which make themselves heard in disturbances of language, and become focused through the problem of what constitutes a proper style and genre for women's writing.

On one level, Schreiner is caught here in a fantasy of identification and of identity: an identity of woman, or for woman, which can transcend the divisions written through the text of *A Vindication*, to integrate reason (the intellectual woman) together with the romantic/sexual woman, and the maternal woman. Hence Schreiner writes of Wollstonecraft's life giving 'such a splendid opportunity for treating of the ideal form of marriage'.[9] But the attempt to take up this 'splendid opportunity' and write the introduction becomes an impossibility for Schreiner: the question of identity is one marked by an uncertainty which repeats itself in the uncertainty of linguistic form.

From very early Schreiner's attitude to the Wollstonecraft project is marked by an ambivalence. In 1888 she wrote to Ernest Rhys, then editor of Walter Scott publishers, that

> It has already cost me about four times as much labour as *African Farm* did, but in one sense immeasurably more because I have gathered into it the result of my whole life's work. . . . There is no side of the sex question, women's intellectual equality (or as I hold inequality with man), marriage, prostitution, in which one has not to speak. My present work is bringing down the immense mass of material I have into condensed form. Sometimes I find by throwing

the thing into the form of an allegory I can condense five or six pages into one, with no loss, but a great gain to clearness.[10]

Two issues emerge from this letter. First, the project quickly seems to become excessive, and this alongside a troubling of the *form* of Schreiner's writing. There is an indication here of the compulsive and totalizing nature of an imaginary identification with a woman's life, and the way in which linguistic form seems to register the uncertainties involved in the establishment of feminine identity within language. Second, there is that ambiguous parenthetical reference to intellectual inequality: is it an inherent inequality, or a present fact of a pernicious social system which could be, and must be, changed? The political language of equality serves to exclude another difficult question, which is nevertheless suggested by the surprise of the parenthesis: the question of difference between the sexes.

Schreiner never completed her Wollstonecraft project; the unfinished manuscript consists almost entirely of a sketchy and crude evolutionary narrative which relies upon the racist figuring of African womanhood to speak an unmediated 'truth'. This truth then supports a history which determines the place of Africans and women within it, while providing the potential for feminist protest in the West. However, many of the themes here did find their way to publication in the form of *Woman and Labour*.[11] This text might unproblematically be identified as the much-cited 'sex book' of Schreiner's letters, except for the long and detailed claim made in its introduction that it in fact constitutes a fragment of a much longer work destroyed during the Anglo-Boer war. I mention this firstly to draw attention to the anxiety which the introduction seems to betray regarding Schreiner's ability to find textual form for 'all her thoughts', and secondly because of the controversy aroused by the denial of Samuel Cronwright – Schreiner's husband – that the longer book ever existed. I have neither the time nor the evidence to attempt an adjudication of this disagreement and nor do I think adjudication the most appropriate or important response. Rather I wish to draw attention to the terms of Cronwright's case against his wife: his assertion that her 'capacity for stating hard, objective facts was often conditioned by her powerful imagination',[12] with the latter rendering her incapable of the book described in the introduction to *Woman and Labour*. That would have required 'hard, exact, systematic reading and study, . . . a kind of labour she was incapable of'.[13]

The importance of this episode lies, on the one hand, in the too easy equating of femininity and fictional writing (here revealed as an imagination which excludes the woman from the very possibility of systematic thought); and, on the other, in the anxiety which elicits from Schreiner such a detailed introduction, with all its disclaimers and apologies. Both issues relate to a disruption of form in Schreiner's text. In the Introduction to *Woman and Labour* she writes:

> In addition to the prose argument I had in each chapter one or more allegories; because while it is easy clearly to express abstract thoughts in argumentative prose, whatever emotion those thoughts awaken I have not felt myself able adequately to express except in the other form.[14]

In a letter to the journalist W.T. Stead, Schreiner laments her inability to give voice to her ideas: 'I can't express myself satisfactorily didactically'.[15] The strange locution of the sentence suggests both a recognition and a misrecognition: a recognition of the failure to express herself satisfactorily, and a misrecognition that tries to confine that lack of satisfaction to didactic expression.

But Schreiner is indeed correct to locate her difficulty here, because in a sense she is on the precarious edge of the critical terrain set out for her. Much of the critical response to Schreiner's work has concentrated on precisely her inability to sustain a form, an assessment which often sees the compulsion to express herself didactically as spelling the danger of aesthetic failure. 'It is only as a novelist, and only so far as she was one'[16] that Schreiner was successful – she was not one, or rather she was a failed one, when that compulsion is visible, revealed in the disturbances of traditional, or readerly, textual form.[17] It seems then, that if it is fictionality that Schreiner cannot keep out of her putatively didactic text, it is also fictionality – where it is revealed through the rents in her text produced by the incursion of 'endless dissertations on philosophy, art, evolution, allegories and whatever interests her'[18] – that warrants the severest censure from her critics with regard to the fictional writing itself. But the very instability of Schreiner's identity as a writer – witnessed through the search for an adequate form – is itself a threat to another kind of fiction: the certainty with which women and men establish themselves as subjects in language.

If, as I have suggested, Schreiner's attempt to write an introduction to Wollstonecraft's *A Vindication* can be read as a submerged history of the writing of *Woman and Labour*, then it is clear that that text, if not incomplete in the way Schreiner herself suggests, is certainly limited in a way that Schreiner could not acknowledge, by the terms of evolutionary science which she employed. For it is femininity and fiction which are the most important terms to emerge from the earlier project, and I want to suggest that the form of Schreiner's allegories and stories is in fact disruptive of the certainties of cause and effect so rigorously claimed and espoused by evolutionary science.

The text which is of particular significance in reading this fragmented terrain of Schreiner's 'sex work' was not published until after her death, although it seemed to be one of her favourite pieces. She writes of it at length in a letter to Cronwright, before their marriage:

> I have been working at a book on sex evolution for ten years. Last year I threw most of it (or it threw itself) into the shape of a curious story. A man and woman sit discussing a whole night, or till near morning. The scientific view which I have formed comes out in the discussion, but also the individual natures of the man and woman and their relation to one another, which throws a curious side-light on the whole discussion. I do not know whether anyone else will like it. It has given me more bliss than anything else I ever wrote; in fact, I do not think I could have borne life that year without writing it. It ends with the woman asking the man to kiss her, and then she goes suddenly out of the room. For the first time it bursts upon him with a sense of astonishment that she loves him; he waits to hear her return; but she never comes; the next day she leaves for India and they never meet again. You realise this because the story opens with the picture of a woman lying dead on a bed looking very happy and peaceful.[19]

This 'curious story' is 'The Buddhist Priest's Wife'[20] which, I want to argue, sets out a series of promises which it yet recognizes as unachievable. The 'scientific view' which Schreiner formulates from her reading of evolutionary theory bases its understanding of sexual difference upon the fact of women's reproductive capacities. Schreiner elaborates this position in *Woman and Labour* alongside her call for equality of access to education and training, citing it as the basis for women's specific moral and cultural duties. In 'The Buddhist Priest's Wife', however, an identity for women which has somehow to embody both those terms, equality and difference, is never fixed. The 'curious side-light' cast by the characters' relation to each other now shines centre-stage. The narrative forces the security offered by individualistic liberalism or evolutionary science into crisis, even as it tries to achieve that securing for an understanding of sexuality and sexual identity.

In their biography, First and Scott comment of 'The Buddhist Priest's Wife' that 'Of all her stories, it is the least abstract or displaced in time, and the most personally revealing; she seems almost deliberately to have avoided an allegorical form.'[21] This reading elides the difficulty of the text in an assertion of the biographical, making the story into Schreiner's wished-for conversation with Karl Pearson. My analysis takes as its starting point the title of the story, 'The Buddhist Priest's Wife'. Rather than situating it at the furthest remove from the allegorical, an attention to allegorical form allows an understanding of this story as articulating some of the key ambivalences which run throughout Schreiner's work. In *The Origins of German Tragic Drama* Walter Benjamin discusses the custom of the double title in the *Trauerspiel* and writes, 'one of the titles always refers to the subject matter, the other to its allegorical content'.[22] The title 'The Buddhist Priest's Wife' shares with that description a dual, or indeed a multiple meaning. The story narrates a visit by a man to the room of the woman protagonist; she is about to leave for India. As they converse, and discuss her planned journey, the man suggests that she might meet and marry a Buddhist priest. He is light-hearted, ironic:

> 'What is taking you to India now? Going to preach the doctrine of social and intellectual equality to the Hindu women and incite them to revolt? Marry some old Buddhist Priest, build a little cottage on the top of the Himalayas and live there, discuss philosophy and meditate?' (64–5)

Again, what gets posed is the question of equality, but here, as elsewhere, it is a troubled image. The ironic scenario imagined by the man becomes a version of the ideal of the intellectual woman which appeared so strongly in Schreiner's engagement with Mary Wollstonecraft's life and writing. What emerges is the possibility of a location for the woman in which she can engage in radical politics, intellectual debate, philosophy and meditation, and at the same time marry. In short, she can become the 'complete' woman signified in Schreiner's enthusiastic espousal of Wollstonecraft's 'ideal form of marriage'. But it is a curious partnership: the man is old, his age threatening any comfortable or conventional imagining of sexual fulfilment. He is also a priest, a teacher of philosophy and meditation – in short, a spiritual master. Desire for a spiritual master constitutes its own particular threat to the ideal of equality between the sexes, but it is the unity of this suggested enterprise which finally exposes its precariousness. Marriage as part of the intellectual and spiritual process becomes the mark of a fundamental impossibility. In so far as it signifies the intervention of sexuality and sexual desire into the arena, it also signifies the failure of any imagined unity and complete identity for women. Philosophy and meditation might well be the staple fare of Buddhist priests, but they are not accessible to women, and the very suggestion that that inaccessibility could be broached through a sexual relation points to that impossibility. Old Buddhist priests do not marry.

This is the title's function, to allegorise the narrative and, insofar as a title is a promise, this title is the promise of an unachievable promise. Benjamin defines allegory as a void 'that signifies precisely the non-being of what it represents.'[23] 'The Buddhist Priest's Wife' names a void, an impossible identity for woman. The notion of complete womanhood, which emerges through Schreiner's imaginary identification with Mary Wollstonecraft's life, is fictionally opened for scrutiny in a story whose allegorical ungroundedness indicates this as fantasy. Never re-named, the woman of the story is signified by an impossible relation.

Schreiner writes of this story that 'the substance of it is that which I have lived all these years to learn, and suffered all that I have suffered to know.'[24] I have already indicated the text's own refusal of the return to the authenticity of 'lived experience', and want to suggest that it also calls into question its own 'substance', the very possibility of a full representation. Indeed, the very relation between 'experience' and writing is problematised:

'You are always going to get experience, going to get everything, and you never do. You are always going to write when you know enough, and you are never satisfied that you do.' (67)

The failure here directed as an accusation to the woman straddles experience and knowledge. There is either too much (Schreiner's anxiety about finding form for 'all her thoughts') or too little – never the realization of perfect representation.

The notion of substance also returns in Schreiner's characteristic description of the change in form of her 'sex work': 'I threw most of it (or it threw itself) into the shape of a curious story.' The image of 'throwing' suggests a pot thrown on a potter's wheel, which makes this story a kind of container, a pot to contain the 'substance of all I know', the product of ten years work on 'sex evolution'. But it is an ambivalent figure. The process of pot throwing is in no simple sense the creation of a container: the lump of clay forms its shape around nothing; it does not 'contain' anything at the point of its creation at the wheel. It gives no easy model of fullness and plenitude, although it may promise the possibility of being filled, of containing, in the future. So while the figure may suggest Schreiner's desire for a container, her desire to find an adequate form, it also expresses ambivalence and the prospect of a more difficult and intractable problem. That problem might be understood as the *impossibility* of finding an adequate form, a questioning of the notion of 'adequacy' at all. For that adequacy has to answer to something which itself emerges as problematic in Schreiner's engagement with sexuality and 'sex evolution': that there may be no essence, no substance with which to fill the pot, no substantial existence which precedes the process of 'throwing' into a form.

The story itself covers familiar ground: the conversation of the man and the woman is about the similarity and difference between the sexes. The woman insists upon an inescapable law for women, 'of her nature and of sex relationship', a law which means that the sexes are at their most radically different at the point of 'the personal and sexual' (72), while intellectuality provides a possibility of absolute identity between them. In *Woman and Labour*, Schreiner secures this demarcation, the 'very narrow, but important region' where 'sex as sex' plays its part, through reproduction and maternity.[25] But here, whatever reference to 'naturalness' the woman protagonist makes, she does not ground it in motherhood.

Rather, the major references to children concern paternity – the man's wish for a child, his anxieties about succession and inheritance. The woman responds to his query regarding women's feelings for children by saying 'Yes, at times a woman has a curious longing to have a child'. (69) This 'curious' (the *OED* gives its meaning as 'Strange, surprising, odd') recalls the earlier letter to Cronwright, where Schreiner refers to 'The Buddhist Priest's Wife' as 'a curious story', and describes the relation between the man and the woman as casting a 'curious side-light'. These repetitions underline something which escapes the limits and terms set by the 'scientific view' to suggest instead an oddness: the 'law of nature' which the woman evokes in her description of sexual difference fails to secure maternity within its jurisdiction. The curiousness of a woman's longing for a child does not find its way to join that 'law of nature', but rather links the instability which it marks in the field of 'sex relationship' with an instability in representation, in writing, where 'the whole subject of sex, as far as my ten years' work at that subject have yet brought me'[26] is thrown into the form of a story. So the form of the representation becomes indissociable from the question of what constitutes the difference between the sexes.

But I must return here to the crucial attempt to hold apart intellectuality and sexuality which constitutes the fragile basis of the claim to sexual equality. That attempt fails and becomes the gap in Schreiner's work between politics and desire, between the wish for equality and the refusal to relinquish what appears to stand in opposition to it. The woman, in a long passage, explains the difference between men and women as the impermissibility for a woman of ever showing her sexual love for a man:

> You may seek for love because you can do it openly; we cannot because we must do it subtly. A woman should always walk with her arms folded. Of course friendship is different. You are on a perfect equality with man then; you can ask him to come and see you as I asked you. That's the beauty of the intellect and intellectual life to a woman, that she drops her shackles a little; and that is why she shrinks from sex so. (73–4)

The man's response to the woman's account of sexual difference is an effective effacement of her as a sexually desiring and desirable woman through reading her speech as a theory of equality: 'If all women were like you, all your theories of the equality of men and women would work. You're the only woman with whom I never realise that she is a woman.' (74) If the woman isn't a woman for the man then she must, in some sense, be a man: in speaking of difference, she erases her own difference for the man who turns out to be the object of her desire.

The most acute and painful points of the woman's impossible position between equality and difference centre on a moment when resolution is offered – then, I would argue, witheld – through a plot of the transcendence of death. The passage I quoted above – which ends with that ambiguous 'and that is why she shrinks from sex so', continues:

> If she were dying perhaps, or doing something equal to death, she might. . . . Death means so much more to a woman than to a man; when you knew you were dying, to look round on the world and feel the bond of sex that has broken and crushed you all your life gone, nothing but the human left, no woman any more, to meet everything on perfectly even ground. (74)

Dying, or doing something equal to death, is the perfect realization of a dissolution of sexual difference, where the woman can 'drop her shackles' in an absolute equality that signifies the death of her femininity. The final sentence would read as a support for this: 'nothing but the human left, no woman any more'. The syntax of the sentences, however, remains obscure. The 'perhaps' and 'she might' could also be read as answering to 'and that is why she shrinks from sex so': in dying or doing something equal to death, the woman might at last be able to end that shrinking from sex. The ellipsis in the text after 'she might' would then signify the failure of this moment, the recognition of the continuing impossibility of finding a language with which to speak sexual desire. And this ambiguity is not entirely closed down in the following sentence where death seems to emerge so strongly as transcendence. Death, supposedly the great leveller, is still posed here as a matter of sexual difference: 'Death means so much more to a woman than to a man'. But the very telling of that privileged relation cannot stay on course: from the pronoun 'you' at the beginning of the sentence, the final verb turns out to be the infinitive 'to meet'. It reveals a fantasy of endlessness, endlessly meeting everything on even ground, an endless deferral of death. So death as transcendence turns out to be a fantasy of the transcendence of death and there is no resolution of the problem of sexual identity.

At the beginning of this essay I said that I would try to indicate how the questions of sexual politics – equality, femininity –

returned Schreiner to colonial politics and her own position as a colonial subject. Reading *Woman and Labour*, hailed as 'the Bible of the Women's Movement',[27] acts as a salutory warning – if one were needed – against a presumption of a common language of liberation. Like the abandoned Wollstonecraft introduction, it too seeks to make the African woman occupy a space which can secure the place of the white, European middle-class (feminist) subject within a telos of civil progress and enlightenment. So, within that text, Schreiner's most acute anxieties around a feminist discourse – anxieties which arise in part out of the contradictions forced through her espousal of evolutionary science – hunt for relief and resolution at the cost of the African woman. Schreiner could of course be left there: a 'racist feminist' or, perhaps, the 'broken winged albatross of white liberal thinking'.[28] But I would argue that it is important that she is not – and perhaps particularly so for a white, European feminist. For while it is easy enough to identify and condemn the racism of Schreiner's texts, and perhaps even use them as a comforting index of change, it is a more difficult and painful task to follow her fantasmatic imaging of the colonial scene and her own place, as a white woman, within it.

In reading one of Schreiner's stories, I have tried to show how an instability in her writing is indissociable from an uncertainty about sexual identity. But there is, of course, one silent figure in the story of whom I have not yet spoken: I might name that figure the Buddhist priest, or perhaps India. I want to suggest that in this 'throwing' of her 'sex work' into a story which continually seeks but eludes resolution, Schreiner returns to a scene of cultural difference which disrupts her rooted images and fantasms of Africa.

The object 'Buddhism' is the one 'created' by nineteenth-century Victorian discourses which, in their location in the West as a textual object, could figure in Schreiner's imaginative landscape.[29] Within that landscape, 'Buddhism' comes to function as the name of the Other of European identity which escapes from, or disrupts, the remorseless and optimistic discourse of progress and civilisation. A ruthless industrialization, the divisions and conflict of sex and race, are lost or salved in a seeming stasis of philosophy and meditation. 'Buddhism' and 'India' pose for Schreiner the possibility of a different location, one which refuses identification as a site in urgent need of the redemptive incursion of Christianity. And while this might allow her to elide the imbrication of a 'civilising' Christian mission with a capital-istic and violent imperialism, it also allows her to at least partially dislodge the fixity of her fantasies. So against the representation of African women as devoid of agency in *Woman and Labour*, there is the possibility of Hindu women's revolt. And if the movement I am suggesting, from India to Africa, seems too great a move to claim for Schreiner, I would appeal to the European object 'Buddhism' again, and point to the widespread European belief that Buddha was originally an African.[30] By that route Schreiner re-encountered a questioning of colonialism.

It is certainly not for the finality of a political direction that Schreiner can be read today. Rather her literary body can be read most eloquently and, perhaps, usefully, as a troubling of representation which shows itself as always implicated in the problem of identity and politics. Her failure to resolve those issues may remain the most important lesson she can offer.

## Acknowledgements

This paper was presented in March 1990 to a conference held at Somerville College, University of Oxford, entitled 'Literature in Another South Africa' and I am grateful for responses to it. I would also like to thank Jacqueline Rose for her comments on a longer version of this piece, and Martin Murray for helpful suggestions concerning a couple of tricky terms.

## References

Abbreviations for letters:
O.S. – Olive Schreiner
H.E. – Havelock Ellis
K.P. – Karl Pearson
S.C.C.S. – Samuel C. Cronwright-Schreiner

1. Rive, R. (ed.) (1988). *Olive Schreiner Letters Vol. 1 1871–1899*. Oxford, Oxford University Press, p. 136. Letter O.S. to Mrs J.H. Philpot, 18 February 1888.
2. Letter O.S. to K.P., 26 October 1886, in Rive (1988), p. 111.
3. Letter O.S. to H.E., 2 May 1884, in Rive (1988), p. 40.
4. Wollstonecraft, M. (1792, rpt. 1985). *A Vindication of the Rights of Woman*. London, Dent, p. 203.
5. Walters, M. 'The rights and wrongs of woman: Mary Wollstonecraft, Harriet Martineau, Simone de Beauvoir', in Mitchell, J. and Oakley,

A. (eds.) (1976). *The Rights and Wrongs of Women*. Harmondsworth, Penguin, p. 306.

6. Wollstonecraft (1985), p. 6.

7. Jacobus, M. 'The difference of view', in Jacobus, M. (ed.) (1979). *Women Writing and Writing about Women*. London, Croom Helm, p. 15.

8. Kaplan, C. (1986). 'Wild nights: pleasure/sexuality/feminism', in *Sea Changes: Culture and Feminism*. London, Verso, p. 45.

9. Letter O.S. to K.P., 11 October 1886, in Rive (1988), p. 106.

10. Letter O.S. to Ernest Rhys, early 1888, in Rive (1988), p. 136.

11. Schreiner, O. (1911, rpt. 1978). *Woman and Labour*. London, Virago.

12. Cronwright-Schreiner, S.C. (1924, rpt. 1973). *The Life of Olive Schreiner*. New York, Haskell House, p. 354.

13. Cronwright-Schreiner, S.C. (1973), p. 356.

14. Schreiner, O. (1978), p. 16.

15. Cronwright-Schreiner, S.C. (ed.) (1924, rpt. 1976). *The Letters of Olive Schreiner*. Westport, Hyperion Press, p. 163. Letter O.S. to W.T. Stead, 1899.

16. Jacobson, D. 'Introduction', Schreiner, O. (1883, rpt. 1971). *The Story of an African Farm*. Harmondsworth, Penguin, p. 17.

17. Barthes, R. (1974). *S/Z*. Trans. R. Miller. New York, Hill and Wang.

18. Rive, R. (1972). 'An infinite compassion', *Contrast*, no. 29. Cape Town, 29, 34.

19. Letter O.S. to S.C.C.S., 4 January 1893, in Rive (1988), p. 217–8.

20. Schreiner, O. (1923). 'The Buddhist Priest's Wife', in *Stories, Dreams and Allegories*. London, Unwin. (Hereafter cited in text.)

21. First, R. and Scott, A. (1980). *Olive Schreiner*. London, Andre Deutsch, p. 191.

22. Benjamin, W. (1977). *The Origin of German Tragic Drama*. London, New Left Books, p. 195.

23. Quoted by de Man, P. (1983). *Blindness and Insight: Essays in the Rhetoric of Contemporary Criticism*. Minneapolis, University of Minnesota Press, p. 35.

24. Letter O.S. to W.P. Schreiner, September 1892 in Rive (1988), p. 208.

25. Schreiner (1978), p. 195.

26. Letter O.S. to W.T. Stead, March 1892, in Rive (1988), p. 201.

27. Brittain, V. (1933, rpt. 1978). *Testament of Youth: An Autobiographical Study of the Years 1900–1925*. London, Virago, p. 28.

28. Gordimer, N. 'The prison-house of colonialism', in Barash, C. (ed.) (1987). *An Olive Schreiner Reader*. London, Pandora, p. 223.

29. Almond, P.A. (1988). *The British Discovery of Buddhism*. Cambridge, Cambridge University Press, pp. 7–14.

30. Almond (1988), pp. 20–24.

Amanda Bell

# 6

## Feminism, class and literary criticism

### John Goode

## I: Droit de seigneur

In the interval talk during the 1990 Glyndebourne production of *Le Nozze di Figaro*, Simon Rattle, who was concerned to stress that the chief feature of the production was the use of authentic instruments which he felt clarified the score's dissonances, implicitly indicated an even more striking feature. He illustrated the relationship between score and singers first by discussing Marcellina, whose aria in Act IV is a strong protest against the oppressive perfidy of the human male. Then he showed how the matronly patience of the Countess could be turned into passionate anger. Susannah's performance was positioned in relation to those two, and neither Figaro nor the Count were mentioned. Thus the opera was to be derived from the apparently least important soprano part and focused on the women as a group. You would not think from the discussion that the dramatic world was ruled by its eponymous hero, or the social world by another man, Almaviva. It was certainly, though not explicitly, a production strongly influenced by feminism.

In part, to be sure, this reflects the opera (though one handbook at least asserts that Marcellina's aria is normally omitted in production). First, it is emphasized in relation to Beaumarchais' text. In the play, Marcellina's attack on men is split between the recognition scene (III.xvi) and the end of Act IV where it only briefly recurs. In the first of these, it emerges as a somewhat absurd outburst in three speeches which become increasingly passionate. Marcellina is said to be 's'échauffant par degrés' in the first and is 'exaltée' by the third (Beaumarchais 1957: 322–23)

– 'carried away by her own eloquence' according to the English translator, who wants us to be under no illusion that there is any substance to Marcellina's rhetoric (Beaumarchais 1964: 176). So it is embedded in a display of character and arises out of the general *mêlée*. In Da Ponte, on the contrary, it is a much more startling and impressive outburst, for Marcellina only reveals her 'feminism' when she has to choose between loyalty to her new-found son and her belief in Susannah's innocence based solely on her solidarity as a woman. The effect of this in the opera is to reduce Figaro himself to the same level of irrational absurdity as the Count, as his ironic air 'Aprite un po'quel' accui' emphasizes. In Beaumarchais, Figaro agrees with his mother and is allowed to hold the audience with general speeches about the times. In Da Ponte, he has become part of the dénouement in Act IV. Marcellina's address to the audience in Beaumarchais only ironizes women who, she says, will fight one another if there is cause for rivalry but when personal interest does not aim them against one another are drawn ('toutes portées') to support their poor oppressed sex. In the opera, Marcellina sings an observation about the perfidy of men. In the play she shows women passively carried by passion from one posture – rivalry – to another – solidarity. This contrast works through in other details. Thus the instant and unquestioned alliance between Susannah and the Countess is broken off momentarily in Beaumarchais by the servant's admiration for her mistress' ability to lie, a gift of 'l'usage du grand Monde' (III.xxiv, 1957: 304). Beaumarchais' target is the social system, not the war of the sexes. Da Ponte/Mozart are concerned also with hierarchy, but much more with the gap between the way women are construed and how they see things themselves. This is not surprising if we think that *Così Fan Tutte* is to follow.

But in one major respect play and opera coincide, and indeed the opera emphasizes what is less obvious in the play, and that is the relationship between the two comic resolutions of male *amour propre* and social oppression. The absurdity of male desire is exposed by dramatic intrigue on stage, and, in the final act, the Count, who has spent the whole play/opera thinking that he desires Susannah, gets turned on by his wife simply because he does not know it is her. Moreover, as I have said, the universalized jealousy of Figaro and the resentment of Bartolo are shown to be utterly subjective. These exposures take place through dramatic disguise, concealment, plot and revelation. Throughout the play male desire is shown to be ludicrous and childish by Cherubino (a complex case of cross-dressing made more imponderable by his/her soprano voice in the opera). A rich comic texture satirizes gender difference and resolves it in the provisional utopian manner germane to the genre.

The class issue, however, is different. This is a drama about the *droit de seigneur;* the fundamental concern is with the power of patronage. Figaro can only get his way through cunning and wit, and then only up to a certain point. However cleverly he tricks the Count into sticking to his decision to give up the *droit de seigneur* (voluntarily, of course – there is no question of it being taken away, and, as a result, no question of a loss of real power as all the praises sung in honour of his decision confirm), Figaro ultimately runs up against an economic determinant. He needs money to release him from his bond to Marcellina. The Count will only give that money in exchange for Susannah's favours. The feudal right which has been officially abandoned is continued by economic pressure. The resolution of this, especially in Da Ponte/Mozart, is not dramatic but narrative and romantic. In a scene of farcical unrealism, Figaro reveals the strawberry mark which discloses him as a gentleman and the son of Marcellina. The birthmark, the story of kidnapping and the parody of Oedipus are all stale romance devices. And whereas in Beaumarchais, Bartolo and Figaro are far from overjoyed by his discovery (thus qualifying it with a certain 'realism') Da Ponte/Mozart have all three – mother, father, son – sing a most happy trio while the Count stands by distraught by his exclusion. It is all absurd, and it occurs so soon and so abruptly that we are left in no doubt that the final dénouement, which is the exposure of the *amour propre,* is the serious concern of the drama. Thus whereas the women achieve equality (of a sort) *dramatically* by the development of character, the servants are only rescued by the fact that their chief spokesman turns out to be a gentleman after all. It is not surprising that Michelet found the play unrevolutionary, nor that it is said that Da Ponte plays down the political subversiveness. I do not actually think this is true, however. What he does is visibly abandon one half of the class/gender differential system which constitutes the dramatic basis of the opera. And the marginalization of Figaro in the fourth act confirms this. The Glyndebourne production brought this out very fully. Not only does Marcellina become the keynote woman, but Figaro is a much less dominant character than the Count whose passions are disclosed with an evil intensity. This was a production threatened with rape.

I draw two seemingly contradictory lessons from this. First, the fact that this production can be so recognizably feminist without, it seems, being conscious of it (since Rattle was concerned with its authenticity) tells us something about the degree to which feminism has altered cultural perceptions even at a level where 'establishment' values are pervasive. On the other hand the social implication seems to be less privileged: Peter Hall's staging was pretty and luxurious, and there was no sense of the *Ancien Régime* being oppressive. This is partly no doubt because the class issues in Beaumarchais are more related to feudalism than capitalism and indicate that gender difference works on a larger, longer time scale.

But the other possibility is that feminism has become the victim of a certain legitimation. For, after all, if the class relations of Beaumarchais have changed, so have the gender relations: oppression of women today is not the same as it was in the eighteenth century. What the Glyndebourne production was responding to was not the contemporaneity of the specific sexual mores of the *Ancien Régime* but the general and translatable fact that in late eighteenth-century society, as in ours, women are systematically oppressed. We could equally make the same transfer of class relations, and indeed the shift within the play from legal to economic power inscribes this on the surface. Beaumarchais, Da Ponte and this particular production each progressively weighs the scale of gender down in relation to that of class. The eighteenth-century authors maybe see it as only soluble through a history that cannot be presented, only represented through the intrusion of another time into the spectacle. The twentieth-century audience has less interest because the dissonances of actuality are more audible on the level of gender.

This, if it is true, is surely a new situation. Twenty years ago, the culture reflected a complex but intense concern with social inequality. From *Roots* and *Saturday Night and Sunday Morning* to *Cathy Come Home* the long revolution towards a society free of class oppression was the central issue. The oppression of women got on to the progressive agenda by a polemical rebuke – women, the *longest* revolution. Capitalism is not now on the wane, but has taken new forms which can accommodate a limited sexual equality. The television is full of advertisements which joke about equal opportunities. We must not exaggerate; opportunities for women may have increased but that is a long way from equality. There may be women on the stock market, and some men have been forced to dress in pretty uniforms and serve fast food. But in the two equal opportunity institutions in which I have recently worked, it is women who clean the male urinals, and the revived sweating system in the garment industry is dominantly serviced by female workers. The opportunities are more equal for some than others.

But this makes it important not to lose sight of the class issue, for the oppression is most effective when it is compounded by economic power. I am far from saying that middle-class women are liberated. The physical environment with its lack of child care facilities, its vast residual imbalance of gender distribution of responsibility and educational opportunity, is underwritten by a culture which still throws unwarranted psychic burdens on women of all classes. If I had to choose, I would rather be a (moderately) poor male than a rich female. Independent of each other as the two forms of oppression are they must both be kept in view. And that means not only not ignoring one of them, but not overlaying one with the other by metaphor or some other rhetorical link. It even means, as this is what happens in the real world, playing them off against one another as enemies. Literature is a privileged site of these issues because it rehearses them in a controlled space. Narrative and metaphor offer tempting connections which as readers we should be prepared to resist.

## II: Men in feminism

I have probably already angered many feminists who will question my right to deliberate on these matters. I am trying to write about the oppression of women, its relation to the oppression of the working class and the implication of this for literary criticism. I cannot claim any real experience of either form of oppression, though I have more direct links to the latter than the former. I do try to practise socialist and feminist criticism, but whereas socialists are nothing if not unfashionable, feminists have established a certain power base in academic life, and it is not surprising that men who ally themselves with the feminist movement are accused of a certain opportunism (for example, Todd 1988). So I had better account for the temerity of my intervention. I became interested in literature as a function of class displacement. Literary texts were both a means of entry into the dominant culture and a way of retaining a critical option. By 1964 when I got my first university post I was working within an ideological framework dominated by Lukács, E.P. Thompson, and Raymond Williams. The specific situation of women is something that barely crossed my mind (unforgivably, it has to be said, since there was plenty of evidence all around me including that provided by my own practice). By amazing good fortune, I worked in a Department of English which also had Juliet Mitchell and Margaret Walters, precisely at the advent of what Terry Lovell has called 'the second wave' of British feminist thought. One of my first publications appeared in the same issue of *New Left Review* as the original text of 'Women, The Longest Revolution'. It is not surprising that I assimilated some feminist ideas. In the 1970s, Juliet Mitchell and later Mary Jacobus invited me to write for collections they were editing. I accepted these invitations without really thinking that I was climbing on to a bandwagon, but I did benefit by being asked to talk at the George Eliot centennial at Rutgers in 1980. Here I met Elaine Showalter, Sandra Gilbert, Nina Auerbach and many others, and realized that feminist literary scholarship was already strongly developed, and that any participation of mine in this field from now on should be more in the nature of moral support than active intervention. This was certainly emphasized by the fact that when Women's Studies were set up at Warwick males were rightly, in the context, excluded from participation. On days of self-flattery, I like to think that as soon as feminism showed signs of being a bandwagon in literature departments, I got off. Obviously, feminism has continued to affect my criticism, but if I need feminism, it does not need me.

This embarrassing autobiographical digression seems necessary as general self-justification in the light of the self-conscious rhetoric of most of the male contributions to that bizarre text, *Men in Feminism* (Jardine and Smith 1987), and of the more excruciating appropriations which have happened in the last decade. I accept that the central preoccupation of feminist criticism should be, as Showalter defines it, 'gynocritics' (1979: 26) though as Lovell has pointed out (1987: 132) this needs to concern itself not merely with women's writing, but more specifically with 'woman to woman writing' that is liable, as she argues, to be 'coded out of "literature"'. Besides solidarity, men can contribute little to this. They can, of course, try to read male texts in a feminist perspective without critical cross-dressing. But there is another

periphery here marked by women's writing which is not specifically 'to woman' but which is a meeting point – vexed and
incomplete as all literary articulations must be – of competing
forms of oppression. So that if here I am waving a banner saying
'what about the workers?', on its reverse, facing the other crowd,
is 'the woman pays'.

## III: An unhappy marriage

Revolutionary socialism, after the terrible trauma of 1956, experienced a revival during the sixties, which coincided with a
feminist revival. By 1983 revolutionary socialism was beleagured
and on the edge of its present total (though temporary, as I
believe) eclipse. The success of feminism was no more than a raft
some socialists were trying to climb aboard. It is clear now that
the socialist movement of the sixties and seventies failed to take
account of the feminist movement in a productive way. The long
series of debates between marxism and feminism were conducted almost exclusively from the feminist position and it is not
surprising that the most potent, though disputed, image was of
the unhappy marriage. Terry Lovell writes that marxism and
feminism talk past one another (Lovell 1987: 161) and the
impression created by her recent anthology is that the situation
described by Sally Alexander in the opening essay, 'Women,
Class and Sexual Difference in the 1830s and 1840s' is that not
much has changed in the last 150 years (Lovell 1990: 28–50). Perry
Anderson's magisterial review of the intellectual disciplines
ghettoizes feminism in a section of its own (the last) and disposes
of it with an embarrassed avuncular simile – 'something like a
transverse current moving, as it were, across the wider flow'
(Anderson 1990: 135).

But, of course, it is precisely the context of the *New Left Review*
in which the debate in its present phase was inaugurated by Juliet
Mitchell, 'the significance of [whose] work for British socialist
feminism' as Terry Lovell puts it, 'cannot be over estimated'
(Lovell 1990: 5). What began in 'Women, The Longest Revolution' as a rebuke to the exclusivity of class analysis, had become,
by the time of *Psychoanalysis and Feminism* a much more direct
challenge to classic socialist theory. Scrutinizing and revising
Freud and rescuing him from biologistic appropriations or
anarchist salvationism, Mitchell proposes that in kinship relations, patriarchy is a meta-discourse, within which capitalist

ideology is but a particular expression. Our access to this meta-discourse is through psychoanalysis, whose main function is to establish gender difference (Mitchell 1974: 409). The strategic proposal is not that socialists should alter their politics to account for gender difference but that it is possible to pursue two autonomous revolutions – the social revolution in the economic base of capitalism and the cultural revolution in the superstructure of ideology.

This becomes known as dual systems theory (for example Sergeant 1981) and is vigorously debated on a number of levels. Much as I would love to enter this debate, I do not suppose anybody but me would benefit from it. There can be no doubt that certain positions are inscribed for men and women irrespective of the particular formation of their societies, and indeed it is precisely because borrowings can be made that these positions and the codes they are fixed by can seem to be (if not are) non-socially specific. Thus chivalry can be made to serve the sanctification of the nuclear family, a form within which it has no place historically. There is also no guarantee that a less oppressive mode of production will in itself alter the oppression of women. And this has to be because such values are constitutive of the self (which means the subject aware of itself as subject). Unless they are biologically determined (which would not make sense) they must be determined by a very deep-seated cultural transmission. Psychoanalysis, which postulates an unconscious in which all the desires which have to be repressed in order to serve cultural needs are deposited, must have a role in unmasking these strategies. I think the arguments that Elizabeth Wilson mounts against the exclusive privileging of psychoanalysis have some grounds but I do not find that they relate to what Juliet Mitchell actually writes. Mitchell does not argue, for example, that psychoanalysis shows gender to be so utterly determined that it might as well be biology. On the contrary, she is arguing that patriarchy, which is what psychoanalysis uncovers, is highly vulnerable. Psychoanalysis is not, after all, a process of knowledge. It is a practical activity. Nor, on the other hand, do I have any sense that it is thought that the 'cultural revolution' could come even if the social revolution were entirely abandoned (Wilson 1986: 157–161). Surely the lesson of Stalinism is rather the opposite. Slapping a different mode of production on an unchanged culture is both violently repressive and, as we now see, doomed to failure.

Nevertheless, I do not think that *Psychoanalysis and Feminism* was intended to be a bible. On the contrary, its conclusions are deliberately circumspect. The unravelling of patriarchy and capitalism is an analytic strategy motivated by the perception that in, say, writers as diverse as Engels and Marcuse, the welding of them together results in patriarchy always being seen within capitalism. This could no longer be said to be the case. There is a great deal of writing which now presents capitalism as merely a special case of patriarchy, the danger of which is that it emulsifies the relationship between them. Mitchell's later retrospective essay is explicitly alert to this: 'by setting up the opposition of the sexes as dominant, we helped to produce the ideological notion of a "classless society"' (Mitchell 1986: 45). It is not surprising that any marriage between marxism and feminism is likely to be unhappy. Both know only too well that it is an oppressive institution. A more abrasive relationship between the two might have more realism.

For this, in the present situation, we need to focus on what Juliet Mitchell strategically marginalized in 1974, the interaction of the two forces in a specific historic formation. This is indeed happening within British historiography. Barbara Taylor (1983) has unscrambled the gender/class tensions within the working class in the age of Chartism. Mary Poovey (1989), in a remarkable sequence of specific studies of parturition, divorce and nursing, investigates 'the ideological work of gender' in mid-Victorian England. Above all, Leonore Davidoff and Catherine Hall (1987) have investigated the role of gender difference in the formation of middle-class culture in early-Victorian England. These texts show that at specific historical points the categories of class and gender cut across as well as reinforce one another and that it is at those points of tension and repressive reconciliation that the complex interactions show themselves. They show that the closer you look at the actual history, the more variegated and volatile are the interactions of economic demands and ideological strategies.

But this does not invalidate a longer view in which cultural divisions transgress economic structures. A class structure needs but is tested by gender difference, and the residual patriarchy which forms the individual's psychic position is at once threatened and appropriated in the actuality of history and how people experience it. In this telescopic view, capitalism is the latest instance of what has motivated all known human history, strategies for dealing with scarcity. Among these capitalism, by its very nature, primarily selects accumulation. It shares with its predecessors, however, the need to deal with scarcity by forms of human selectivity – the most tried and trusted of which is oppression of specific groups. The most efficient and affable form of oppression is to activate one oppressed group against another, and nothing could be more convenient for the ecology of selective practices than that such groups should experience such oppressions in radically different and exclusive forms. This prescribes active solidarity, but language is too vulnerable to premature utopianism. It should also strive to recall the past and represent the present. On the level of theory, feminists and socialists should learn how to quarrel, and socialist feminists in particular have to learn how to quarrel among themselves. That this is a well-developed though highly-fraught area of intellectual debate, Lovell's anthology fully demonstrates (1990: 71–169). But it is important for the understanding of literary texts, which float up from variable depths and on different currents.

## IV:  Insisting on the letter

The first level of the problematic of reading is that 'literature' is a construct that arrives and is developed (dialectically, not genetically) with the developing domination of capitalism and the industrial bourgeoisie. This gives rise to contested readings. The novel lies outside 'literature' for a long time but once it is incorporated, we can never again return to the primitive reading of the cultural production situation of novels in the eighteenth and nineteenth centuries. This is not a question of canonicity but of reading practices. Terry Lovell (1987: 133–150) has shown that 'literature' is linked with the extension of higher education to women (as in theory it was to have been for the working class as well). We can write general histories of the class/gender implications of extended literacy and its cultural significance, but our reading of these texts is always going to be within a definite institutional framework. Even non-canonical phenomena – popular fiction, movies, advertisements – are assimilated into the interpretive process, which assumes that the text does not really know what it is saying. Like analysands, they need to be interpreted. Both the texts that make it to the academic couch and the qualified readers who – whatever their origins – have the resources to study them are inevitably separated from working-class experience.

The question is whether such privileged texts can do more than embody the oppression of women as a specific class expression. There are two answers to this – one is basically 'no' but they can by their silence help us to translate the specific gender oppression to other specific gender oppressions. Thus, for example, Boumelha on *Shirley* does not try to challenge the Thompson/Eagleton position that for all its gender radicalism, it retreats into a bourgeois myth, but shows that it remains audibly silent at this barrier, leaving the last word to the servant (Boumelha 1990: 99). There is a second kind of answer, like Nancy Armstrong's, which argues that fiction displaces politics to domesticity and thus that in the gender conflict the real subtext of the plot is played out (Armstrong 1989: 4).

One way through this impasse is the further restriction that literary texts by their very nature tell lies. Boumelha complains, in her essay on George Eliot, that too much feminist criticism relies on a naive realism (Boumelha 1987: 25). One of the striking developments of the last decade has been to see the text less as representational than as functional. Texts do not embody real relations but display the imaginary relations by which those real relations call the subject into being. Thus it is not for what they represent that texts must be read but for what they omit or expose in a disturbed way (Belsey 1980: 129). The dominant aesthetic of organic form has to be inverted. In this way there is first a departure from the classic realist text and a new evaluation of fantasy, but there is also within the 'realist' text a subtext which does not say what it means, but reveals the meaning it is designed to conceal.

There are two difficulties here. In the first place, far from inverting prominent critical modes this merely seems to me to confirm them. There never was a genuine canon of literary studies, though it is often convenient to deal with a recurrent body of texts as though it were so. We must not forget that an enterprise such as *The Great Tradition* which sets out to establish a body of sacred texts, is consciously contesting a perceived dominant category. Nor does it privilege representation and realism, though later Watt's *The Rise of the Novel* appears to (I say appears because Watt does not offer representation but a kind of readerly consensus as the mark of formal realism). The organic form or moral fable is also a kind of subtext and the more subversive subtext of later feminist criticism is only displacing one paradigm (of identity) into another (of difference). I say 'only' and it would be wrong to underestimate that inversion. One uneasy silence in my argument is about contemporary French feminism whose re-interpretative energies are undeniable, though whether we can resist what Janet Wolff calls 'any lingering essentialism' (Wolff 1990: 62), without resisting the whole enterprise, is not easy to judge. We see in American deconstruction how pluralism and open-ness can be depoliticized.

More importantly, it is not sensible to confuse representation with narrowly defined realism. If we see texts as merely expressive we have to move from the text to the author, which is a circular process – since how can we find the author except in the text? But we can usefully, though admittedly with analogical imprecision, think of a text as having margins, that is markers which identify the conditions on which a text distances itself from language in general. This relates to the specific mode of production of the text, and it is interesting that Wolff (1990: 108) has recently, in calling for a greater integration of textual analysis and the institution by which texts are produced and consumed, recalled Eagleton's phrase 'literary mode of production'.

But production does not stop. *Villette* has a marginal but concise place in *The Great Tradition* but, since Kate Millett selected it as the only female novel to discuss in any detail (1972: 140–147), it has become the patient of many readings. Is it produced in conditions of the Victorian novel or the Feminist Tradition?

The relativity of production may be, however, the way through the dilemma of representation and expressivity. Texts would not be expressive if they were not representative or even representational. Lovell has noted how the history of the novel is poised strangely between formal realism and the Gothic, but these two are not so far apart. The portrayal of unromantic daily life is of course completely illusionistic. Neither *Pamela* nor *Emma* represent anything that really happened. Instead it is the condition of realism that it contains a negotiable world within a definite frame – as Balzac, accusing his reader of sitting complacently in his armchair at the commencement of his obscure Parisian tragedy, acknowledges. It is only a kind of snobbery that suggests there is not this same mix of motives when we pick up *Emma* as when we watch *East Enders*. The recognizability is part of the pleasure. Equally fantasy is not escapist. If it did not represent something real it would lose its compensatory value. Gothic terror is not merely a frisson but an education. The point is that both kinds of text offer narrative and the important point about narrative, as Boumelha, making a more useful distinction between Romance and *Bildung* suggests, is that they are teleological, offering 'socially ratified closure' to 'utopian expansion' (Boumelha 1990: 20). On this basis, feminist reading becomes a question of unmasking what is resistant to narrative closure. Boumelha's own reading of *Villette* is a subtle and expressive deconstruction of the way in which the novel forces upon its reader 'the strangeness of narration itself' (1990: 103).

This strategy reveals a site in which the divided discourses of class and gender can interact, but it has dangers. The most cogent argument against my claim that the 'literary text' is constituted as a fixed area within which class can be subordinated to gender is Kaplan's 'Subjectivity, Class and Sexuality', which precisely maintains that by its nature as 'a heterogeneous discourse' literature can be read as 'an imaginary though temporary solution to the crisis of both femininity and class' (Kaplan 1985: 164). Visibility and frailty thus open up the awareness of something (the class insistence on gender difference) otherwise 'absolute and impregnable'. How exactly does that 'both' get constructed? For Kaplan (who uses few examples), it is through a resort to the Althusserian appropriations of Freud – condensation and displacement. This arises from the general limitation of feminism to a function of the Enlightenment project. Wollstonecraft situates feminism within rationality and thus the liberal coherent subject. Literature demolishes that by the heterogenous admission of other discourses: 'Female subjectivity, or its synechdotal reference, female sexuality, becomes the displaced and condensed site for the general anxiety about individual behaviour which republican and liberal political philosophy throw up' (Kaplan 1985: 165). The number of hermeneutic steps that have to be taken here is very worrying. In the first place we have to assume that female sexuality (which in turn is mostly represented by 'romantic love') is a synechdoche for female subjectivity. I can only say that, as a man, I would never allow anybody to do this to me. My sexuality is obviously part of my subjectivity but I would strongly resent being identified by my capacity to fall in love. Indeed no *Bildungsroman* with a male protagonist would work in that way. Even the hero of *Le Rouge et le Noir*, who makes a career out of falling in love, has a second room in his ego for diplomacy. Secondly, that sexuality is colonized by general ideological anxiety, which in turn is truncated into individual behaviour. Interpretation of this kind fuses distinct factors whose relationship is never stable.

If gender is cultural, however, so is narrative. All novels use narrative but they are only a tiny manifestation of the totality of highly developed narrative practices. The clearest motive of narrative seems to be, as Levi Strauss defined myth, to explain something in a culture which cannot be explained rationally. It is a just-so story – do not ask why, here is how. Realism at its most abstract level is crucial to this – for our culture, gender is explained entirely by narrative. It has no cause other than the history of its formation. Eve, the mother of mankind, was made to be the helpmeet of man from his spare rib. Through her, mankind fell from his paradisal state and she was thus condemned to the pain of childbirth. In the Judaeo-Christian tradition which was widely believed well into the nineteenth century, no biological reason for gender is offered. Biology becomes important only when the narrative fails. Boumelha (1990: 13) writes that Darwin, Marx and Freud all offered narratives and although this is true, it is also true that they set out to demolish the more convenient narratives of bourgeois society – genesis, Lamarckian teleology, supply and demand, the narrative coherence of dream and waking. The origin of species turns out not to be originary, the market turns out to be a specific historical structure not an eternal law.

This makes narratives by definition double-edged. They are modes of legitimation but they would not be necessary if they did not have questions to be answered; you do not need to make laws against acts that people are unlikely to commit. Thus, by their readability, they are also the means of recognition. It is not merely the *defects* of fictional coherence that open up the ideological closure, it is the fictionality itself that discloses a problematic in the ideology, otherwise you would not need to tell stories about it. That may be a reason, for example, why there is so little fiction about the labour process itself (indeed not much real documentation either) because there does not need to be a story about work. You work for a living if you need to because otherwise you would starve (this is ideologically, not absolutely true). Why women can't work for a living or only work at certain useless tasks like being a governess, why marriage has to be monogamous, permanent, and exogamous and why women have to take the name of men – these are not self-evident. They are matters of history. History, if it is indeed what hurts, is not a simple undialectical limit of desire. It is rather the set of conditions within which needs and desires may come to be partially accommodated. This is not to deny Boumelha's concept of excess, merely to take it structurally into the narrative project.

If this is the case, and I recognize that it resists a whole line of argument deriving from deconstruction and its penumbra, then we do not ask of bourgeois literature that it should somewhere reintegrate the abrasive contradictions of gender and class, not even in the transformed text of interpretation. Bourgeois culture can recognize rank but it cannot recognize class since class is part of the economic structure. Ideologically, a man's a man for all that, but of course it cannot think that a woman is a man too, though there is no reason why not. From at least *The Rights of Woman* to *Daniel Deronda* that contradiction is unmasked by argument and narrative. On the other hand, the woman's story in certain privileged texts meets its own class boundaries and it is in these that the relationship between class and femininity is deployed. They are the texts, I shall argue, that look back to childhood when gender is in the proces of formation. This double instance makes *Middlemarch* the key text, though a comprehensive account would need to consider much debated precedents such as *Frankenstein* and *Wuthering Heights*.

## V:  It would have required a narrative

In her suggestive exploration of women intellectuals within Victorian patriarchy, Deirdre David writes: 'All intellectuals of both sexes can trace their genesis, in the most general terms, to a matrix of cultural and social values, but the woman intellectual in the Victorian period possessed a less firm sense of lineage and affiliation with a tradition than was the experience of the male intellectual' (David 1987: 226). As it happens, I do not think the sense of lineage and affiliation of most male intellectuals would stand much scrutiny. Carlyle, Ruskin and especially Arnold were after all desperately trying to construct such a lineage (what could be more minimalist than the touchstone?). But it is true as a relative statement – coherence is even harder for the writers David investigates than for their male counterparts. This implies that we should turn the statement on its head. Women intellectuals have a more strong sense of the disorganic forces within their situation.

I want to question the apparently transparent metaphor of the matrix, clearly used by David as a mathematical term but recalling by its contiguity its biological etymology. Yes, we have one mother, but it is not from her that we derive our cultural and social values. These not only do not come from a unitary source but specifically come from contesting sources whose task is to neutralize one another. The utopian function of the traditional intellectual (who, in the English case at least, is not assigned to but has to seek this role) is to organize that contest into an acceptable coherence (ritual, dance, catharsis). But s/he can only aspire to this through the recognition of the originating dispersal. This is why so many major Victorian male writers felt themselves prone to or threatened by their own femininity, and why the most knowing and unaccommodating of them, Arthur Hugh Clough, defrocked genesis, matrimony and masculinity. *The woman intellectual is the paradigmatic case.*

We must attend to texts that represent the class-specific expression of the gender division. These will expressly not be woman-to-woman texts but texts that inscribe femininity at the boundaries of class culture. Thus if *Villette* assumes a central place in feminist criticism, *Middlemarch* will have to be restored to its frontier. This is confirmed by its remarkable critical history. There is a certain point at which it might be seen as the canonical text – morally motivated, organically structured, naturally available for discussion. The two dominant tendencies in British criticism, Cambridge scrutinism and Oxford liberalism, both claimed it as their own. If Leavis thought of Eliot as 'a peculiarly fortifying and wholesome author' (1962: 139), thus making her the *All Bran* of English Literature, W.J. Harvey would also cite *Middlemarch* – along with *War and Peace*, and taking his authority from C.S. Lewis and Iris Murdoch – as one of the 'normal' novels of which the 'liberal' says 'Yes, this is the world' (Harvey 1966: 16, 182–83).

*Middlemarch* has paid the price of this assimilation. By the time Barthes' ideas arrived in England, MacCabe had it as the example of the classic realist text, situating the reader as unproblematic subject in dominance with access to a metalanguage by which the mere minds within the text could be ironized (MacCabe 1978: 16), and Zelda Austen was defensively trying to explain 'Why feminist critics are angry with George Eliot' (Austen 1976: 549).

Showalter saw Eliot as less radical than Charlotte Brontë and proposed rescuing a woman's novel ('the fall of Dorothea') from *Middlemarch* (Showalter 1977: 131; 1980: 306). The end of organic form and the end of realism on the one hand, the rise of radical feminism on the other, both made *Middlemarch* look like a monument to dead ideas.

Of course that was in the 1970s. The last decade has seen a recuperation. Hillis Miller and Lodge have shown that the authority of the narrator is not unquestioned and various writers, notably Gillian Beer (1986) and Jennifer Uglow (1987), have reclaimed Eliot for the sisterhood. I think something has got lost in this double restitution, however. Certainly the pluralist text of Lodge – though it certainly is closer to what actually happens than MacCabe's selective reading – does not pick up what for me is the most striking and positive thing about the novel, and that is its absolute concern for truthfulness and straight looking, within a strong awareness of its difficulty. In other words I certainly think there is an authority claimed by the text, though not the authority assumed in MacCabe's understanding of realism. This is partly because I resist the compression of knowledge and power into a single mode of oppression. As for the feminist reclamations, I think that there is some wishful thinking involved even in Gillian Beer's meticulous contextualizing, which significantly focuses on the unrepresented history of feminism that closes the gap between the time of the story (the 1830s) and the time of the narrating (the 1870s) (1986: 147–199).

We must start from a text which does operate a hierarchy of discourses and does not concern itself with the emergence of the female subject. Penny Boumelha again anticipates my position here, showing that Eliot's novel eschews 'transcendence by the individual' and 'uses a relentlessly materialist vocabulary' to affirm this. I need however to develop this insight to apply to the whole structure of the text (Boumelha 1987: 30).

If 'Realism' is a useful term to apply to nineteenth-century fiction, following it is true the retrospective celebration of Lukács, it can be said to be identified with Balzac and Stendhal in France and Gogol and Tolstoi in Russia. In so far as it has an idea of itself, it is exactly opposite from the descriptions of MacCabe and Belsey. In fact 'classic realist' must be a contradiction in terms since 'classic', if it means anything at all, must refer to the possibility of ahistorical aesthetic structures which realism, evolving at its simplest level, from Cervantes, actually seeks to subvert. Even *Anna Karenina*, which seems to offer itself as an almost natural narrative, opens with a self-conscious comparison between happy and unhappy families and occasionally materializes Levin's reflections (as when he appears wrapped in furs early in the novel). Balzac is certainly challenging the reader's predisposition to literary convention in *Père Goriot* and when Stendhal asks whether the word 'hypocrite' surprises us he is questioning the whole basis on which we receive character.

'Realism' as a project undeniably posits an authorial distance but that distance is problematized and secular. When George Eliot in Chapter XV of *Middlemarch* contrasts her position with Fielding's capacity to involve generalizations in an armchair drawn to the front of a proscenium arch, she is disavowing three classical principles: a belief in human nature as a universal, a belief in the capacity of the author to speak in his own right as a man of sense, and a belief in the demonstrative capacity of the stage to show appearances that coincide with the reality. Lydgate's discovery of science, which is the subject of the chapter, exactly parallels this distance. He moves from the vapid generality of a gentleman's classical education to the dusty particularity of research which knows that neither sign nor category have any status in the object of knowledge. This particular web which has so often been taken for a totalizing principle in the novel has to be unravelled by the act of writing. Of course, like Darwin's tangled bank it does not disclose *itself* as a set of connections. If there is an ecology it must be researched.

This has two implications for the argument of this essay. Firstly, it suggests that *Middlemarch* is deeply suspicious of the lying discourse of literature, specifically metaphor and narrative. Both of these are related to the situation of woman in social organizations and are, of course, not merely literary but social. Lydgate here in Chapter XV is viewed by Middlemarch itself as 'a cluster of signs' and by himself as someone betrayed by woman, someone with a narrative already closed. Within the wider text, not only is Rosamund's swan-like neck conferred on her at a dinner party by gossip, but also the opening image of Miss Brooke is presented to us before she has any kind of history. More importantly, narrative is the unreliable chain that ties women into marriage since it is only through the necessary prolepsis of romance that marriage choices can be made. Both Dorothea and Rosamund make up stories of their future, but this is not a straightforward irony, since how else can they be expected to choose men?

Dorothea's inferences may seem large but really life could never have gone on at any period but for the liberal allowance of conclusions, which has facilitated marriage under the difficulties of civilisation. Has anyone ever pinched into its pilulous smallness the cobweb of pre-matrimonial acquaintanceship? (Eliot 1986: 22)

This is a clear attack on the binding contract of marriage which makes an imaginative inference into an iron law: 'I am always at Lowick'. 'That is a dreadful imprisonment' (382).

The novel also deploys both metaphor and narrative in the interests of truth, but this leads us to its two specific conditions. First, its historicity. The only moment when the shared misery of the novel impinges on consciousness is when Dorothea appeals to Lydgate and he, years afterwards, remembers the cry from soul to soul, within that embroiled medium. Of course this recall comes too late to be of use to either of them, but it establishes the precise nature of the reader's privilege. We are not enabled to see the error and limitation of the protagonists because of some subject-engendered privilege, merely because we are no longer caught in that history. We have to make judgments on what the characters do – not to judge would be to treat the lives of people as objects of consumption (which, of course, is partly inevitable if we read about them) but judgment is at our peril for we live within our own embroiled medium and we only see the embroil-ment of others with any clarity. That is why, I think, for all its historical distance and its class boundaries, *Middlemarch* goes on bearing meaning to its readers, (who have more sense of actual life than some academic critics). When Eliot does come, at last, in *Daniel Deronda*, to write about her own time, she has given it up for lost.

Secondly, in so far as it claims for itself a certain scientificity, *Middlemarch* does not belong to the natural history discourse of Balzac but to the discourse of experiment. Experiment operates by exclusion. One of MacCabe's demonstrations of the novel's arrogance is the end of Chapter XXXIX when Dagley, drunk, is dismissed to benightedness. MacCabe fails to quote, however, the end of the chapter:

Some things he knew thoroughly, namely, the slovenly habits of farming, and the awkwardnesses of weather, stock and crops, at Freeman's End – so called apparently by way of

sarcasm, to imply that a man was free to quit it if he chose,
but that there was no earthly 'beyond' open to him. (433)

The irony doubles back on itself. However unbenighted
Dagley might become, there would be no earthly 'beyond' open
to him. But the novel does not pursue this. What is more
important is that it comes in the very chapter that, in reply to
Ladislaw's 'that is a dreadful imprisonment', Dorothea answers 'I
have no longings'. Clearly there is a connection between the
economic and the ideological determinants here, but it cannot be
said that the former substitutes for or displaces the latter since the
connection is visibly repressed. There are other moments when
the novel seems to encounter its own boundaries. Thus in the
very chapter in which Mrs Garth questions Dorothea's woman-
liness (538), Caleb, confronted with the peasants' fear of rail-
ways, is reduced to silence for he 'had no cant at command'(546).
All round the text is a silence that acknowledges a world beyond.
Later in the novel, fraught with jealousy of Ladislaw and
Rosamund, Dorothea looks out and sees a poor man and woman
walking each with a burden, 'the manifold wakings of men to
labour and endurance' (777). This will give her a general courage,
but the 'manifold wakings' pass out of the story. Clusters of
signs, narratives, are controlled by far-reaching enquiry, but it
knows exactly how far it goes – not into the life of Brassing or the
tenant farm or the nomadic labourer. The historical project is
specific.

I have argued elsewhere that the specific movement in George
Eliot's fiction from the dualistic pictorialism and memorialization
of *Adam Bede* and *The Mill on the Floss* is in *Romola* because it makes
marriage the narrative opening (Goode 1983: 44). Marriage for
Eliot is not the privileging of the domestic over the public life but
the arena in which public and private meet. We need, I think, to
see a definite historical sequence which investigates this meeting:
first, at the onset of the modern world, the Renaissance, in
*Romola*, then at the emergent dominance of Eliot's own middle
class, the 1830s, the time of the Reform Bill, and finally, her own
time, the threshold of Imperialist expansion and extra-European
consciousness. In this sequence, if I am right, it is not *Middlemarch*
that is the anomaly but *Felix Holt*. This novel sets out most
explicitly to deal with class relations and it is the focus of the most
concentrated political complaints about her. Williams's critique,
for example, focuses on *Felix Holt* a good deal (Williams 1970:

83–88). *Middlemarch* returns to the same period, and effectively cancels *Felix Holt*. What redeems the latter novel, of course, is the story of Mrs Transome. The issue of gender subverts the project, leaves it looking lifeless. The stated project, that there is no private life that is not determined by a wider public life, is never realized in the text since the question of reform is simply personalized, and change merely weathered. What threatens to disrupt this is the story of the critical wife and dominant mother. The relationship of political and gender issues is inverted in *Middlemarch*. Reform here is marginal, almost there merely to provide a seam connecting Miss Brooke to Middlemarch and a pretext for the presence of Ladislaw.

Davidoff and Hall have enabled us to see what a central and accurate historical decision this is. They show a number of things which illuminate the actual project of *Middlemarch*. First, that the question of marriage and the gender roles it displays is a new issue in the years 1780–1850. Second, that this question is constitutive of middle-class identity and that it is in process during that time, so that to deal with it is not to displace actual politics – it is a political sphere (and not in the dubious sense in which the personal is claimed to be political, but in the sense that it is an important public arena). Third, that it requires the redefinition of masculinity and femininity. This applies in a very detailed way to masculinity as it is perceived in *Middlemarch*. Davidoff and Hall register, for example, a shift in the evaluation of gambling as an index of manly occupation to accounting, and then argue that accounting is rooted in estate management. (Davidoff and Hall 1987: 20, 201). The story of Fred Vincy, who has to learn not only not to gamble, but also to keep books at the hands of the estate manager Caleb Garth, exactly fits.

But more important is the complex way in which femininity shifts from partnership to equality within separation, and how this is bound up with the pursuit of leisure and retreat. Out of this emerges a fourth crucial point and that is that there is no static class identity, that consequent culture includes rural and urban families and ranges from rich to middle income families. The remarkable coherence of the middle class is not to be found within the class-specific politics of the franchise, free trade and industrial development but within marriage.

This may lead to a revision of Juliet Mitchell's perception of the historical relationship of kinship ideology to the capitalist relations of production. On a detailed level, it confirms her point that liberation can be as limited by the freedom of consumerism as it can by the work ethic. Davidoff and Hall show that the work ethic and the cult of leisure are not contradictory but flow into one another. But at a deeper level it may show that capitalism and kinship are not contradictory of one another in the way she surmises though, of course, they are contradictory in so far as exogamy and the gift are redundant in a community which has mobility and the machinery of accumulation. Mobility and machinery of accumulation are not of course overnight blessings and in particular it would seem that only in a socialist society could you do without marriage in the base since it is necessary for the privatization of childcare, and the inheritance of wealth.

It does not need to be shown of course that marriage is at the core of *Middlemarch*. The first words of the novel proper, 'Miss Brooke', are a sign of the exchangeable identity of the woman: 'and how should Dorothea not marry?' What we have is a comparative anatomy of marriage in which various models – father/daughter, brother/sister, master/slave – are deployed against one another. We might even schematize this by seeing the two main marriages as manifesting a new ideology of partnership in old pre-bourgeois conditions (since Casaubon is both squire and rector) and the old ideology of wife as furniture in the new conditions of professional self-reliance. Certainly this social, class-specific inflection is related to an older resilient patriarchy. Eliot anticipates Mitchell, as she does Davidoff and Hall, in the opening pages which stress how Dorothea is constructed not by one absent father, but three, since not only is her biological father dead, but her social father effeminate, and her spiritual father, Mr Cadwallader, irresponsible, so that she does act as a dutiful daughter in seeking to seduce another father, Casaubon. Vincy too is notable for his absence of imagination, a coarse mirror in which the beauty of Rosamund cannot properly see itself. The cultural level, however, is manifest by the class-specific and historically distanced project which sets it in motion. I am far from suggesting that the text resolves the relationship of class and gender. Literary texts only ever resolve things rhetorically. In fact it is the refusal to fuse class and gender that makes *Middlemarch* such an uncompromised text.

But this does not differentiate my reading from the Boumelha/ Showalter rescue of the woman's novel from the text, which would finally have to rescue Dorothea from her second marriage, and may be not allow Mrs Bulstrode to return to hers without a sense of loss. I return to the absurd prolepsis, the pilulous smallness of the pre-matrimonial acquaintance which constitutes the ideological basis of the novel. The best marriage in the novel is Mary's and Fred's. It is, of course, very marginal and, consciously - I think, made within visible literary conventions (Fred is the victim of great expectations, and the whole Rigg episode seems like a mystery not pursued). In two ways, Mary and Fred escape the constraints of the real patriarchal world. First, Caleb is far from absent, and can act as a substitute father for the incompetent Mr Vincy. Secondly, they have grown up together – they are siblings.

This gives marriage in the novel a dialectical possibility, since it is not merely a prison characters move into through lack of knowledge. Dorothea, who marries her father, learns through this to become the 'critical wife'. In the formation of middle-class, as opposed to aristocratic, domination, marriage has a potentially progressive as well as regressive role. Specifically, it is by the awareness generated by her bad first marriage – the realization that you cannot rely on fathers to teach you Hebrew, which would be access to the written secrets of the culture – that Dorothea learns to identify herself (by a written protest to her dead husband's instructions) and (as part of this) to recover her own childhood. For that is what her relationship with Ladislaw is, first that she is to him not a picture, image, portrait of a lady, but a voice (and a voice waiting to be released, as the Cleopatra is revealed to be the Ariadne), and secondly that the voice is contacted through an *exchange* of looks. The gaze of the opening, of Middlemarch, of the reader, is vicariously via Ladislaw returned. He is indeed one of the few visible males in fiction. What male readers find hard to take is that he is actually pretty – an attractive sexual object. But what is more important is that once they have found one another Dorothea and Ladislaw can become like children. There are many ironies here, to be sure, not the least of which is that Eliot with her historical distance as well as her historical imagination, knows that the mythic potential of the couple is sibling more than exogamous.

This sketchy account of the novel does not do justice to the complex textual realization which makes of marriage so dynamic a process working through the text. Thus on the margins of a feminist history proper of fiction – which focuses on the madwoman in the attic, on hysteria, on the incomplete suppression of female subjectivity – the history of the interaction of class and gender is inscribed not merely in the bourgeois novel but in the novel most consummately about being bourgeois. For the way to become fully part of 'the involuntary palpitating life' by which Dorothea sees her connection to the manifold wakings of men to labour and endurance is to enact the complex history of marriage by which the bourgeoisie institutionalizes its domination. The terms on which this development can take place include the suppression of that further class struggle between the bourgeoisie and the working class, but it is not a silent, naturalized suppression. It is marked at the boundary of Dorothea's consciousness and deferred by the novel's historicity.

## VI:  The tragedy of the dispossessed

Davidoff and Hall's research finishes in mid-century. When Eliot reached her own time in *Daniel Deronda* capitalism was already a world force, complicated by empire. The hegemony that both Gwendolen and Deronda have to deal with is a triplicate mastery of gender, class and race, and the objects of that mastery therefore are embroiled in their own divisive contestation. Daniel's bitter confrontation with his mother and the desolate last encounter of Gwendolen and Daniel are fraught with that internecine struggle. Class, gender and race are frequently cited as a totality, but this novel shows them to be opposed and athwart. The concept of a matrix of the subject is even more of a mask. Motherhood at the end of this novel is the source of nothing other than self-denial, unacceptable to the hero with new lands to occupy, redemptive for the heroine who is not a special case. I use 'redemptive' ironically, for what Gwendolen is told to return to is conformity to the image of motherhood that Daniel refutes.

We are entering with this novel the realm of the modern – urban, global, self-conscious, ironic. The frontier of women's history and class struggle is not merely complicated by the new boundaries drawn by globalization of capitalist exploitation, it is placed in another dimension. This does not mean, of course, that there are no texts which explore this frontier after 1880: Hardy's fiction, for example, can be seen as an uneasy negotiation of sexuality and class (see Boumelha 1982) and both George Egerton ('Gone Under', 'Wedlock') and Katherine Mansfield ('The Garden Party', 'Life of Ma Parker') explore this abrasive contiguity. Nevertheless, as modernity becomes more ineluctable, a certain aesthetic totality becomes less easy to sustain. This is not due to the loss of the unitary subject which one glimpse at the the first chapter of *Middlemarch* will show never existed. What is lost is the capacity of either mobility or pivotability to be agents of narrative continuity. If we take urbanization as the common denominator of modernity, mobilization and zoning are two contradictory conditions which make those forms of privilege unexceptional and therefore incapable of providing perspectives. What the great British modernists have in common is that they privilege obscurity (transitive and intransitive) in order to have access to modernized experience. So that whereas the function-ality of the pre-modern protagonist derives from whatever provisional and contingent unity the plot confers on the subject, Clarissa Dalloway, Bloom and the separate generations of Brangwens owe their narrative agency precisely to their sever-ance. That is why it is not difficult to marginalize any of them in an aesthetic derived from a totalizing politics. What is important about such texts is the productiveness of the transformation of ideological material they represent, and in these terms it is precisely the sense of the war between determinants that constitutes the basis of their effectivity. Thus while I don't think that Molly Bloom can be recuperated for feminism ('Penelope' is not feminine writing but a parody, though see Henke 1990: 126–163 for a different view), or that Clarissa Dalloway can be made an honorary member of the working class, I do think that the specific and limited agency constructed by these texts is one that socialists and feminists should hold precious.

The implications of modernism for feminism are analysed with remarkable succinctness by Janet Wolff. Arguing that the defi-nition of the modern and the nature of modernism derived from the experience of men (to which we should add 'bourgeois') she goes on to say that women nevertheless had their own experience of the modern world and are as involved in the revolution of literary and visual languages as men. She concludes that modern-ist strategies are not intrinsically progressive, but that it is for us to insist on 'the radical potential of the deconstructive strategies of modernist culture' (Wolff 1990: 57, 63). We could make the same case for the working class, though its access to modernism is very limited. But they will not be the same case, and neither will the case of imperialist subjects. On the contrary, they will certainly contest one another, as Woolf contests Lawrence's phallocentrism, and Lawrence contests Joyce's petty bourgeois self-consciousness and Joyce contests their English imperialism. Needless to say (and it has already been said by others) each of these writers forces the reader to see what is being obliterated by the contestation, which is why you can see how important feminism is to Lawrence or how Woolf constantly brings the reader up against the working world in, for example, *Jacob's Room* (on this matter in general see Beer 1987). But what is just as important as these qualifying statements is that the texts of the modernist movement bear witness to the intractability of the contradiction between different levels of exploitation.

One way of handling this is to resort to cultural materialism, which I take to be a development of Althusser's relative autonomy. All levels of social interaction are grounded in material relations of power and exploitation and not in a way that can be reduced to a single paradigm, notably that of capital and labour. Gender and imperialism are therefore sites of struggle in themselves, and more significantly, the arena of cultural practices as a whole – even when making no direct reference to the three political arenas – is one in which the struggle can be unmasked; Lovell's study of fiction and her extension of the argument into the relationship of English studies to the containment of the emancipation of women is a notably valuable case. It is not difficult to show that the global and panoramic aspirations of nineteenth-century writers are at best illusory and, like all illusions, are sponsored by the hegemony. In this case, the modernist writers can be presented as carrying on their own cultural revolution rather than betraying someone else's.

I recognize the need to rescue modernism from the homogenized negation we find in Lukács and later variants on the one hand and some of the unremitting representationalist feminist critiques on the other, but it leaves me with a double anxiety. First, it is political. Capitalism is a more diverse and adaptable productive system than its predecessors, and it can therefore make space for many specific emancipations. During the immediate post-war period, when the Unions were strong, it enabled some improvement in the workforce. In the wake of advances in birth control and other advances in medical technology, it could adjust to the feminist revival. And it also handled decolonization without being radically damaged. All these adjustments, however, do not take away the fundamental condition on which capitalism relies – the production and exchange of commodities. Commodities can only exist as commodities on the basis of differential values and therefore of competition. There must always be, as the East Germans are now finding out, losers. The aggregate degree of oppression has never diminished under capitalism. It simply moves around. And it will always seek to displace itself, which is why class oppression is always passed on to gender or race and why gender and race in their struggle to ameliorate will always ignore economic misery if possible, and even create their own parodic exploitations. There is no sequence in this. There is a finely balanced ecology of misery. Only a society based on the exchange of use values in respect of human needs and abilities would change this. There is no site of struggle that has not been determined by a wider site of struggle.

The great classics of modernism eschew the panoramas of nineteenth-century fiction not because they have woken up to the illusory nature of the unitary subject (which was at best a transitive strategy and at worst always disintegrating) but because they need to speak for obliterated energies in search of different forms of totalization. But this leads to my second anxiety, which is methodological. It is certainly convenient to speak of the texts of 1910–1940 as radically different from their nineteenth-century forbears, because although the texts of Wells, Bennett and Galsworthy are also different, they are not different in the same way. That is why I use the term 'modernism'. 'Modernism', however, is sometimes opposed to 'realism' and sometimes to 'Victorian', and this must make us see immediately that it is at best a very leaky category. 'Modernity' to which 'modernism' is an aesthetic response is around from at least the 1840s, before 'realism' gets into English as a term applicable to the novel, and this latter does not have sufficient coherence to define either an aesthetic programme, or even a retrospectively constructed category, without great elaboration. What needs to be stressed for the present argument is that the changes in literary method that we see in the development of the novel are continuous within parameters defined by an authorial project of demystification. In terms of the relationship between feminist criticism and class conflict this means looking more attentively at the origins of the feminist novel itself.

By 1910, there is, of course, a good deal of conflict between feminism and the labour movement. But this is not before the loss of a generation which held them together, and this is a significant moment in literary history. I am not only thinking of Beatrice Potter (later Webb) and Annie Besant, but of the remarkable group which centred on Eleanor Marx in the 1880s. Marx herself, of course, translated Ibsen and most significantly *Madame Bovary*, and her lecture on 'Shelley's Socialism' stresses the influence of Mary Wollstonecraft and Mary Shelley on the poet's 'perception of woman's real position'. 'The woman is to the man as the producing class is to the possessing' (Aveling and Marx Aveling 1947: 13). But more specifically, for our purposes, we need to attend to two novelist friends of Eleanor Marx, one neglected, the other underestimated, who have to work their way through the given conventions of the broadly mimetic narrative in order to articulate the relationship defined in this comment.

The first of these is Margaret Harkness whose 'realistic story', *A City Girl*, was published in 1887, and whose even more extraordinary second novel, *Out of Work*, 1888, has recently become available from the Merlin Press (1990). Both of these texts – which come out of a critical reading of Zola – bring the issue of the exploitation of women into the immediate arena of, in the first case, urban poverty, and in the second that of unemployment and the unemployed riots of 1886 and 1887. *City Girl*, as the title signifies, seems the more obviously relevant since it takes a working-class girl as the focus of the double exploitation of women and the working class (see Goode 1982). But *Out of Work* is both more experimental formally and a more forceful illustration of my general point that the exploitation of women and the exploitation of workers are also in tension with one another. The pressures on 'the pretty methodist', Polly Elwin, to reject her pledge to the unemployed hero are fully realized, so that when he calls her 'little hypocrite' he also leaves the marks of his male violence on her wrist. More significantly, Harkness borrows the gamine convention in the Squirrel who ironically becomes, as Bernadette Kirwan observes, a substitute mother (Law 1990: xvii) to the hero. But before we are told that he has crawled back to his original mother's grave in the countryside to die, we are given a scene in which the Squirrel becomes aware of the cosmic but unfathomable female wisdom of the Sphinx and hears the song of 'the wraith Suicide' which echoes the last words on the cross. The Squirrel is drawn into 'the strong embrace' of Father Thames and is no longer 'a waif and stray' (Law 1990: 268).

What is remarkable about this novel is the way that the fragmented story embodies the relegation of what Kirwan terms 'sociable relations' (xvii) to the realm of the casual poor who by definition constitute no community – the Squirrel literally loses

Jos in the stream of homeless poverty. Equally, Polly rejects him
when she bumps into him on his way from a night in Bow Street
police cell to 'the doss house' as she turns the corner of
Commercial Street (218). This is in every sense an urban novel, a
totally modern experience in which 'the utter loneliness' (267) is
what men and women have in common. It is not a modernist
novel and it is permeated by a strong but pessimistic Christianity,
but it negotiates the boundary of gender relations and class
relations in an important way.

The other text of this period which reworks the conventions of
the novel in order to cross without negating the boundaries of
exploitation is Olive Schreiner's *The Story of An African Farm*. This
is not, of course, a neglected text and on the face of it it is less
concerned with the interaction of feminism and socialism than
that of feminism and Darwinism and feminism and imperialism.
It is not trying to represent the formation of social relations: the
farm is very isolated and more like the microcosmic world of
*Wuthering Heights* than even a provincial world as distanced as St.
Oggs. Nevertheless, the novel is situated in a larger political
world, for the downfall of the precarious idyll is brought about by
the parodically self-made Bonaparte Blenkins, who brings specious evangelicalism to the farm, and who reaches the height of his
power after catching Waldo reading the chapter on property in
Mill's *Political Economy*.

The critical questions that arise here are not about the importance of this text but about its pessimism and its incoherence. At
the end of her chapter on 'The Feminist Novelists' which includes
a strong account of Schreiner, Showalter quotes a story from
*Lolita* of a monkey given an easel whose first painting shows the
bars of its cage. I find the irony of this more telling against
Nabokov than against the feminists who 'elevated their restricted
view into a sacred vision' (Showalter 1977: 215), though there is
no doubt that both Schreiner and Egerton, and, as we have seen,
Harkness deploy the discourse of cosmic pessimism against what
is perhaps a failure to see a clear programme of action. In this text,
however, it is precisely the sacredness of the prison bars – or at
least their unpassability – that generates its solidarity. It is
because Waldo and Lyndall come together at the boundaries of
their subjective experience that they articulate a totality that lies
outside the individual life and outside the particular emancipations of religious doubt and feminist awareness. In this sense
Gregory Rose, who begins as a courtier and ends as a transvestite

nurse, is as much the embodiment of the novel's radical ideology as Waldo's stranger or Lyndall herself (a suggestion implicit in Showalter 1977: 152).

Because it deals with forms of oppression as separated experiences (Lyndall's question to Waldo is unanswered), and yet as coherent manifestations of oppression as a whole, the novel has to build itself not on subjectivity (which it parodies by inverting the pivotal, mobile agency of earlier novels, making the male pivotal, and the female mobile). Rather it has to build a structure out of gaps and barriers and occasional transmissions, whose only unitary source is the shared oppression of childhood. Doing this, it becomes not only the foundation novel of the African feminist tradition, as Holtby, Dinesen and Lessing recognize, but, certainly, one of the foundation texts of the modern novel in general. Gilbert and Gubar (1989: 53) correctly place it against the cultural agenda activated by imperialism, but still accuse it of incoherence, anachronistically dividing it between Victorian convention and modernist experiment. This makes experiment sound gratuitous or even wilful, and they tend to extract from the novel a new *Wuthering Heights* in which, strangely as cause for lament, male potency is lowered. Schreiner herself, however, made it clear that the 'incoherence' is programmatic. Echoing Eliot's dismissal of Fielding's generality as theatrical, she takes it further:

> Human life may be painted according to two methods. There is the stage method. According to that each character is duly marshalled and ticketed; we know with an immutable certainty that at the right crises each one will reappear and act his part, and when the curtain falls, all will stand before it bowing. There is a sense of satisfaction in this, and of completeness. But there is another method – the method of the life we all lead. Here nothing can be prophesied. There is a strange coming and going of feet. Men appear, act and react upon each other, and pass away. When the crisis comes the man who would fit it does not return. When the curtain falls no-one is ready. When the footlights are brightest they are blown out; and what the name of the play is no-one knows. If there sits a spectator who knows, he sits so high that the players in the gaslight cannot hear his breathing. (Schreiner 1889: vii–viii)

This is not the same as Eliot's 'embroiled medium' nor as Woolf's 'luminous halo', but it clearly comes between them. Of course it is marked by the cosmic pessimism of its time, as Eliot is marked by positivism and Woolf by Bergson. What is more important is that it shares with them the need to break with previous supposedly realist practice in the interests of the new realism, though the failure to finish *From Man to Man* suggests that Schreiner found no way through the problems posed by the fractured narrative of the earlier novel. A full analysis would show, however, that it is not her incompetence which the provisionality of that text shows, but her unflagging ambition to present new forms of female consciousness in face of the evolving structure of global capitalism. It may be that we had to wait for *The Golden Notebook* for that, a text that no one would accuse of incoherence. Between them, Winifred Holtby, who also tried to find new totalizations of competing forms of oppression, recognized in her review of *From Man to Man* that the separate parts of Schreiner's work addressed themselves to 'the tragedy of the dispossessed' (Brittain, Holtby 1985: 201). That tragedy is large, endlessly changing and rarely given to peripoetic unity, but it sometimes has reluctant spokespersons in literary texts. It is for readers to make its voices heard, and to value those texts which will not hide its discords.

## References

Anderson, Perry (1990). 'A culture in contraflow', *New Left Review* 182, 85–137.

Armstrong, Nancy (1987). *Desire and Domestic Fiction: A Political History of the Novel*. New York, Oxford University Press.

Austen, Zelda (1976). 'Why feminist critics are angry with George Eliot', *College English* 37, 549–61.

Aveling, Edward and Eleanor Marx Aveling (1947). *Shelley's Socialism: Two Lectures*. Manchester, Leslie Preger.

Beaumarchais, Pierre Augustin Caron de (1957). *Théâtre Complet*, edited by Maurice Allem and Paul Courant. Paris, Bibliothèque de la Pléiade.

—— (1964). '*The Barber of Seville*' and '*The Marriage of Figaro*', translated with an introduction by John Wood. London, Penguin Books.

Beer, Gillian (1986). *George Eliot*. Brighton, Harvester Press.

—— (1987). 'The body of the people in Virginia Woolf', in Sue Roe (ed.) (below), 85–113.

Belsey, Catherine (1980). *Critical Practice*. London, Methuen.

Boumelha, Penny (1982). *Thomas Hardy and Women. Sexual Ideology and Narrative Form*. Brighton, Harvester Press.

—— (1987). 'George Eliot and the end of realism', in Sue Roe (ed.) (below), 15–35.

—— (1990). *Charlotte Brontë*. Hemel Hempstead, Harvester Wheatsheaf.

Brittain, Vera and Winifred Holtby (1985). *Testament of a Generation*, edited and introduced by Paul Berry and Alan Bishop. London, Virago Press.

David, Deirdre (1987). *Intellectual Women and Victorian Patriarchy*. Basingstoke, Macmillan Press.

Davidoff, Leonore and Catherine Hall (1987). *Family Fortunes, Men and Women of the English Middle Class, 1780–1850*. London, Hutchinson.

Eliot, George (1871–2). *Middlemarch*, edited by David Carroll (1986). Oxford, Clarendon Press.

Gilbert, Sandra and Susan Gubar (1989). *No Man's Land. The Place of The Woman Writer in the Twentieth Century. II: Sexchanges*. New Haven, Yale University Press.

Goode, John (1982). 'Margaret Harkness and the socialist novel', in Gustave Klaus (ed.), *The Socialist Novel in Britain*. Brighton, Harvester Press.

—— (1983). '"The affections clad with knowledge": woman's duty and the public life', in *Literature and History* 9, 33–51.

Harvey, W.J. (1966). *Character and the Novel*. London, Chatto and Windus.

Henke, Suzette A. (1990) *James Joyce and the Politics of Desire*. New York and London, Routledge.

Jardine, Alice and Paul Smith (eds) (1987). *Men in Feminism*. London, Methuen.

Kaplan, Cora (1985). 'Pandora's box: subjectivity, class and sexuality in socialist-feminist criticism', in Green and Kahn (eds), *Making a Difference. Feminist Literary Criticism*. London, Methuen.

Law, John (Margaret Harkness) (1990). *Out of Work*, introduction by Bernadette Kirwan. London, Merlin Press.

Leavis, F.R. (1962). *The Great Tradition*. Harmondsworth, Penguin Books.

Lovell, Terry (1987). *Consuming Fiction*, London, Verso.

—— (1990). *British Feminist Thought*. Oxford, Basil Blackwell.

MacCabe, Colin (1978). *James Joyce and the Revolution of the Word*. London, Macmillan.

Millett, Kate (1972). *Sexual Politics*. London, Sphere Books.

Mitchell, Juliet (1974). *Psychoanalysis and Feminism*. Harmondsworth, Penguin Books.

—— (1984). *Women – The Longest Revolution*. London, Virago Press.

—— (1986). 'Reflections on twenty years of socialism', in Juliet Mitchell and Ann Oakley, (eds), *What is Feminism?*. Oxford, Basil Blackwell, pp. 34–48.

Poovey, Mary (1989). *Uneven Developments*. London, Virago Press.

Roe, Sue (ed ) (1987). *Women Reading Women's Writing*. Brighton, Harvester Press.

Taylor, Barbara (1983). *Eve and the New Jerusalem*. London, Virago Press.

Schreiner, Olive (1889). *The Story of An African Farm*, by Ralph Iron [Olive Schreiner]. New Editon, London, Chapman and Hall.

Sergeant, Lydia (ed.) (1981). *The Unhappy Marriage of Marxism and Feminism*. London, Pluto Press.

Showalter, Elaine (1977). *A Literature of Their Own. British Women Novelists from Brontë to Lessing*. Princeton, New Jersey, Princeton University Press.

—— (1979). 'Towards a feminist poetics', in M. Jacobus, (ed.). *Women Writing and Writing About Women*. London, Croom Helm, pp. 22–41.

—— (1980), 'The greening of Sister George', *Nineteenth Century Fiction*, 35.

Todd, Janet (1988). *Feminist Literary History. A Defence*. Cambridge, Polity Press.

Uglow, Jennifer (1987). *George Eliot*. London, Virago.

Williams, Raymond (1970). *The English Novel from Dickens to Lawrence*. London, Chatto and Windus.

Wilson, Elizabeth, with Angela Weir (1986). *Hidden Agendas. Theory, Policy and Experience in the Women's Movement*. London, Tavistock Publications.

Wolff, Janet (1990). *Feminine Sentences. Essays on Women and Culture*. Cambridge, Polity Press.

*Anna Hopkins*

# 7

## Fellow-travelling with feminist criticism

### *Rick Rylance*

This essay, like Lear's kingdom, comes in three parts. It is firstly an account of how a male critic, sympathetic to feminism, comes to terms with that role in the contemporary academic context of literary studies. The second part looks at ways in which gender issues are examined in the writing of the 1950s and early 1960s. The relationship between the two parts is personal and generational. I use the analysis of this writing to say something of the difficulties experienced by my generation of critics on gender issues, and to indicate why it is, I think, feminism speaks powerfully and helpfully to us. The third section of the essay returns to the contemporary situation and comments more fully on recent varieties of feminist criticism.

## I: The success of feminism

Over the past twenty years literary study has changed in many ways. Largely – though not sufficiently – this has been for the better. The social base of the literary academy has widened as new kinds of teacher have entered the profession; the tone and accents of its delivery have been tuned differently; and the range of social experience to which critics address themselves has more fully responded to the range of social experience offered by writers. But, of all these developments, it seems to me the most significant has been the extension of gender consciousness. This has happened almost entirely because of the impact of feminism.

Though related, these developments are not homologous. The attention given to social class, for instance, has not, until quite recently, been matched by interest in the situations of women. It has been quite common for women to complain that, when agendas are prepared, it is often they who disappear into another category or onto another page (for discussion, see Middleton 1989). However, this has not quite been the case in literary studies. Indeed it is probably true that more sustained attention has been given to writing by and about women over recent years than to writing by and about any other traditionally-ignored group. The women's presses have got many works by women back on the shelves and this has been of major importance, as has the relative welcome accorded to them in the educational establishments. A comparison of this situation with that of 'working-class' writing, for instance, indicates the relative affluence of attention enjoyed by writing by women. It is hard to buy, and therefore to teach, writing produced out of the mainstream in class terms, and there has been correspondingly little theorization of it – partly because recent marxism has confined itself to critical inwardness and the same old canon.

This perhaps reflects the backgrounds of its intellectuals, as well as its disconnection – compared to feminism – from a broad-based social movement. But the comparison does pose an interesting question on which I wish to focus in the first part of this essay: why has feminism been so successful in literary studies when this popularity is out of step with the general situation? Though, in temerously describing literary feminism in this way, I do not mean to underestimate the difficulties of many women, teachers and students alike, or ignore structural conditions. The problems set by competing demands and responsibilities, inhibitions to access and lack of confidence and esteem, as well as the routine prejudices of predominantly male institutions, persist as part of the texture of everyday educational life (for recent discussion see Thompson and Wilcox 1989 and Kauffman 1989). Women continue to be marginalized organizationally. Using data largely from the late-seventies and from the universities, Terry Lovell concluded that, though women 'are key agents in the transmission of cultural capital' in literary studies, they 'are still unable to take full possession [of it] in their own right' (Lovell 1987: 151). Recent findings tend to agree. A general study has argued that while higher education institutions do not actively discriminate against women, their culture makes it significantly more difficult for them to succeed (Thomas 1990). As I write, another study has just revealed an organizational 'hidden curriculum' which discriminates against the careers of women in the college sector (Herzfeld 1991), and they are drastically under-represented in my own institution. Of 18 full-time staff teaching on the English degree programmes, only three are women. The shifting of this gross imbalance must remain a major priority if feminism is to have the kind of impact at an organizational level that it has had at the curricular level.

However, there are good reasons why literary studies have been particularly accessible to feminism in Britain. First, unlike the situation obtaining elsewhere, many women have successfully produced the writing – both imaginative and critical – which defines the discipline's concerns. This is a historical circumstance. It is tempting to speculate that, excluded from other careers, intelligent women in the nineteenth century looked to imaginative writing (rather than science, philosophy, formal scholarship or the other arts) for creative intellectual work. This was partly because there was no need for formal training, partly because of the gender composition of the readership for such work, and partly because of the relatively open access to publication (compare the situation relating to exhibition in the visual arts or performance in music). George Eliot's career indicates something of this. *Middlemarch: A Study of Provincial Life* can be seen as an innovative form of imaginative sociology, crossed with a massively-informed interest in the advanced science and thought of the day. Yet it is unlikely that Eliot could have built a career as a free-lance intellectual like her partner G. H. Lewes or her friend Herbert Spencer. Even in a fledgling discipline like psychology, in which both these men were radicals, and which was relatively free from conservative institutional pressures, it was women of family or markedly traditional outlooks (such as Marie Blaze de Bury, E. Hamilton – daughter of Sir William – or the contradictory feminist Frances Power Cobbe) who joined the debates. It is improbable that a woman with the daring convictions (let alone personal history) of a Mary Ann Evans could have intervened in a free way: hence, in part, the novelist George Eliot (Rylance 1990).

Secondly, this major, though until recently underestimated, contribution by women has been backed by another historical factor: the overwhelming presence of women students. From its beginnings, English was seen as a discipline peculiarly fitted to ladies (Palmer 1965; Doyle 1982; Baldick 1983). Subsequently, the majority of students reading English have been women, though these courses have been largely administered by men. The ambiguous energies of this situation have inhibited, but also galvanized, the development of feminist approaches in a discipline founded on a patronizing response by Edwardian men to demands for female education, and in a profession which has traditionally recruited women into lower status positions.

Thirdly, and relatedly, literature speaks powerfully and directly to the experiential and political concerns of women. This, again, is a matter of historical opportunity. For, as I shall argue in the second part of this essay, it was literature that was particularly able to articulate a gendered account of the world in the late 'fifties and early 'sixties when there were no public languages available for such work. It is no accident that feminist activists like Kate Millett and Germaine Greer had a markedly literary turn to their work. Literature itself, and the analysis of literature, can offer a relative discursive freedom in negotiating experience. The lack of alternative languages makes literature particularly appropriate for gender-conscious responses. Many students come to degree study of literature looking for courses that respond directly to their concerns as gendered subjects.

Literary feminism, therefore, has been able to take advantage of a number of structural factors to advance the claims it makes on the ethical and political legitimacy of its general case. The forms of inquiry and production within the discipline, the existence of a traditional clientele for literary study among women, and the adjacent shifts in educational provision across the system, have all played a part. These factors, as well as the slowly increasing number of women in the profession as teachers and managers and the particular reconceptions of the discipline they have proposed, make it important for men to make a positive response. In Britain women's studies courses have not flourished and feminist concerns therefore have energetically continued within the more traditional disciplines. Though the case for a separate disciplinary base for feminism remains a good one (it is carefully argued by Messer-Davidow 1989, for instance), co-existence in 'mixed' departments will continue. And if men accept (as I do) the justice of feminism's claims, then it would seem not just politically legitimate, but also necessary, given that women continue to be under-represented, for men to articulate these views in teaching, policy discussions and administrative councils.

But the subject is controversial, and political exigencies can encourage a complacent ventriloquism which ignores practically the problems it recognizes formally, so that apparent concern masks continuing discrimination. At the same time men have an anxious relation to feminist ideas. In *Men In Feminism*, edited by Alice Jardine and Paul Smith, a range of related issues are addressed by women and men largely from literary backgrounds. Often they focus on the paradox identified initially by Stephen Heath. Existing feminism, Heath argues, can put men in a double bind. It demands they change, but also excludes them from discussions (Heath 1987: 1). There are a number of possible responses to this. One would be to say 'tough', and this seems to me valid for easily-graspable reasons. Men have a long history of appropriation and no-one should want feminism hi-jacked, or turned into something else. This is the fear concerning 'gender studies', or the move to see feminism as another branch of theory (Showalter 1983 and Todd 1988: ch. 7). In addition, there is a rough historical justice in the idea that men are now excluded from the main debates – though it may be, as in many conflict situations, that it is the useful, rather than the hostile, who are excluded. The argument then turns around definitions of utility, and these, given the broader cultural and institutional implications, are very complex indeed. Either way, it's best to accept, as Heath says, that we are dealing with a political and not an existential situation.

Nonetheless, such considerations are personal, and it is often urged by feminists that the point of any male involvement is for men to change themselves. Heath's discussion is again helpful. In literary criticism, he argues, feminism is not just a matter of method. It unsettles men in a way that is both dispiriting and alarming (though eventually constructive one hopes), and this is the point. Men need to learn to be feminists (a political position), and not women (see also Moi 1989). Men need to work with and against their own gender difficulties, which means coming to understand their own, as well as women's, history.

## II: The world we are losing

I was born in 1954 and went to university in 1973. Looking back, I see an extraordinary naivety about gender issues. I read Germaine Greer while in the sixth form, but I also read Alistair Maclean, Ian Fleming and Chairman Mao's little red book. Feminism seemed roughly in line with my libertarian outlook, and so I notionally supported it and thought no more about it. I thus continued to behave as a male of my generation; that is, I was largely oblivious to the grain and texture of gender relations. Partly this was a matter of callowness, partly a matter of (distinctively male) arrogance, and partly a matter of the extraordinary silence that prevailed on gender issues. There was little public language for such things, and the history of that thoughtlessness, that long male unconscious, is still with me and many of my sex and generation. It was an extraordinary hole of not-seeing, of having neither perceptual nor conceptual vocabulary. It is also, therefore, a reservoir of stubborn and destructive attitudes.

Subsequent studies, by Rowbotham (1973 and 1990), Sinfield (1989: ch. 10), Wilson (1980) and others, have filled-in the picture. Feminism, like the concept of social class, had ceased to be necessary in the 'fifties, it was claimed. There was living equality, each according to his needs. Men went to work, women ran the home. It was for this that each nature was best fitted. The consequences of this were felt in a refusal to look at the realities of women's domestic lives, and substantial – and persisting – inequalities in job opportunities and rates of pay. Its realities were also found in double standards in sexual attitudes, in attitudes towards the family, in political and cultural access, and in educational expectations. Overarching all this was the lack of any language with which to articulate gender relations in alternative ways – thus the widespread inability to think about the problem at all. Without alternative modes of comprehension and imagining, difficulties remain naturalized, and much of the writing by women in this period is concerned with the difficulty of speaking in a situation of effective ideological obliteration. For Betty Friedan, in *The Feminine Mystique* (1963), women's experiences were 'The Problem That Has No Name', and Tillie Olsen's symptomatically influential essays begun in 1962 were called *Silences* (Olsen 1980).

It is worth pondering some examples of these silences to perceive their extent, and also to glimpse the inventive ways in which women understood and responded. (I mix British and American examples in what follows to reveal shared concerns.) There is an early poem by Adrienne Rich in *A Change of World* (1951) entitled 'An Unsaid Word'. In it a woman learns that her language is to be defined by her man's needs. The poem works by articulating an ideological commomplace, only to startle the sentiment at the close:

She who has power to call her man
From that estranged intensity
Where his mind forages alone,
Yet keeps her peace and leaves him free,
And when his thoughts to her return
Stands where he left her, still his own,
Knows this the hardest thing to learn. (Rich 1975: 3)

The poem uses two heroic stereotypes: the male foraging alone while the sympathetic woman waits to mop his brow. The refusal to dramatize a conclusion, however, jeopardizes the heroism with a tone of sad sacrifice, and underlines the heroine's predicament. Her word cannot be said, nor, for that matter, can any word of communication between them. The concern with unsaid words is widely evident in this collection: 'An Uncle Speaks in the Drawing Room', but his reactionary bombast is unrefuted; Aunt Jennifer, in the famous 'Aunt Jennifer's Tigers', silently creates a vivid expressive life through her embroidery, while her outer life is squashed by 'The massive weight of Uncle's wedding band'; finally, in 'Afterward', Rich later changed the ostensibly universalizing pronoun 'his' in the last line to 'her', to reveal the submerged gender politics of a poem about a disappointed life frustrated to suit others (1975: 2).

These marvellously adroit early poems are unrepresentatively subdued. In 'When We Dead Awaken', an essay of 1971, Rich related this to the sexual politics of the period of their composition. Their formality, like asbestos gloves, allowed her to handle materials for which the 'fifties had neither language nor appetite. The result was a representative psychological splitting which is both the subject of poems like 'Aunt Jennifer's Tigers', and the condition of the writer:

beneath the conscious craft are glimpses of the girl who wrote poems, who defined herself in writing poems, and the girl who was to define herself by her relationship with men. (Rich 1975: 94)

This offers stark alternatives – articulation or men. Later, of course, Rich developed new, innovative forms for the analysis of this experience and this was common among women during the 'sixties. Doris Lessing's *The Golden Notebook* (1962), for instance, also dramatizes the barrier between private feeling and public articulation. The novel therefore questions available forms (the realist narrative, the alienated subjective monologue) and leaves

the heroine struggling to reconcile a life split and compartmental-
ized, lacking a culture which can offer a coherent, adequate,
accepted language.

*The Golden Notebook,* of course, is about more than the gender
issue, and it depicts the crisis in language at more formally-
recognized political and cultural levels too. But the fragmented
experiences the novel presented spoke powerfully to women in
the 'sixties (Taylor 1982), and its struggles with fictional form
have been a leading issue in much subsequent women's writing.
Which forms will articulate experiences the available languages
cannot negotiate? The answer has often been to rewrite, or, in
Adrienne Rich's term in 'When We Dead Awaken', 're-vision'
existing material. Older forms, particularly those more congenial
to women's experiences, were rewritten, like Angela Carter's
reworkings of fairy stories and motifs from children's literature
begun in the late 'sixties. But this problem troubles writing by
women from top to bottom, and even in more orthodox, less
fiercely engaged writers, there is a struggle with available
materials. Much poetry by British women in the 'fifties, for
instance, deals with religious or spiritual experience. But the
dense meditations of Elizabeth Jennings (the best-known example), Anne Ridler, Ruth Pitter or Frances Bellerby often reveal
a collision between private feeling and public form. Ruth Pitter,
for example, who wrote a column for *Woman* magazine on
domestic management and rural living, uses forms drawn from
the often-sentimental women's journalism of the period to
contest male attitudes, or to offer images of female success which
are ambiguously related to accepted norms (Pitter 1990).

Frances Bellerby also plays between different levels of meaning
to contest perceptions of female domesticity. The poem 'The
House' (1958), for instance, is, typically, a poem about loss. It
begins in the nursery – 'Listen, children, to a fairy tale' – in, as it
were, a mother's routine; and it ends reassuringly, 'they could
always go home' (1986: 90–91). But on the way the tale is
contested ('the story is too pretty to be true'), and the poem's
fugitive organization does not allow it to settle into received
understandings. The poem's 'home' is, at one level, Heaven.
Characteristically, though, this is not explicit, thus creating the
effect of a subjectivity not quite confident in its own convictions.
This ambiguity continues as the sense of loss comes and goes.
Bellerby was badly disabled after a cliff fall, so the poem may be
about a stoical recovery from injury. It is also about the loss of

childhood innocence, and the entry into a baffling and inhospitable world, but this too is problematic. Bellerby's marriage failed, and the couple decided to part in 1942. After years of married silence she stared to write again, and 'The House' can be read with this in mind. It is a poem about a generalized loss of voice and confidence, and it indicates the condition I have outlined: the inadequacy of the languages available to women. Bellerby's ostensibly happy ending ('they could always go home') is thus fraught with uncertainties, for peaceful domesticity is a world without dimensions for a woman, and the reassertion of the fairy idiom can be read, not as regained certainty, but an ironized version of the good life. The final stanza is poised between ostensible certainty and oblivion: 'the dead banished/ soon the dreamers from hope's curious kingdom,/ and quite soon those dreamers forgot their dream.'

British writers of this period tend to be more accepting than their counterparts from abroad like Rich, Lessing or Sylvia Plath. But the same themes are widely evident. An early Plath poem, written between 1952 and 1956, is entitled 'Female Author'. It is a gaudy sonnet, picturing a solitary woman in Baudelairean or modernist decadence, like a voluptuously-dressed model in a Matisse – a motif also reworked by Anne Sexton (see for instance 'The Nude Swim', Sexton 1981: 183–84). In these left-bank scenarios, in effect a woman looks at a man looking at a woman:

> All day she plays at chess with the bones of the world:
> Favored (while suddenly the rains begin
> Beyond the window) she lies on cushions curled
> And nibbles an occasional bonbon of sin. (Plath 1981: 301)

The sonnet's resources are significantly unused (there is no turn towards a resolution of the problems raised), and, like Anna Wulf in *The Golden Notebook*, this artistic woman is trapped in male-centred events, stationary in a room, imprisoned by guilt. At the close, the price is not just her own corruption, but the inability of her writing to get any grip on the world outside: 'lost in subtle metaphor, [she] retreats/ from gray child faces crying in the streets'. She has no language, as she has no appearance, other than the 'female-author' style. Nor can she, the ending suggests, connect with her own childhood. As in Bellerby, there is no organic connection between child and adult. Patriarchy means the abandonment of the ways in which one's own desires and hopes are represented to oneself. Significantly, the woman poet watching the male portrait of a female author has no discernible voice – a situation mirrored by even the favourable responses Plath's work received. These concentrated on her praiseworthy rendering of psychotic conditions, and remained silent about the political features of her work.

'Female Author' is almost a successful poem. Its failures – slips in tone and diction – are tied to its theme; it cannot work with these dependent languages without succumbing to them. It is not, that is to say, written in the innovatory voice of her later work. But the later work draws its energies from the same problem of finding a language for women's experience. The poems revolve around silences: the monologues directed towards domestic implements, mute babies or Tate and Lyle tins; the problem of finding a vocabulary for unacknowledged atrocity; the self-policed silence of women in male culture. One poem intended for *Ariel*, and ironically dropped by Ted Hughes, is entitled 'The Courage of Shutting-Up'. It is both abrasively violent and grimly accepting of a world in which women have no language other than recorded monologue, 'disks of outrage'. With marvellous metaphoric virtuosity, the grooves on the record become the rifling of a gun barrel, and the record-player needle becomes that of a surgeon or tattooist. The body is thus over-written with crude male fantasy: 'the same blue grievances,/ The snakes, the babies, the tits/ on mermaids and two-legged dreamgirls' (1981: 210). It is a trophy world depending on the dismemberment of its ostensibly-valued object.

Plath, like Lessing, connects the sexual politics of the period to imperialism. The woman in 'Shutting-Up' becomes herself a trophy, 'Hung up in the library with the engravings of Rangoon'. The reference is precise. Burma gained independence from Britain in 1948. Thereafter, as in most post-imperial states, there was protracted political turmoil exacerbated by American manipulation of international aid and the Korean War. In 1962, when the poem was written, some kind of solution had been arrived at, and the newspapers, as Plath wrote her poem, were full of General Ne Win's take-over of power (which he has held since, being one of the aged dictators who didn't fall in 1989–90). Ne Win's policies were Albanian. Burma rejected American aid, and withdrew from the world, pursuing, as the final lines of Plath's poem have it, 'An obstinate independency/ insolvent among the mountains'. The poem is as startling in its intellectual reach as it is depressing in its conclusion. Its world, like that of

*The Golden Notebook,* is the Cold War; its behavioural model is a silent chain of violence; its vision is an obstinate, insolvent independence in which violence turns inwards. As we now know, the female psychological scenario of 'The Courage of Shutting-Up' became the general political scenario of Burma under Ne Win.

There are few more uncompromising and searching examinations of post-war life than those in Plath's later work (and the general political context of this is too little remarked). Plath links the absence of women's access to language to regimes of violence and inhibition, and she was not alone in so doing. Women found little access to popular or official records. They had nothing of their own, even in the newer narratives. What for instance became of all the 'Scholarship Girls'? The male mode – in Richard Hoggart, Raymond Williams, Tony Harrison – is well-known. It is a standard story of the period. But what of their female class-mates? Recent memoirs have adjusted the picture, and not only among the consciously-politicized women of the various Virago books (Heron 1985; Maitland 1988; Wandor 1990). Terry Jordan's collection, *Growing Up in the Fifties,* resumes some commom themes. 'Hazel', for instance, remembers modelling herself on Sophia Loren, but recalls that 'I think the things I was most attached to were things I made myself, the things I was proud to have done. Mostly these were clothes, but I also wrote poetry' (Jordan 1990: 19). One poem was about a love affair. 'The sex was insinuation only, nothing specific and nothing rude about it.' But her mother was horrified and her husband burst into tears.

This world of difficult expression is, perhaps surprisingly, also visible in some popular romances of the period, a form in which the majority of women writers worked (Light 1986). Jean Plaidy's best-selling *Light on Lucrezia* (1958), for instance, has an interesting Author's Note which asks us to understand Lucrezia Borgia as a victim of male perfidy and violence. The Note begins:

> After delving into the lives of the Borgias it is difficult to understand why Lucrezia has been given such an evil reputation. It could have been because many of the writers of the past believed, with reason, that lurid sensationalism was more acceptable than truth. To the more intelligent reader of today, this is not so; and a bewildered girl, born into a corrupt society, struggling to maintain her integrity, is, I

think, a more interesting and convincing figure than an evil
and sordid poisoner. (Plaidy 1968: 5)

A list of eighteen volumes of historical research, with biblio-
graphic details, follows.

It is odd to read a historical romance guarding against 'lurid
sensationalism', but the form is being used very seriously in *Light
on Lucrezia*. The title is carefully-chosen: the book illuminates a
misunderstood subject, but also requests us to understand the
pressures placed on a woman, to be light in our judgements. It
describes a corrupt, vicious political world in which men pull the
strings. It is, in fact, a world similar to that of Lessing and Plath.
In it Lucrezia struggles (as Plaidy says) 'to maintain her integrity',
but the language remains the language of the victim, and the
heroine's qualities emerge in terms of female frailty and sub-
mission (the Note talks of 'this serene and gentle girl' and so on).
Plaidy cannot imagine a vigorous independent heroine, but she
does pull some interesting tricks, and the opening neatly reverses
some stereotypes. A very young man, the unfortunate Alfonso,
journeys to meet his betrothed, the fearsome Lucrezia. His
trembling apprehension is not robustly male, but characteristically maidenly. This dramatizes the problem of Lucrezia's
reputation, and dismantles myths about male desire. When we
encounter Lucrezia, she is similarly maidenly and we are made to
think, not only about received images of her, but also about the
psychology of power. *Light on Lucrezia* essentially describes the
Cold War world: psychopathic brutality on the one hand, and
maidenly victimization on the other. This way of seeing things
imagines movement and energy as violence, and goodness as
passivity (essentially 'female'), or the violent resistance to violence (the essentially 'male' John Wayne or James Bond film). The
same pattern is evident, for instance, in Ted Hughes's Cold War
poem 'A Woman Unconscious' from *Lupercal* (1960), and in many
'Angry' texts, most strikingly *Look Back in Anger* itself. The male
glamour attached to this energetic violence is a difficulty with
much of the literature of the period.

Yet the response in works by men is often more complicated
than one would first assume. Plaidy's romance, like other
'female' romances of the period, produces challenging images of
women (Light 1987). But male romance is sometimes surprising
too. Here is a slight abbreviation of the closing moments of Ian
Fleming's *Goldfinger* (1959):

Bond said firmly, 'Lock that door, Pussy, take off that sweater and come into bed. You'll catch cold.'

She did as she was told, like an obedient child.

She lay in the crook of Bond's arm and looked up at him. She said, not in a gangster's voice, or a Lesbian's, but in a girl's voice, 'Will you write to me in Sing Sing?'

Bond looked down into the deep blue-violet eyes that were no longer hard, imperious. He bent and kissed them lightly. He said,

'They told me you only liked women.'

She said, 'I've never met a man before.'

. . .

Bond smiled down into the pale, beautiful face. He said, 'All you need is a course of TLC.'

'What's TLC?'

'Short for Tender Loving Care treatment. It's what they write on most papers when a waif gets brought in to a children's clinic.'

'I'd like that.' She looked at the passionate, rather cruel mouth waiting above hers. She reached up and brushed back the comma of black hair that had fallen over his right eyebrow. She looked into the fiercely slitted grey eyes. 'When's it going to start?'

Bond's right hand came slowly up the firm, muscled thighs, over the flat, soft plain of the stomach to the right breast. Its point was hard with desire. He said softly, 'Now.' His mouth came ruthlessly down on hers. (Fleming 1961: 222–23)

In one sense this is just foolish, but it is revealing. Pussy Galore represents two ignorant cliches of the period: that lesbianism is a social disease, and that women's natures are half sexual innuendo, half domestic pet. Bond, therefore, is the commanding partner and the woman is a child. But Bond's language is actually rather fraught. In fact there are two languages. There is the language of the sexual tough with its masterful register, which is now rather comical: Bond is firm, has a passionate, cruel mouth, fierce eyes, and so on. But, like David Owen, he can be tender too. He kisses lightly, offers TLC and sympathy. The two languages appear in a final oxymoron, 'He said softly, "Now." His mouth came ruthlessly down on hers.' The adverbs softly and ruthlessly are ill-matched.

Obviously all this comes within an offensive framework and draws on a long history of male romance of this kind: women are childish victims and have no business being lesbians or master-criminals. But I also think that, in its confusions, this is a representative male discourse of its period. It is as if the male stereotype won't work for Fleming, and needs supplementing. As a result he has no way of describing sexual relations other than confusedly. The same problems are widely evident. If women had no ready language with which to describe gender politics from their vantage, then men too are often in difficulties for different but related reasons.

Philip Larkin's poem, 'Deceptions', from *The Less Deceived* (1955), for instance, deals with a rape victim whose story he found in Mayhew. The poem is concerned in tone, with significant extensions of sympathy. But there are also troubling shifts in direction and a reluctance to offer a female perspective for this woman's experience. The poem has an epigraph from Mayhew in which the woman's story is given in her own words. The first line then reads 'Even so distant, I can taste the grief . . .'. One immediately thinks the poem is to be a dramatic monologue with the woman speaking. But it is quickly apparent that it is not, and the poet's troubled commentary makes up the rest. The title refers to the victim's deception (she has been drugged), and to the self-deception of the rapist whose desires are not satisfied (Larkin 1977: 37).

'Deceptions' is a disturbing poem for a number of reasons (for further contextual comment see Featherstone and Rylance 1989). First, it begins with sympathy for the victim but ends with the perpetrator's disappointment. Second, its formal strategy cancels the woman's voice. And, third, by evading the violence, it fails to come to terms with the psychology of the act for either party. The poem's hesitant, concerned rhetoric ('I would not dare / console you if I could . . .') complicates the matter, but remains complicit with the structure of male discourse. This has two features. Firstly, events are seen in male terms and the woman is silenced. This response is the leading element and reveals a gross failure of imaginative sensitivity and moral concern typical of the male blindness to which I alluded at the opening of this section.

But there is also a second element which involves a lurking sense that really this isn't good enough, that a different kind of response is needed, a different kind of language. Often this is barely articulated, and emerges only as contradiction. In Alan

Sillitoe's *Saturday Night and Sunday Morning* (1958), Arthur Seaton's attitudes to women are violently and plainly contradictory. Within pages he will abuse women, then identify with them; will treat them as objects, then think this kind of thing:

> Arthur, in his more tolerant moments, said that women were more than ornaments and skivvies: they were warm wonderful creatures that needed and deserved to be looked after, requiring all the attention a man could give, certainly more than the man's work and a man's own pleasure. A man gets a lot of pleasure anyway from being nice to a woman. (Sillitoe 1985: 50)

The framework is still male-centred, and women ('creatures') are only seen in relation to men, but the attitudes cut across prevailing ideas somewhat.

Such passages are occasional, and always circumscribed by the dominant matrix, but they reflect a sustained ambiguity in male attitudes which are related to the absence of any language for such concerns. If, from a woman's perspective, it seemed there was no vocabulary at all, some male writers also perceived the inadequacy of the dominant language to articulate needs which went beyond those the period demanded and authorized. David Storey's *This Sporting Life* (1960) is such a case. A novel about Rugby League may seem unpromising for such an argument, but this is the point. Arthur Machin is a man's man: violent, manipulative and frankly cynical about the needs of others, his career as a sporting adventurer seems rosy. Yet the book is haunted by a sense of loss which is brought into focus as Arthur's career dwindles into injury. Generically, the novel plays against the upwardly-mobile, I've-had-my-ups-and-downs-but-battled-through manner of the (still largely male and working-class) sporting autobiography for which there remains a formidable market. The opinionated cheerfulness of these books contrasts sharply with the down-beat tone of Machin's narrative. Arthur spends as much time on his knees as on his way to the top.

Arthur consciously plays to cultural models. He is Tarzan or the Big Ape (his nicknames), the King Kong of Yorkshire rugby. His regular reading is aggressively and self-consciously masculine, and he uses it to buttress his sense of identity, especially at moments of guilt or confusion. His fantasy heroes are boxers, street-wise detectives and de-mobbed adventurers:

> I sat at the bar and got out *Tropical Orgy* – a moonlit night on a

calm tropical sea, and Capt. Summers had just come on deck after leaving his sample 'fully satisfied and utterly contented' in his cabin below. A boat came alongside to collect the contraband, and Capt. Summers took out his dark little .38. I found I wasn't blaming myself. I wasn't all that responsible, I told myself. Don't tell me she's that innocent. She's been married. I wouldn't have tumbled like that if I hadn't thought. . . . Still, I didn't feel safe till I saw Maurice and the girls come through the door. (Storey 1962: 97)

The real woman in this passage is Mrs Hammond, Arthur's landlady, with whom – though he would not put it in this way – he is in love. A page earlier he has sexually attacked her.

Arthur has no language for love. His relations with Mrs Hammond consist of violence, money, showing-off and utterly ineffectual efforts to communicate more seriously. Like Arthur Seaton in Sillitoe's novel, Machin swings between violence and a more sensitive attempt (which can never quite be verbalized) to understand and relate. 'I looked at her afresh. I'd never seen her much as a person. She didn't want to be seen' (Storey 1962: 68). Storey here captures something of the lack of a language to communicate feelings in a characteristic late-'fifties register. The man doesn't see, the woman doesn't want to be seen as, an independent person. Therefore, as a typical man of his circumstances and generation, he treats her as an object. This is the sexual attack mentioned earlier:

She relaxed for an instant, then suddenly stiffened. I pulled her back from the bed and folded my hands round the front of her body. I'd never felt such a loose jointed shape before. She jumped about and shouted something particular. I held her tight and didn't make a sound. All the time I reminded myself of the ugliness of her face, of her terror. I was half stunned by her lack of excitement. Her head twisted every way as she went on yelling something I didn't understand. I seemed to be fighting the bed itself. I couldn't understand why she hadn't expected it, why she didn't give in.

Then suddenly I felt sick, retching, put off by the sight of that shabby underwear. (Storey 1962: 96)

'A loose jointed shape', 'the bed itself', 'yelling something I didn't understand': Arthur dehumanizes the object of his desire. He cannot hear her, nor cope with the failure of his solipsistic desires and fantasies (she does not reciprocate, she has no glamorous underwear), or the moral dimensions of his action ('suddenly I felt sick').

This seems a remarkable diagnosis by a man of the pathological gender relations of his period, and it is useful to recall that Storey's next novel, *Flight into Camden* (also 1960), is a first-person narrative by a woman. (As I indicated earlier the attempt by a man to offer a woman's perspective is exceptional in this period.) Usually read only as a piece of 'working-class' naturalism, *This Sporting Life* is an intelligent inquiry whose sexual politics bear some thought. If the novel has the sadness of tragedy (and in that respect it is a quite typical post-war account of working-class life), then the tragedy in large part springs from the chaos it portrays in gender relations: the lack of a woman's voice, the lack of a shared language for feeling, and above all a set of male attitudes which have since been described more explicitly by feminists like John Stoltenberg. Stoltenberg is concerned with the way male objectification of women depends on the absence of an ethical language. His analysis is worth quoting at length to close this section at a point which is both within, and beyond, the condition with which it opened.

> Needless to say, trying to delineate the ethical meaning of sexual objectification is very difficult. On the one hand, there is no tradition of public and truthful discourse about men's sexual response to their perception and treatment of people as objects. There is scarcely even a vocabulary. And on the other hand, trying to think about sexual objectification in a conscientious way can make the mind want to give up, go blank, and shut down. Trying to unlock and unblock the function of sexual objectification, particularly on women's lives, can be to risk recognising too much that is too deeply disturbing. Trying to think about the reality and experience of sexual objectification can be like struggling to untie a knot that has been pulled too tight over too many years by too many hands – and like having one's own fingers bound up someplace in the knot. (Stoltenberg 1990: 51–52)

## III: A common language?

Some of the changes introduced by feminism are illustrated by placing Stoltenberg's essay alongside Storey's novel. Though they focus on similar problems, the language and address has changed. Storey's is an account of a world without adequate language, Stoltenberg's is of frailty in language and motivation. Feminism, that is, has made conscious what was not, and made the dark speakable. It has offered a descriptive vocabulary, and an effective moral and political position.

However, does this mean that what is being developed is a common – implying genderless – language? The answer must be 'no'. There is not only the danger of male appropriation, and the political need for women to sustain their own movement, there is also the question of the terms of analysis. A man may construct the field differently; he may use different concepts and forms. Many women claim this is determining: there are male modes of comprehension, analysis and language, and there are female. To write about feminist problems in a male mode will inevitably twist the account.

This question has been of great importance in literary studies, though the hypothesis of a distinctive female language remains controversial (Cameron 1985). Many follow Elaine Showalter's distinction in her influential essay 'Towards a Feminist Poetics' (1979). Showalter divided feminist criticism into 'the feminist critique' and 'gynocriticism'. The distinction is partly historical, though the two co-exist. The former criticises traditional, sexist representations of women in literature and criticism. This is followed by the definition of the distinctive features of women's writing. In gynocriticism the critic studies female culture: the relatedness of women writers, the particular circumstances in which they write, the forms and modes they use, the particular female experiences they record and explore (Showalter 1979). In practice gynocriticism has two forms: a largely American form which examines these topics mainly historically (and whose best-known representative is probably Showalter herself), and a French form which, drawing on psychoanalytic and post-structuralist theory, develops the idea of 'écriture féminine', a particularly female form of writing and exploration. Showalter's account has been widely adopted, and many feminists see a more or less fundamental distinction between the two modes (Kaplan 1985: 53; Jones 1985: 96; Stimpson 1987; Gilbert and Gubar 1989: 146–47).

Showalter has argued that the move from a protest-based (and therefore in some sense male-orientated) criticism, to a woman-centred criticism, marks the beginning of a mature feminist criticism, with a distinctive method and defined object of study (1987b: 39). If this is so, there is an axiomatic problem for men in feminism at this level, because it is not probable they will have the imaginative or intellectual familiarity with relevant experience and modes of apprehension to undertake worthwhile work. This does not mean that there is a biological difference in modes of understanding: it simply points to an experiential fact which has historical, cultural, educational and personal dimensions. Both politically and professionally, therefore, it seems best that men should exercise great care in approaching this area of feminist concern and research.

In recent work Showalter has played down tensions between the various feminist criticisms. She has stressed the diversity and interaction of the French and American modes while continuing her own historically-grounded approach (1986, 1987b and 1989). The new taxonomy stresses co-operative, non-aggressive models for intellectual and literary development, in contrast to male competition-based theories – Harold Bloom is her example, Stanley Fish would be mine (1989: 363). In one sense this is compelling, though it perhaps understates the difference between her own work and that of French feminists. This turns on the issue of historicality, and mirrors quarrels between historicists and textualists elsewhere. Showalter's work is committed to historical difference within the overall project of understanding the persisting dynamics and problems of women's culture. As in the title of a recent essay (1989), she studies assimilation and autonomy, and this kind of dialectic runs throughout her work. Gynocritical culture is subject to its historical relations with the general culture. Hence her analytical habit of negotiating between ostensibly opposed conceptual pairs: tradition and difference in *A Literature of Their Own*, the women's movement and 'the old patriarchal institution of literary criticism and theory' (1986: 7–8), 'the theoretical and the personal', 'spontaneity and methodology' (1986: 4 and 12). In practice the negotiation is conducted through the dense analysis of historical occurrence.

The question of historical understanding in French feminist theory, though, is more ambiguous. In a recent piece, Hélène Cixous writes that:

It happens that at a certain moment of my life I found myself in the midst of women's History. That is not where I was when I began to write in 1966. In 1968 there was the explosion of women's History but I wasn't in it. Then at a certain moment I couldn't not be in it. It was impossible for

me not to take it into account; to refrain from speaking of it
was impossible for me morally and politically and thus I
found myself in it and proceeded as far as I could go.

But in the domain of women nothing can be theorised. No
science can say anything about it. The only thing one can say
is that writing can, not tell or theorise it, but play with it or
sing it. (Cixous 1989: 11–12)

It is unclear why History is capitalised here, but it is clear that
Cixous can neither accept, nor utterly disclaim, the historicality of
her own work and subjectivity – though the tendency, and the
yearning, seems to be to delocate them. In this writing, motives,
purposes and agency seem deeply obscure. The preference for
passive constructions, multiple negatives and a fugitive, occulted
sense of subjectivity make the going difficult. Political tasks and
determinations seem resented, as does the frustration of a
withdrawal from the world. Yet, it is argued, this is not the point.
Such writing gains access to a female subjectivity which is
trans-individual. The features of it I find problematic are those
which most closely render what is projected as a distinctive and
special female experience. My scepticism, therefore, might be
because I have, as a man, always been in some sense at home
with patriarchal discourse which this style aims to transcend.

However, my scepticism persists because I find the theory
contradictory. On the one hand the argument is made with
reference to the special biological and cultural situation of
women. But, on the other, it is universalized, either through
analogy or through utopian appeal. When Cixous, in her
influential 'The Laugh of the Medusa' (1975), analogizes the
situation of women to that of black people the discussion loses
focus. Does this include patriarchal black people? Cixous, though
wishing to transcend historical and cultural norms, resumes a
habit in French radical thought which is in practice genderless.
Sartre, for instance, analogized the French working class to an
idealized 'negritudinal' experience he had derived from the
Martinicans, Césaire and Fanon.

I can see the political desire for theories which offer women a
distinctive subjectivity remote from patriarchy, just as I can
understand Sartre's desire for exotically redeemable images of
the French proletariat during the struggles over Algeria and the
Fifth Republic. But it is difficult to sustain the claim that this
stands outside history or (in the words of 'The Laugh of the

Medusa') that 'In woman, personal history blends together with the history of all women, as well as national and world history' (Cixous 1981: 252–53). I cannot understand this other than as a historically-specific activist rhetoric; that is, the ultra radicalism of the May events. Her disclaimer, quoted above, that she has subsequently freed herself from a temporary thraldom to History, is implausible. The manner and texture of her ideas seem to me, as with much post-structuralist theory, to be modulated versions of that late 'sixties rhetoric touched, of course, and inevitably, by twenty years of subsequent experience, including the relative success of feminism.

Cixous' thinking, that is, is as historically located as my own, or anyone else's, and our politics are conditioned by that. 'The Laugh of the Medusa' seems to me marvellously organized and rhetorically effective, and I have some sympathy with its politics. But I have difficulties with its mode of understanding and analysis. Nonetheless, this does not prevent me welcoming it. This is because I cannot believe in a world absolved from history. The same grounds that lead me to reject Cixous' analytical manner, lead me to welcome her writing; the same grounds that lead me to conclude, from Showalter's definition of a distinctive female centre to feminist research, that men should be wary of treading there, also leads me to think that the kind of work I attempted in part two is worth doing. That is, to understand the historical and cultural sources of one's situation by studying writing by women and men in particular times and contexts.

If I want a model for this I might look to the philosopher Alasdair MacIntyre. In *After Virtue* and other works, MacIntyre argues that contemporary ethical and political culture is made in the intersections of sometimes overlapping, sometimes competing, communities of values. There are no means of arbitrating among these from standards beyond them, though it is likely that such standards will be on offer within each community. However, the apparent relativism of this position does not – contrary to some post-structuralist thinking – make belief suspect. This is because, in particular value communities, values have a functional and creative efficacy. In my view, post-structuralist theory underestimates the creative function of value communities because, in deconstructing texts, it pays too little attention to the detailed transactions of historical experience in particular communities; that is, how values thrive or fail as specific activities not textual features. (It is then an interesting question why deconstructionist values should have become so powerfully influential at this historical juncture.)

The values represented by feminism now form a powerful community. In this sense feminism does provide a common language, a discursive community which rests on roughly-shared assumptions, but which retains the necessary gender distinctions, and the political choices that follow from them. Feminist literary criticism offers a range of methodological options and modes of analysis. It also offers, for men as well as women, a range of choices about these methods and values which are effective both as critical approaches and choices about living. Decisions about these will often be, in large part, political decisions, and men need to be particularly vigilant in this respect. They will also be part of revisable and extending learning. But the difference feminism has made is to have changed the debate within the academic discursive community for the better, to have provided a language for the exchange of ideas about values and the recognition of human experiences, and to have organized important political pressure for the establishment of that language. That is why this fellow travels with it.

## Acknowledgement

I would like to thank the following for advice, reading and comment on this essay: Judith Boddy, Kate Campbell, Kelvin Everest, Simon Featherstone, Aleid Fokkema, Felicia Gordon, Kim Landers, Sharon Ouditt and Nigel Wheale. Writing is always a collective learning, one hopes, and I have benefitted from this small, immediate audience both now and for the future.

## References

Baldick, C. (1983). *The Social Mission of English Criticism, 1848–1932.* Oxford, Clarendon Press.
Bellerby, F. (1986). (ed.) Anne Stevenson, *Selected Poems.* London, Enitharmon Press.
Cameron, D. (1985). *Feminism and Linguistic Theory.* London, Macmillan.
Cixous, H. (1981). 'The laugh of the Medusa', in (eds) E. Marks and I. de Courtivron. *New French Feminisms: An Anthology.* Brighton, Harvester, pp. 245–64 (originally published 1975).
—— (1989). 'From the scene of the unconscious to the scene of history',

in (ed.) R. Cohen, *The Future of Literary Theory*. London, Routledge, pp. 1–18.

Doyle, B. (1982). 'The hidden history of English Studies', in (ed.) P. Widdowson, *Re-Reading English*. London, Methuen.

Featherstone, S. and Rylance, R. (1989). 'The poetry of Jack Clemo and the way we read today', *Ideas and Production*, 9/10, 105–24.

Fleming, I. (1961). *Goldfinger*. London, Pan.

Gilbert, S. and Gubar, S. (1989). 'The mirror and the vamp: reflections on feminist criticism', in (ed.) R. Cohen, *The Future of Literary Theory*. London, Routledge, pp. 144–166.

Heath, S. (1987). 'Male feminism', in (eds) Jardine and Smith, *Men in Feminism*, pp. 1–32.

Heron, L., (ed.) (1985). *Truth, Dare or Promise: Girls Growing Up in the Fifties*. London, Virago.

Herzfeld, E. (1991). 'Women "face hidden curriculum"', *Times Higher Education Supplement*, 19 April, p. 6.

Jardine, A. and Smith, P., (eds) (1987). *Men in Feminism*. London, Methuen.

Jones, A.R. (1985). 'Inscribing femininity: French theories of the feminine', in (eds) G. Greene and C. Kahn. *Making a Difference: Feminist Literary Criticism*. London, Methuen, pp. 80–112.

Jordan, T., (ed.) (1990). *Growing Up in the Fifties*. London, Optima.

Kaplan, S.J. (1985). 'Varieties of feminist criticism', in (ed.) G. Greene and C. Kahn. *Making a Difference: Feminist Literary Criticism*. London, Methuen, pp. 37–58.

Kauffman, L., (ed.) (1989). *Feminism and Institutions: Dialogues on Feminist Theory*. Oxford, Blackwell.

Larkin, P. (1977), *The Less Deceived*. London, Marvell Press.

Light, A. (1986). 'Writing fictions: femininity and the 1950s', in (ed.) J. Radford. *The Progress of Romance: The Politics of Popular Fiction*. London, Routledge, pp. 139–166.

—— (1987). 'Towards a feminist Cultural Studies: middle-class femininity and fiction in post-Second World War Britain', *Englisch Amerikanische Studien*, 1, 58–72.

Lovell, T. (1987). *Consuming Fictions*. London, Verso.

MacIntyre, A. (1981). *After Virtue: A Study in Moral Theory*. London, Duckworth.

Maitland, S., (ed.) (1988). *Very Heaven: Looking Back at the 1960s*. London, Virago.

Messer-Davidow, E. (1989). 'The philosophical bases of feminist literary criticisms', in (ed.) L. Kauffman, *Gender and Theory: Dialogues on Feminist Criticism*. Oxford, Basil Blackwell.

Middleton, P. (1989). 'Socialism, feminism and men', *Radical Philosophy*, 53, pp. 8–19.

Moi, T. (1989). 'Men against patriarchy', in (ed.) L. Kauffman, *Gender and Theory: Dialogues on Feminist Criticism*. Oxford, Basil Blackwell.

Olsen, T. (1980). *Silences*. London, Virago.

Palmer, D.J. (1965). *The Rise of English Studies: An Account of English from its Origins to the Making of the Oxford English School*. London, OUP.

Pitter, R. (1990). *Collected Poems*. London, Enitharmon Press.

Plaidy, J. (1968). *Light on Lucrezia*. London, Pan.

Plath, S. (1981). *Collected Poems*, (ed.) T. Hughes. London, Faber.

Rich, A. (1975). *The Poetry of Adrienne Rich*, (ed.) B.C. Gelphi and A. Gelphi. London, Norton.

Rowbotham, S. (1973). *Woman's Consciousness, Man's World*. Harmondsworth, Penguin.

—— (1990). *The Past is Before Us: Feminism in Action Since the 1960s*. Harmondsworth, Penguin.

Rylance, R. (1990). 'Psychological Theory in Cultural Context 1850–1880'. PhD Thesis, University of Leicester.

Sexton, A. (1981). *The Complete Poems*. Boston, Houghton Mifflin.

Showalter, E. (1979). 'Towards a feminist poetics', in (ed.) M. Jacobus. *Women Writing About Writing About Women*. London, Croom Helm.

—— (1986). 'Introduction: the feminist critical revolution', in (ed.) E. Showalter. *The New Feminist Criticism: Essays on Women, Literature and Theory*. London, Virago, pp. 3–17.

—— (1987a). 'Critical cross-dressing: male feminists and the woman of the year', reprinted in (ed.) Jardine and Smith, *Men in Feminism*, pp. 116–32 (originally published 1983).

—— (1987b). 'Women's time and women's space: writing the history of feminist criticism', in (ed.) S. Benstock, *Feminist Issues in Literary Scholarship*. Bloomington, Indiana University Press.

—— (1989). 'A criticism of our own: autonomy and assimilation in Afro-American and feminist literary theory', in (ed.) R. Cohen, *The Future of Literary Theory*. London, Routledge, pp. 347–69.

Sillitoe, A. (1985). *Saturday Night and Sunday Morning*. London, Grafton.

Sinfield, A. (1989). *Literature, Politics and Culture in Postwar Britain*. Oxford, Blackwell.

Stimpson, C.R. (1987). 'Introduction' in (ed.) S. Benstock, *Feminist Issues in Literary Scholarship*. Bloomington, Indiana University Press, pp. 1–6.

Stoltenberg, J. (1990). *Refusing to Be a Man*. London, Fontana.

Storey, D. (1962). *This Sporting Life*. Harmondsworth, Penguin.

Taylor, J., (ed.) (1982). *Notebooks/Memoirs/Archives: Reading and Rereading Doris Lessing*. London, Routledge and Kegan Paul.

Thomas, K. (1990). *Gender and Subject in Higher Education*. Buckingham, Open University Press.

Thompson, A. and Wilcox, H., (eds), (1989). *Teaching Women: Feminism and English Studies*. Manchester, Manchester University Press.

Todd, J. (1988). *Feminist Literary History: A Defence*. Cambridge, Polity.

Wandor, M., (ed.) (1990). *Once a Feminist: Stories of a Generation.* London, Virago.

Wilson, E. (1980). *Only Half-Way to Paradise: Women in Post-War Britain, 1945–1968.* London, Tavistock.

# 8

# Mary Kelly and Griselda Pollock in conversation

*Introduction: Margaret Iversen*

The conversation transcribed here between art historian Griselda Pollock and artist Mary Kelly was staged before an audience and recorded. The event was not, however, open to the general public, but restricted to two groups that had gathered in Vancouver in June 1989 – some to attend the 'Summer Intensive in the Visual Arts' at Simon Fraser University, that year led by Mary Kelly, others to take part in a series of seminars conducted by Griselda Pollock at the Vancouver Art Gallery. The relative intimacy of the occasion explains the spontaneity and informality of the discussion. In one way this makes the conversation more accessible, but in another way it is more tied to that particular occasion – a great deal is assumed by the participants. It therefore requires some introduction and contextualization.

This was by no means a first encounter; Pollock and Kelly have been having just this sort of conversation privately for many years. These exchanges, and others like them, have proved mutually beneficial. Pollock's critical/historical work has been inflected by her close contact with contemporary women artists, while Kelly's artistic practice is thoroughly informed by feminist theoretical writing and art historical research. Indeed, in Kelly's case, any neat distinctions between theory and practice, or writing and art, immediately break down. Her work is not an illustration of feminist theory, but rather a contribution to it in a discourse which includes images and texts. The conversation was also facilitated by their sense of being engaged in the same project – the feminist critique of patriarchal social structures and institutions of cultural production, as well as the collective effort to imagine a different future. Because the conversation was 'closed' it could also be 'open' in the sense that it did not have a definite agenda, and also in the sense that it responded to questions and comments from the floor. For both reasons, it lacks an elegant formal structure. However, two distinct themes emerge: the problem of finding a non-reductive but demystified language for describing artistic working methods and the vexed question of postmodernism and feminism. With a view to an interdisciplinary readership, I will first introduce the two discussants and their respective projects, and then briefly comment on the matter of the conversation.

Griselda Pollock is best known for the forceful argument she and Rozsika Parker put forward in their book *Old Mistresses: Woman, Art Ideology* (1981). Here they insisted that it is not enough for feminist art historians to retrieve the work of unjustly neglected women artists and insert them into the existing framework of art history, because that very framework is structured around certain stereotypes of masculinity and femininity and wedded to concepts of art and artist that systematically exclude women and their contributions. Art history's fundamental concepts and habitual procedures were shown to constitute an ideological practice. The appropriate response to this is not to supplement the canon of great male artists with an equal number of female ones, but rather to interrogate the historical production of the canon and the formation of the discipline's notion of artistic greatness. In other words, *Old Mistresses* brought elements of a Marxist critique and the strategies of a social history of art to bear on the crucial question posed by Linda Nochlin: 'Why are there no great women artists?'

The book includes a chapter on twentieth-century feminist art practice and, although it is generously inclusive, it is not uncritical. For example, Judy Chicago and others are criticized for the way in which they attempt to validate female experience and sexuality. The resonances these artists set up between, say, flowers and female genitalia may strike a positive chord for many women, but their work is wide open to appropriation in a cultural context which already positions women as closer to the body, nature and sexuality. Pollock favours an art practice, like Mary Kelly's, which works to unsettle ideological constructions of femininity. She expands on this theme in her response to the 1984 Difference exhibition, 'Screening the Seventies' (1988). The article is also an effort to shift the discourses around feminist art practice away from post-modernist deconstruction and closer to the tradition of a dissident marxist-modernism. In the essay, she recalls the late 1970s adaptation of Brechtian aesthetics and that moment's call for distantiation or for disidentificatory practices which were thought necessary because vision can 'only confirm ideologically sanctioned perceptions of the world . . .' (Pollock 1988: 165). She cites a 1975 article by Stephen Heath in which he declares that 'reality is to be grasped not in the mirror of vision but in the distance of analysis'. This assumption has clear consequences for feminist art practices. By adopting collage or montage or scripto-visual techniques, one could present the conditions and causes of women's oppression instead of simply reproducing its appearances.

Mary Kelly's work is a model of this complex and reflexive art practice, except that, as I will suggest, she is interested in reassessing the psychoanalytic conception of identification and perhaps in retrieving it in some form as a possible ground for women's pleasure in relation to representation – it might serve as the basis for some viable alternative to the dominant voyeuristic scopic regime. The possibility of a specifically feminine form of visual pleasure was, after all, one of the themes of her major work, *Post-Partum Document* (1973–78), which dealt with the mother–child relationship in psychoanalytic terms. There she proposed the possibility of a female form of fetishism witnessed in a mother's desire to cling to traces, tiny vests or hand molds, of a pleasure now lost.

The conversation reprinted here makes reference to Mary Kelly's recently completed project *Interim* (1984–89). It is an extended project which takes the 'middle-aged' woman and her cultural invisibility as its theme and explicitly turns on the issue of identification and disidentification in relation to representation as well as to other people. Kelly began her project by sifting through cultural artefacts (like women's magazines) and by recording conversations with many women in order to find out what positions we habitually take up and what ones are fantasized. She asked what points of attachment, what ego-ideals are in circulation for us. The resulting project turns out to be both a critique of the limitations imposed on women by the restrictions of the available images and discourses, and a positive re-evaluation

of identification as a specifically feminine basis for visual pleasure. She suggests that identification need not be a matter of
stabilizing an illusory sense of coherence in a single mirrored
ego-ideal. Rather, patterns of identification turn out to be
shifting, unstable, slippery. True, many of the sites offered for
feminine identification are less than inviting. In the section called
*Pecunia*, for example, we meet the self-sacrificing mother and the
wife whose object of desire is a clean toilet bowl. But even here
desire is invoked in relation to these sites and vision is not
chastized (figure 1). Rather, images and imaginary scenarios are
presented in a sort of grisaille: in *Corpus* instead of the female
body, a photo-positive of a garment is attached in Plexiglas so
that it has a ghostly, 'mediatized' presence (figure 2). In the
accompanying anecdotal text panels, emotional investment is
invited and then gently undercut, often with humour (figure 3).
Patterns of identification are put in place and then set adrift
through a dialectic of desire and reflection of it (see also Bryson
1990 and Iversen 1988).

In the course of conversation, Mary Kelly makes some revealing remarks about her own processes of art-making which have
important implications. She is attempting to invent a demystified language to describe artistic creativity – that is, a
language which by-passes the traditional use of such categories
as authorship, originality, expression, intuition and genius.
These concepts are still deeply entrenched in the discourses of
Fine Art, despite relentless critiques. Kelly's account of the way
she goes about finding appropriate forms and materials, or
suggestive visual metaphors, cuts across the concept of style as
an all-over signature (e.g. Abstract Expressionism) and at the
same time calls into question art practices which rely on unmediated appropriation of commodities, media or art images.
The conversation circles around the theme of the irrationale of
artistic production while resisting recourse to mystical notions of
intuition. The various references both Kelly and Pollock make to
Kristeva and Lacan are an effort to understand the unconscious
dimensions of making a work of art, including the artist's desire
to be received by a specific ideal audience.

This salutary deflation of the myths surrounding the artist-
genius is balanced by Kelly's efforts to resist the recent tendency
to level distinctions between sign and object, commodity and art.
Thus she curated an exhibition in London, *Beyond the Purloined
Image* (1983), which advocated an art practice different from the

uninflected appropriation of high cultural precedents (Sherrie Levine) or of commodity images (Jeff Koons, Haim Steinbach). Instead she suggests a strategy of 'de-appropriation' or 'de-colonization' which wrests signs away from one context and re-positions them in another. To use the most obvious example, in *Corpus* the endlessly fetishized image of the female body is re-imagined according to women's desires and fears concerning their own bodies. This project of re-articulation is necessarily complex and, as Kelly says herself, 'demands . . . a rupture in the paradigm of single, rather seamless artefacts' (Kelly 1990: 61). This explains the importance she attaches to the nature of her work as an extended project.

The other important theme which arises in the conversation concerns postmodernism and feminism. It is launched by a distinction Griselda Pollock makes between those artists who continue to work within a paradigm of modernist 'dis-affirmative' practices (deliberate painterly awkwardness, primitivism, automatism, use of 'inartistic' materials and so on) and those who insist upon a more radical breach with modernism, emphatically signalled by the non-use of paint (photo-text, video, performance). Earlier on in the discussion, Kelly had briefly outlined a history of art since the sixties in which she noted with regret the disappearance in the eighties of conceptualist art and discourses on art and the return to more traditional practices, particularly a kind of painting aiming to valorize that which lies outside the compass of linguistic signs. Pollock returns to the theme, but does so in the context of T.J. Clark's debate with Greenberg and John Roberts' use of that debate in an article called 'Painting and Sexual Difference' (1990). Roberts outlines the case for a 'feminist/textualist' strand of practice with reference to Kelly's work. He seems to find it an unduly severe self-imposed exile from the high ground of modernist culture and is more sympathetic to feminist artists who see their work both in, and in contest with, the mainstream. This implies 'that feminist consciousness in painting is no less bound up with the determining conditions of modernity or representation than the work of men' (Roberts 1990: 179). Pollock objects to the way the argument ascribes to feminist artists terms that are current in the debate about the meaning of modernism – high and low, avant-garde and kitsch. Feminist art practice must be understood as a specific intervention countering patriarchy and not as a general political disaffirmation of culture.

This prompts Mary Kelly to respond on a number of different levels. First of all she is highly dubious about any global notion of 'feminist art practice' – there are only feminist interventions in art practice. And these interventions are strongest when they don't stop at opportunistic thematizing of women or sexuality, but shift the ground of debates in both the women's movement and contemporary art practice. Further, she insists that any notion of feminist art practice which embraces painting and other media blurs crucial differences – in sympathetically accommodating diverse practices, there is a danger of blunting the strategic edge of a particular practice. The debates around postmodernism, feminism and art practice in the United States are, she thinks, very productive because they don't just cede feminism a corner for their opposition to the dominant culture. On the contrary, the theory at the very heart of the debate is shaped by (mainly French) feminist thought.

It becomes clear that the difference in emphasis between Kelly and Pollock is partly owing to their different positions: an historian feels a responsibility to represent the range of contemporary debates about art practice, while an artist must be committed to a strategic position. Yet there also seems to be at stake here a version of the on-going debate on the left over the value of completing the 'Enlightenment project' (Habermas 1983) in the face of the postmodernist critique of its totalizing rationality (Lyotard 1986). Although both Mary Kelly and Griselda Pollock would agree that the history of modernism is the history of the systematic exclusion or marginalization of women, one sees the strategic value of joining forces with those radical critiques of modernism found in the discourse of postmodernism, while the other is wary of that discourse's sometimes virulent anti-marxism. Pollock's commitment to socialist feminism makes her more sympathetic to the still vital theorizing on the politics of culture in the tradition of the Frankfurt School, even though that tradition has signally failed to acknowledge satisfactorily the importance of the women's movement. She would perhaps be happier with Janet Wolff's notion of 'modified modernism' than with postmodernism (Wolff 1990: 205). Yet Pollock's remarks towards the end of the conversation, where she points to the difficult contradiction of being committed to the project of modernity in a postmodernist world, would seem to be an effort to bridge this divide.

## References

Bryson, N. (1990). 'Interim and identification' in Mary Kelly, *Interim*. New York, New Museum of Contemporary Art, 27–38.

Habermas, J. (1983). 'Modernity – an incomplete project' in H. Foster (ed.) *The Anti-Aesthetic: Essays on Postmodern Culture*. Port Townsend, Bay Press, 3–15.

Iversen, M. (1988). 'Fashioning feminine identity', *Art International*, 2, 51–7.

Kelly, M. (1983). *Post-Partum Document*. London, Routledge and Kegan Paul.

—— (1990). 'That obscure object of desire' (interview with H. Foster) in *Interim*. New York, The New Museum of Contemporary Art, 53–62.

Lyotard, J.F. (1984). 'Answering the question: what is postmodernism?', in *The Postmodern Condition: A Report on Knowledge*. Manchester, Manchester University Press. See also A. Benjamin (ed.), (1989) *The Lyotard Reader*. Oxford, Oxford University Press.

Parker, R. and Pollock, G. (1981). *Old Mistresses: Women, Art and Ideology*. London, Pandora Press.

Pollock, G. (1988). 'Screening the seventies: sexuality and represen-tation', in *Vision and Difference: Femininity, Feminism and the Histories of Art*. London, Routledge and Kegan Paul, 155–199.

Roberts, J. (1990). 'Painting and sexual difference' in *Postmodernism, Politics and Art*. Manchester, Manchester University Press, 166–181.

Wolff, J. (1990). 'Postmodern theory and feminist art practice', in Roy Boyne and Ali Rattansi (eds.), *Postmodernism and Society*. Basingstoke, Macmillan, 187–208.

The conversation took place at the Vancouver Art Gallery in June 1989. The event was organized by Judith Mastai Ed.D., Head of Public Programmes at the gallery. She also extensively edited the transcribed event which anticipated the exhibition at the Van-couver Art Gallery of Mary Kelly's *Interim* in May–July 1990. Two Vancouver-based artists intervene in the discussion: Landon MacKenzie, a painter who teaches at Emily Carr College of Art and Design; and Sara Diamond, whose work consists primarily of photography and video installations.

## *The conversation at the Vancouver Art Gallery, June 1989*

### Positioning the exchange

*Griselda Pollock:* According to the logic of this evening, as part of the seminar series that we've been doing here, it seemed highly

She wanted her *and* she
wanted all of her clothes.

**Figure 1.** Mary Kelly, *Pecunia* 1989. Detail from 'Soror' Section 3 of *Pecunia*. Silkscreen on galvanized steel. Vancouver Art Gallery. Photograph: Trevor Mills.

appropriate that the end point of our discussion should be around practice, questions of art-making, and the context of art-making.[1] Because of the whole theoretical enterprise into which feminism has launched us, feminist cultural practices have been such a rich and vivid place for development of theory that

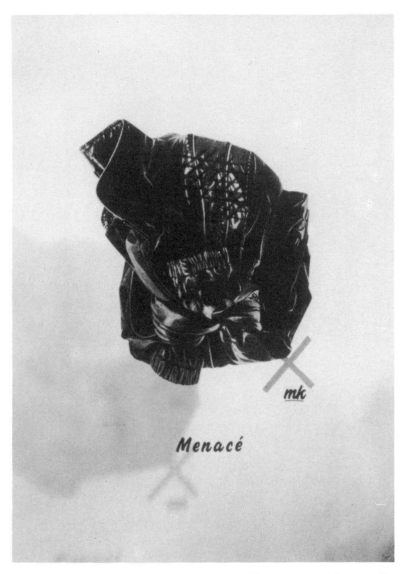

**Figure 2.** Mary Kelly. *Corpus* 1984–85. Detail from 'Menacé' Section. By permission of The New Museum of Contemporary Art, New York.

they can easily be taken over by theory, and left there; rather than being rigorously attacked, taken hold of, used and explored, with both respect and disrespect. The idea is to see what theory does for us in terms of practice.

**Figure 3.** Mary Kelly. Installation view at Vancouver Art Gallery with *Corpus* and *Historia*. Photograph: Trevor Mills.

Now, my practice as an art historian is as a writer about art. But I refuse to let the division exist between 'artists who make art' and 'some kind of witness or supplement who is called upon to provide the discourse when necessary'. I couldn't do the kind of art history and art writing that I do without having been part of a community which had both intellectuals and practitioners of various sorts in constant conversation with each other. A writer has to have a means of talking to artists who are engaged more obviously in practice, for these are overlapping practices.

It's been my experience that there isn't a rigid split between theory/practice, writers/artists – a division which has been such a bugbear of studio experience for so many years. For instance, in many institutions, the studio staff don't want to have too much to do with the people who talk about art and so a dialogue is not encouraged. So this isn't a set-up where I'm the art historian and here is the artist and there is a division. It is a conversation.

## The practice of making art

*Griselda Pollock:* Something that does particularly interest me about the practice of making art is the process of thinking about the forms of things. One of the things I'm fascinated by in your work, Mary, is how carefully the formats, the forms, the physical appearance, the aesthetic dimensions are thought through. On so many occasions I hear Mary's work described in terms of the theory that it seems to deploy, of the sense of it being difficult or theoretical or distancing. Yet it seems to me that there is a massive amount of consideration of the experience of the work as something that you engage with on many, many levels. I'd be interested in the decisions you make about art. At the moment you're going through the process of thinking out the next two parts of *Interim* and your calculations are an area that I find extremely interesting.

*Mary Kelly:* First of all, it's not such a comfortable position to be involved in a practice of writing as well as a visual practice of art, because this became rather unfashionable in the eighties, after that moment, in the late sixties and early seventies, when part of the so-called conceptual art project was for artists to take control over all the levels of reception of the work. There was then much more writing. But there wasn't a lot of writing by women. I remember this very distinctly, being kind of confrontational with people like *Art and Language*,[2] and very definitely engaging with someone like Joseph Kosuth. I thought, 'If women don't do that – make this critical overview – then their work will not have the kind of presence that it needs to, historically'.

But towards the end of the seventies, as everyone knows all too well, when the postmodern debate emerged, and then consolidated around the revival of more traditional practices, artists made a very self-conscious effort not to talk about their work. Now, if you do talk about the work, people automatically think you're not visual: that's a product of a particular moment. I'm just trying to put it into an historical perspective. It's not always been like that. You can go right through history and see that there are moments when artists were assumed to be articulate and other moments when they were not. And certainly it's around the re-establishing of the expressive moment, a particular kind of painting which valorizes what's considered to be something outside of the written or spoken forms of linguistic signs, that you get that emphasis. I think this is probably underlying the approach to my work that would say it's more engaged in the ideas than the making of it. But for me it's a combined process.

As I've emphasized before, when I speak about it, my way of working is a visualization and a theorization simultaneously. In fact, I usually don't write something about it until afterwards, and I work out the problems, or engage in the debates that I'm interested in, partly as a visual means, and this is not very easy to describe. I'm sorry I have to resort to some kind of essentialism here, but how do you describe a feeling for certain materials, how do you make that translation? It's interesting to see how much the whole idea of metaphor is central to what causes visual pleasure. One of the examples that I could think of, in terms of what was very pleasureable for me in making it, was in the second part of *Interim – Pecunia*. I based it on the greeting card (figure 1). I was very fascinated by this idea. I usually take things from popular culture that initially interest me, and there was a certain look, size, scale and everything to this card which you wouldn't just literally appropriate, but which I wanted to re-present some way. I came up with an idea that would be an all-in-one, folded piece of steel, starting on the wall, attached to the wall, coming out, and then opening up. Just the economy of that – the fact that it wasn't like a card on a shelf, that it wasn't like a book leaning backwards on a podium. It just had that look of the card, but it took on another whole dimension of meanings by the translation into that material. But the shape in itself wasn't enough. The shape was not good enough. I tried a lot of different processes because I didn't want to go to the extreme of enamelling it. Obviously I could create the colours of the greeting cards and the flashy surfaces and I might get, also, the metaphor for a car or a refrigerator or something, which would be good, but that seemed to be too close. It didn't allow something else I needed – another level of associations to do with money, which was the theme of the piece. Finally, after trying some different galvanizing and iodizing processes, we came up with one kind of zinc process, which made the steel look iridescent. It's actually a very cheap process that they use to keep things from rusting; in fact, it has the quality of brass or copper – a kind of mix. So it also had the sentiment – that look of sentimentality of the cards – but it got the other level. When I saw it, when it came back from the metal company, I jumped up and down, after just the day before reaching the lowest possible ebb when I saw the first result of another process. If you're involved in a construction of meaning that's tying together form with content; then, it's primarily the ideas that you're working with that are prompting you to take on the problems of different media.

So, it's not as though I get stylistically attached, or make a particular medium my trademark. That's definitely not what it's about. It's finding the most appropriate thing for each one of the sections, which means there's a lot of so-called visual research which has to be done on each section. I'd just mastered the screen printing and knew how the plexiglas worked and then I had to understand what the steel was like. You couldn't possibly, in my case, use the same means in the second piece that you used in the first, because the first was about the body and about the image and needed that reflective surface, and the second was about something else. I could say, just extending that, that I couldn't possibly, in *Interim*, use found objects the way I did in *Post-Partum Document*. People would say after number VI (the one that I cast on the slates), 'Well, why don't you do a lot of these?' Everybody wanted to buy them. I found it almost impossible to make a one-off work outside of a series that would be something to be sold in its own right. I'm only saying that because I'm trying to describe how integrated this is, as a project and as a process.

## On essentialism, recognition, and an ideal audience

*Landon MacKenzie:* I wrote down your statement – 'I'm sorry I must resort to some kind of essentialism here' – when you talked about going back to the art process. The word 'essentialism' comes up in such a defensive manner in so many contexts recently. I wonder whether there's another term which includes something about making, where there are other factors operating. For instance, when it came back looking like that, you knew you had it, and so you jumped up and down; and when it came back like this, you knew you didn't. You're the only one who knows what you're looking for, and yet you can't always pin it down until you see it. How can we acknowledge that response and suspend the defensiveness around 'essentialism'?

*Mary Kelly:* I think you're suggesting that perhaps you need some way to talk about creative imagination without talking about creative essentialism, and talk about the art-making process, but not necessarily as a question of authorship or style. I was trying to do that, to give a sense of what causes pleasure in the process of making – and also to admit that, at one level, it's pretty hard to talk about it and describe it. But to describe, also, a process that puts that in the service of something other than about creating a transcendent author for the work.

I think probably there are some other ways you could take that up. I don't know if I'd particularly want to, but I used to be more interested in Kristeva's early work and the way that she described certain things that were not necessarily outside of language, but that were pre-verbal experiences which she related to a certain disposition of sound and colour. The caution is not to think of this as outside of language, but as another level of linguistic inscription that's less trackable.

*Griselda Pollock:* I am interested in what you've just said. I was talking last night[3] about the possibilities for formulating languages in which we can talk about some of the processes to do with art-making in a way which is not mystical. What I was trying to say is that notions of aesthetics and harmony have a very suspect ideological relationship, not only in general, but to questions of sexuality with which we are concerned, because they cover over precisely those processess on which Kristeva's theory of the semiotic may give us a handle.

Again, to go back to the theory of linear time,[4] it's not a question of a 'before' or 'after'. You have to hypothesize the basis on which you're going to arrive at the structures. But once you have structures, their bases don't come before; they are dialectically involved in being the conditions of the structure, and also the conditions of the change and transformation of them. So, Kristeva's theory, in the territory of aesthetic practice of literature, poetry, art and music is precisely as all those thresholds and boundaries. All those forms are definitively part of the symbolic and part of culture, but have a different set of exchanges, with the constant and necessary components of all language at both their formal level and the level at which they represent the drives.

*Mary Kelly:* There is a difficulty with this because there is something so fundamental about the process that Kristeva describes; that is to say that the child's first experience of the mother's body as this array of sound and colour, and the space that the mother's word occupies there, being perhaps the founding moment of something like a metaphorical relation. You can say that underlies all art work – there's something just too fundamental about it to be very useful, I think. Your question provokes me to remember this, but also it's available to apply to absolutely everything. So I think I was more interested in saying, given this, what do you actually do with it? What specific use does the artist make of that kind of potential?

*Landon MacKenzie:* I was thinking of a word like 'recognition'; that you're looking for something, you're sieving through. It must be the same when you write a sentence and you know you've got it right. There's recognition. It's the same in a visual process. We're all working against the historic model of things falling into place, the work as a screening of thoughts and images. I think we have to find some way of acknowledging the active recognition. I guess because that involves the subject again, or brings you into contact with something that works in terms of that other layer of language, which comes out of visual experience. Obviously, you can sit down and write about it after. I like the way you said that; you do it, then later you write it out.

*Griselda Pollock:* I find that the process of writing has the same sense of 'recognition', but also the sense of discovery because it's not clear, when you are writing, what you are writing. So it's not that there's a discreteness about the visual and then you write. But what you're describing seems to be a process of constant interaction and exchange. Now, there are certain kinds of mysticisms that go with that, which have come to be represented in 'studio conversations'. For example, people imagine having a conversation with the canvas, interactively, and it feeds back. This ignores the question of who was actually the site of this exchange, the localization of it, which is you as a subject. This connects with the notion that I was trying to work out in *Vision and Difference* with regard to Mary Cassatt and Berthe Morisot, as some kind of general theory for myself. There are certain ways in which we study women artists, for example, and we go along with the assumptions that, because they're women, we should start searching their canvases for certain qualities. And to some extent, I still hang on to the idea that as women they are different. There's something there; and I've got to find a way to find out what it is.

But it's more in the sense that the studio is an arena of performance, of enactment, with these processes of exchange, and something gets put into the canvas which then acts as a representation back to the person who's painting it; it produces a social image of what they've been doing, which then becomes constitutive of a certain kind of knowledge and awareness. So I'm qualifying the kind of 'recognition' of some things which we might be slightly mystical about – that works, that's it, that's perfect, that's lovely – and I think you can get at much more by theorizing about certain processes of pleasure.

This would propel us into the territory of 'the imaginary', which is where things appear simplistically as either good or bad.

The imaginary operates antithetically to this notion of having a theory about the process and practice, which is why this kind of theory so consistently emphasizes studio work or any other kind of cultural work as a practice, because you say, 'Here's an institution or here's a scenario; here's a social space in which social actions are taking place with social materials, very highly specialized, very intensely enacted'. But what is it that you are recognizing that works when Mary jumps up and down? It's not because she's having a pure simple moment of visual recognition. It's because all of these complicated processes have found a signifying form and in that form what you recognize is the sense of a sufficiently rich, metaphoric language to hold the many levels that have been spinning round in a separated form.

*Mary Kelly:* The reason perhaps that I was using metaphor to describe this is because of the group that I've been working with – we've just recently been using these distinctions between metonomy and metaphor, following Jakobson and Lacan – emphasizing them as two axes within language. And certainly it's appropriate in terms of visual language to talk about that. When Lacan describes metaphor as a process by which, momentarily, you make sense out of nonsense, that describes the jumping up and down to me. When you say all these things come into play for at least that moment, some kind of meaning takes place. Of course, one could explore the other axis too. Another feeling that's very common is that you're never satisfied with the work – never satisfied. That places you within the axis of metonomy or desire, which is also very productive to examine in terms of who you really are desiring to speak to in the work.

This is another thing that I've often had to consider when people ask the question about audience. I could say in a strategic way who my audience was, and I always said there was no such thing as a general, mass audience; that I directed it specifically at a certain group. First of all, it was feminists, then it was mothers, then it was artists engaged in critical practices – three overlapping circles and where they met you might have the ideal audience – but then you'd have it spreading out in these three directions. Well I had to admit, as we're pursuing this kind of psychic dimension of this production, that out of this centre of an ideal audience, if you like, there would be very specific women, for me. For instance, with the first part of *Corpus*, when I'd made the prototype for it, but before I'd actually finished the work, I met with that small group and we went over the work.

It was a very special kind of experience because I wanted to confirm this for myself, because I knew that this had been so important in the way the piece had taken shape, but I also wanted to tie it to something that Craig Owens said about his horror at going round art schools and discovering that more and more students rather self-consciously admitted that they were making their work for a certain patron or a particular collector. I think that the level of desire in a work and who you're actually aiming this for is important, because if the one person you're desiring to please means that your strategy is one aimed at the private sector, as Craig has suggested then we've lost the public domain. We've lost the sense of a 'public' for art. For me this is very directly linked to the whole project of history painting or 'picturing' – we're trying to decide on a new way of terming, because it can't be history 'painting', so maybe it can be history 'picturing' – and really, recuperating something of the effort of that work prior to the modern period, where artists actually worked in the public domain.

## On power and 'mastery'

*Sara Diamond:* I want to talk a bit about the experience of power, in the process of producing work, because some of what I feel does coincide with a description of a desire always to make a work different or better – that frustration – but also that sense of having achieved a 'moment' with it. It feels very much like power, like a moment of empowerment, achieved by working through the problem, and then another level where I examine my party structures in the sense that I'm never quite satisfied with the sense of individual power. When I reach a moment where the work seems to come together and speak, I'm always concerned that it has to be checked back against the idea or the theory that I'm trying to work with or, also, against that sense of audience. Then it's a kind of displacement of my power into examining a power outside myself, and some kind of decision around that. It's an exchange of a sort of internal power versus external. And then a decision and then I re-engage with the work.

The other level, for me, has a lot to do with why I ended up being an artist. As a woman, I felt a need to control the basic level of representation, and a continual sense of being empowered by that, which has meant that even though I write, I keep returning to make art work because I become dissatisfied with my writing and I have something to engage in a different level around that experience of power.

*Mary Kelly:* Do you think it's power? That might not be exactly the word I'd use. I know what you're describing, but I might be more likely to talk about 'mastery', for example, rather than the whole dimension of social and political process that would be involved in that idea of power. In psychoanalytic terms you might talk about it as 'mastery', in terms of the desire for control, but the futility of ever really trying to achieve that particular point. I also think women are more apt to admit this in their work.

*Sara Diamond:* I guess what's interesting to me is whether that experience is common in the process of producing art work, or whether it's something specific to working with certain forms at certain points in time. It's a kind of personal empowerment within the process of production, or certain strategies, because I imagine that if one is involved with work that's critiquing dominant language, one might not feel that kind of 'moment'.

## Disaffirmative and strategic practices

*Griselda Pollock:* One of the things I was trying to explore for myself last night was the position or set of arguments that are put forward around the legacy of modernism as it's being re-examined by social historians of art, particularly the Clark debates with Greenberg;[5] all of that which leads to a sense of modernism as a process of taking on existing versions of art, accepted protocols and procedures, and systematically disrupting, destroying them, which leads to this thesis about 'botching'.[6]

On the other hand, there are a series of practices which that group represent as having abandoned the whole legacy of modernism. They have instead taken as their focus of attention the dominant forms of capitalist culture in terms of photography, the cinematic, the media. Critics localize certain main tendencies of postmodernism in this strategy, dumping feminism into it. That's what the John Roberts paper says is the 'anti-painting argument'[7] which basically explains feminist interest in photography as the result of its being democratic, or popular culture. It therefore repeats a basic division which derives from Greenberg's 1939 paper, 'Avant-garde and Kitsch'. Modernism still retains, as its central point, that awkward relationship between high art and popular culture.

Now what interests me is: how do we think about feminism's place in these debates about strategies? Because I don't accept that all kinds of feminist practices, even critical feminist practices, can be classified in that way, but I am interested that one could look at it in those terms and raise those questions about it.

And obviously, feminist art work is always perceived as trying to be 'disaffirmative', disrupting, playing against the grain. And yet it does so by means of studied, formal appropriateness which is easily misrecognized as a kind of fetishized formalism. What we've been talking about so far is that you arrive at certain formal solutions in notions of 'appropriateness' in terms of quite a complex set of strategic calculations, recognitions and the acknowledgement of desire and pleasure.

*Mary Kelly:* This is one thing that I do have a problem with that I want to talk to you about. It sounds like there are all these so-called feminist practices – and there are many, many women working in the same way. I don't think that's the case. I think that there's a particular kind of working process that, probably, is appropriate for each person – and one of the things that I'd be very adamant about in my case is the project nature of the work, and that is a strategy, across the board, as a corrective to the one-liners of the so-called 'new criticality': one is making an intervention. I take up your own saying which was 'Let's not talk about feminist history; let's talk about feminist interventions in art history'. And I think you have to talk about feminist interventions in art practice and not 'feminist art'.

I know that you suggest this in your book[8] but then you slip into 'feminist art practice' again. You have to look at the way feminism is imported into the art world because you're really talking about that kind of intervention in art and not feminist practice. The most common and visible form of this is what I'm going to call 'opportunistic references to sexuality and to the category of woman'. In *The Forests of Signs*[9] you have examples such as Cindy Sherman and Barbara Kruger. The critical discourse around the work, not the artists necessarily, opportunistically imports those references, but is very careful never to mention the term 'feminism': it's the political dimension that remains totally unacceptable in the art world. I'd say we have not gotten anywhere with that. What's happened is that they've been able to use work around the idea of 'woman' or of 'sexuality', as particular themes that certain artists are working with. On the other hand, there are artists (an example would be Nancy Spero) where the positions are very much carried over into the practice, almost as direct quotations.

I would say that both of those kinds of strategies are still very different from the practice that I was trying to describe. It's not just that you're importing the positions or quoting the theory. You're actually making an intervention which shows that you're thinking through the art work, coming up with a visual debate that's contributing in some way to the ongoing debate in the women's movement as well as in the art world. There are other artists who try to do this, like Mary Yates perhaps, but I think it would be more a matter of (to use your terms) the 'specificity' of all of these practices rather than any generalization that you could make about feminism – and I think that this is also a very important point because, after all, what the boys always do is deny, adamantly, any kind of covering term or tendency for their unique production.

*Judith Mastai:* Seeing that you've brought up the John Roberts article a few times, I'd like to raise a couple of questions. First of all, I'm not quite sure that I understand the point you were making about the article in terms of resurrecting a Greenbergian dichotomy between kitsch, or popular culture, and the avant-garde. What, in simple terms, do you think that the scripto-visual represents?

Another question has to do with the business of 'disaffirmative practices'.[10] With these, the list has been constructed, therefore the procedures and the methods of disruption are now known, and so, what the process becomes is, not exactly formulaic, but a lot of 'knowns' being worked out in contemporary situations – as opposed to the modes, the practices, the materials, as well as the disaffirmations, the disruptions, the feminist interventions in our practice – all those are unknowns when you're trying to do that kind of practice.

I appreciate very much the term 'disaffirmative practices', the concept behind 'botching' something on purpose, but I think it's about apples and oranges. One is a total enterprise, starting from almost ground zero, and the other has a social, political, historical context that's been ongoing all this time.

*Griselda Pollock:* This has clarified something important here. If you say, 'What is it that feminism, in its specific disaffirmative practices, is disaffirming?' one might say (and I apologize for this but for the sheer sake of short hand) we're disaffirming patriarchy. We're dealing here with whatever term we have for the

kind of complex social, economic, ideological and psychic processes which we identify as constituting 'the problem' in all its
varied forms. Whereas, what John Roberts and those people are
disaffirming is culture, good art. They're disaffirming culture as
some kind of comfort by trying to show that the forms of culture
and the majority of what the bourgeoisie purchase and consume
is the product and the realization of the culture that condoned the
murder of six million people, the holocaust, or condoned the
dropping of the first atom bombs on Hiroshima and Nagasaki,
and introduced us to the world in which we now have the
potential for one group of people, seriously or accidentally, to
wipe us off the face of the earth.

There is a connection there, and Greenham Common is an
instance of the feminist movement's attempt to try and bring
those two processes into some kind of vivid connection for us.
But it seems to me that putting the two together shows that those
people who were arguing for disaffirmative practices have a
sense of it only disaffirming culture. Whereas, what we have
been trying to explore, is that, in the process of disaffirming
patriarchy and the constitution of sexual difference, we may well
find ourselves operating strategically and calculatedly in certain
domains called culture, even deploying very sophisticated aesthetic processes or techniques, lures and pleasures, for which this
notion of 'botching' doesn't make a lot of sense for a feminist.
That's what I was really interested in. If one explores the logic of
that kind of marxist modernist/postmodernist debate, it enables
us to see more distinctly what feminism is. And, I think, what
Mary is saying, in terms of this intervention, also confirms that
particular point. What John Roberts represents, to go with the
first point of your question – why I brought up the avant-garde/
kitsch – is that they're caught in a cleft stick between funda-
mentally being passionate about modernist culture, just loving
what it can do, and yet being politically in a position where they
have to say they don't like it, because it is the culture that
produced Auschwitz and Hiroshima. So Terry Atkinson then
comes out with this notion of simply going on, you must keep
doing it. You know that there will be poetry after Auschwitz,
there shouldn't be poetry after Hiroshima, but somewhere along
the line you have to do it. And some of that must be important to
feminism because of the overlay of the world we live in. Where
you locate the structures of violence is somehow slightly different, and therefore the answer to that question – 'what is it that

feminist interventions disaffirm?' – isn't modernist culture, but something more structural. And therefore, citing those kinds of art work, the processes and practices which, as Mary says, co-opt notions of sexuality, references to sexuality or voyeurism, the gaze or fetishism, or any of the elements of psychoanalytic theory, without that overall sense of what one's doing it for, how it articulates, appear to the John Roberts of this world as simply failing to disaffirm culture.

*Mary Kelly:* Before you go too much further with John Roberts. I would like to say that he is a critic of absolutely no consequence and I don't think we should be wasting our time talking about his position, because the way this debate has shaped up just recently in Europe is not even as interesting as Greenberg and it rehashes the very same kind of dilemma between high art and low art. And that is so completely out of sync with the more interesting things that have gone on in North America as far as the postmodernist debate in art is concerned. Here, at least there's been some idea that the whole field of postmodernism can't be captured by one tendency. There's writing by Hal Foster and Craig Owens about oppositional postmodernism and some acknowledgement, if minimal, of the way that feminism is based within a wider context of theoretical work in that field. You were referring to Jacqueline Rose's earlier article[11] which points out just how permeated the current discourse is with the radical, mostly French, feminist theories; and how people like Jameson use this without really acknowledging where it comes from, and you could say, 'How did they come to that position?' It was coming very much from the debates that went on at that time in France, that is from feminism – other examples are found in Lyotard or in Ken Frampton's writing on critical regionalism. Its been very far-reaching. We're not claiming a little territory, as it were, a little intervention by feminists in some kind of reserve of popular cultural kitsch. There's a centre or 'totality' of modernism that's been shattered by the things that feminism – feminist theory – I should say, raised. So, why not drop John Roberts, and think about other kinds of critics, and other debates, that actually do have some space to situate a discussion of women artists and feminism?

*Griselda Pollock:* I'm very uninterested in the fact that it's so easy to stay, automatically, within the field in which everybody is talking your own language; and I'm very interested in establishing dialogues with those critical positions which seem so far

removed and incompatible that you might not have any conversation. Now then, there are those people who are happily within
the frameworks of Lyotard and Baudrillard, but there are whole
groups of feminists who are working in areas of art practice in
which that is not what they're based on, and what I am interested
in is making sure that there is a feminist discourse large enough
not to have left the territories of painting. Women who are
involved in painting feel that the only place that feminist debate
takes place is with those who use a certain kind of discourse, a
certain kind . . . .

*Mary Kelly:* That is a terrible problem, because what you're
doing is trying to accommodate all women and accommodate all
feminisms and that's taking the politics right out of the art
practice. I am not sympathetic at all to the woman who stood up
last night and said, 'Well, I'm so happy you talked about gesture
and about paint because I just love to paint and I want to paint.'
You don't need to accommodate that. It's like somebody saying
'Well, I'd like to have socialism but don't take away my summer
home or my BMW.'

*Judith Mastai:* Now you are coming to a very crucial issue
though, because, let us argue for the moment, for the sake of
argument, you can write off John Roberts because he's not an
important critic. The fact is that he does mention the work of four
women artists who are using paint. By writing him off we're
writing off the four women artists he's talking about, under the
same rubric. So where does that leave us in terms of paint?

*Mary Kelly:* I have to finish just one more thing, because I'm
getting worked up if this attempt to accommodate women leads
you to accept forms of painting that aren't very radical. Let's
acknowledge that teaching is one thing, and that the world of art
institutions – which I would define as entertainment – is very
different. I think here we have to acknowledge that we are
involved in a kind of cultural warfare where not everything goes.
When you're teaching you don't set up hierarchial relations to a
particular medium: what you're interested in is the development
of the student. In that sense, you're not prescribing the student's
politics. But in terms of your own practice, that is where you
absolutely lay down the line: there is an argument. If representations have meaning, and we have responsibilities for making
them, these positions really matter. And the difference is that,
within the academic institutions, we have to believe that art is a
teachable craft, so all the Greenbergian formulations about

appropriateness of medium, etc., might apply; but in the entertainment sector – which is what's on right now at the Vancouver Art Gallery or wherever – there is a very different set of criteria (also central to modernism) about establishing artistic authorship, originality, genius. What is most compatible with those kind of demands is a traditional form of practice like painting. So we're not saying that there is no hope for painting; we're saying it is historically very specific, very strategic, what you take up in your practice – and not 'anything goes', and not every woman needs to be supported.

*Griselda Pollock:* I don't accept that by listening to what is actually being said in a range of practices that one is necessarily saying 'anything goes'. What are the arguments available which might propose some kind of radical practices for women in painting? What are the historical legacies of either modernism or marxism or any of the others as they converge across the territory of feminism? There is some set of strategic difficulties. That's one fact which is more available for you to take up because that is where you make your choices. What would you do? In a sense, what surface and what kind of positions would you advance? On the other hand, I think it is really important, without any sense of just either falling into 'anything women do is okay' and 'anything anybody wants to do is okay', to take what people are saying – either at a level of expressing a desire to paint or, institutionally, the pressure to paint – and somewhere along the line, you have to investigate what the implications are in that territory. Otherwise you end up in a situation which I see constantly being re-enacted – where the nature of the feminist interventions is being massively displaced and marginalized by being described in terms of a choice about media.

## On alliances

*Mary Kelly:* We're not talking about a hobby here. We're talking about a very different kind of practice and what you fear about marginalization you might be reinforcing by looking for these threads of feminism that cross all these diverse practices, because the alliance, as I see it, is that I would be much more interested in the work of Hans Haacke or Victor Burgin or even Jeff Wall than I would be in any of the women mentioned in John Roberts' article. I think that the debate lines up more along those lines.

*Griselda Pollock:* That is a position which anybody could observe in terms of the strategies that you've outlined. You don't make women's shows. You make group shows in which the issues that feminism has put on the agenda are explored by those who practise, and that may include men as much as women . . . I don't think that you can cancel out what I'm doing as lending legitimacy or not lending legitimacy. I'm not a critic. My perspective is historical. I'm not in a position of lending currency or political legitimacy to any particular position. I'm interested in what you call 'the cultural warfare'. That kind of cultural intervention has to be engaged in. This may be because of the British situation out of which I have come. There hasn't been a show since *Difference*[12] in 1984 that has seriously taken these questions on board and, even when *Difference* came out, all of two people wrote about it in a major way – John Roberts and me.

There is a kind of silencing, which is interesting because, historically, that is why it has been imperative that you relocate. Some places aren't really interested in certain kinds of discussions. For instance, this kind of debate – could I imagine this happening in Leeds or Cardiff? That may be where I get my sense of 'I have to take the battle now to where those who seem to be in control of critical discourse are'.

I see in the feminist journals a certain kind of discontent. It is the revolt of the daughters against their mothers. And it seems to me that British daughters are far more rebellious than in any other country. Particularly, there is much less generosity to the first generation of feminists than there is in any other country.

The other thing is that there is a very strong formulation of who my potential allies might be, in terms of left critics, which would be those people who are very heavily influenced by Clark, and that tradition must have some currency in Vancouver.

My strategy at the moment is, if consistently a feminist attack on a certain kind of feminist work is being mounted, and if that argument – pro-party – gains currency without being contested (and without an equally probing and intelligent response to the basis of this attack) that field of critical feminist possibilities, as a possibility for critical practices, is lost because the assault is from the feminists, the assault is from the left and we know that, as far as the establishment is concerned, it's not working. Within the American art system (I don't know about the Canadian) where you're located at the moment, I would be very anxious, precisely by what you're saying, because the show *The Forest of Signs* provided a situation where there was currency for a certain kind of work. And even in *Beyond the Purloined Image*[13] you were safe, satisfied to mark out the difference between the Brechtian-inspired critical practices that seemed to be characteristic of British artists, and the Baudrillardian tendencies that seem to me to lead into very murky ideological territory.

*Mary Kelly:* I can see what you're doing. Obviously, in fairness, you're engaging with Roberts because that is being politically responsible. That shapes the debate in England at the moment. But going back to *Beyond the Purloined Image*, which was 1983, every 'good Marxist' believes in the specificity of a particular political, social, geographic location, but somehow that has managed to fall apart, partly because capitalism – everything – is international, or multinational. And in a sense when Thatcher got in, and now she's been in for ten years, the things that began to change in the art scene in England were so dramatic. First of all, the so-called alternative spaces, many of them were closed. And it virtually wiped out all forms of performance, installation and video art, because these were the kinds of centres that showed them. The ICA and Riverside Studios remained. But also the Arts Council, given that there was now a Conservative government, didn't have to abide by any of those things that we had accomplished in the Artists' Union early on. They stopped giving grants, much less getting them distributed equally among women and ethnic minorities. So all of that was scrapped. Now, because (and this is terribly superficial) there is no real ground for modernism in England, or modern art, or collecting of modern art, the private sector is quite small. This I attribute to the historical fact that it never had a proper bourgeois revolution, so that it didn't need the cultural products of the middle class to consolidate it. But when you get such a long period of Conservatism, then you can see that the space for this oppositional practice is disappearing, becoming almost impossible, unless you make an alliance with other kinds of oppositional practices going on as in North America. Or at least outside of Britain. And that was my reason for curating *Beyond the Purloined Image*. It was an attempt to shape that tendency, to prepare for the *Difference* show, which would then bring together the two kinds of tendencies. Because even though there have been Conservative or Republican governments in the United States, they didn't sufficiently damage the industry, so that it would close up around traditional practices. It remains, for economic and other reasons, possible to sustain that kind of art, so you find that this new criticality eventually peaked. And I think that was simply one of the reasons that leads me to emphasize that it shouldn't be just national in its focus, and that perhaps the emphasis, again, on feminisms, shouldn't be national either; if one really wants to get round the whole problem of ghettoization, and see these issues sustained and historicized.

Of course, as you said, you're not primarily a critic, and I'm making a plea for a more radical criticism, but because there are so few women who have your purchase on all of these ideas and can really enter into those debates, you have to perform the functions of critic, historian – the whole thing. Who is there who can cover that in the way that you can?

### Rewriting the history of the twentieth century from a feminist perspective.

*Griselda Pollock:* The project I've set myself is to say, 'Can I write a feminist theory of painting?' I doubt it. But I try to sort out all the terms in which that word operates. Painting is not just a particular medium, but there is a certain amount of desire invested in it, and I'm not going to dismiss that desire until I've worked out what it is. In some sense, it can be examined in the light of this set of practices or set of priorities that feminism might pose for me. It is also something that is incredibly heavily invested in in terms of the legacy of cultural languages and dominant paradigms that we inherit.

Where painting stands to modernism is almost synonymous with a certain set of practices clearly authorized and validated through the major museums. What we're seeing, through the market place, is a whole range of those elements that you've mentioned in terms of authority and authorship and authenticity and expression. There is a massive number of historical and ideological investments which are signified by the term 'painting' which go far beyond that simple thing you know – hogshair brushes or pieces of linen with mud on them. And there's a confusion there between the technical and the institutional.

There's another domain where there are two different cases being made. There's the case for a kind of painting that is the site of figurative explorations which are affirmative in the sense of saying 'these are about my relationship to landscape, to woman, to my babies, to whatever, etc.' And there are also those who pursue painting as a site of some kind of feminine inscription. So there is an enormous amount of confusion if anybody who says, 'you should paint; you shouldn't paint'. All I'm saying is I'm one of those boring people who wants to know what it is that you are saying by using that word 'painting'? And this launched me into an enormous conundrum of different communities using the term, different traditions, etc., and what I was trying to do was to throw some of them into a context with each other, so that we might profitably come to some conclusions.

Now, I suspect it is over-determined that painting is difficult in so far as all the available practices and justifications that I've come up with, in terms of women's use of it, have a certain problem, because women tend to be using painting in order to affirm some sense of women's meanings, whereas those in the account – for instance, go back to Terry Atkinson – use painting, not as a means of exploring certain ideas, but as the site against which to throw the British involvement in Ireland, for instance – the whole question of nuclear war and militarism. Atkinson's gone through using figuration and drawing and narrative and history painting and collage and photography and prints; now he's into taking on non-representational art – abstract art – as a site. Now that's a very different set of practices, which is to say, painting is that legacy which I am going to trample over in my hobnail boots with my father's mining helmet on my head – which is to some extent what's going on – a certain enforced exploration of the culture of the bourgeoisie from a perspective of someone who wants to be involved in cultural production but has other investments of a very political kind. Now, is that an interesting model to look at?

Or is an interesting model to look at, for instance, the Latin American situation that Nelly Richard describes,[14] which seems to raise some of the possibilities in her history of art in Chile in the last 20 years? It's really fascinating because it mirrors exactly what's happened in feminism. You have the quilts and patch-works in the early period of 1973 when there was propagandist, affirming, populist, political art; then came a generation which has forgotten that history, comes back to the European art schools with their paint boxes and paint brushes and has got 'expression'. This is just as interesting, because it's the same trajectory. Now, if I put those together, am I not going to get a purchase for the feminist community, in its diversity, which enables us possibly to arrive at some strategic possibilities for feminist intervention, in that institution, in the art world, which is centralized under American hegemony?

But there are all these peripheries with which we can form interesting alliances which may have some serious effect in both the entertainment sector and the art education sector because we're providing our students with text (what you're suggesting about being in a dilemma, because what you've got comes through the magazines or your art instructors). We need to write feminist histories of the whole lot . . . that's my sense, rewriting this whole history of the twentieth-century contemporary situation from a feminist perspective because you need that knowledge to make those decisions. You may say that's kind of redundant, because we're going to end up with the same conclusion that you've already come to – that you don't paint – it's just not on.

*Mary Kelly:* No, I just said that it was historically very specific, and I think the example you give of Chile is very important, because you can see it's not the medium, it's the context. What I was arguing for was a visual debate, not a dogmatic art practice. I wasn't dismissing the academic institutions; I was just saying, in general, that there are many discourses and institutions, and they aren't always in sync. The perfect example: we're here, meeting – under Judith's education programme, feminism is consolidated, right? But in the collection or in the shows, it's not. These are not necessarily overlapping sites. There's certainly room there to make more demands, but exactly what happened in terms of art education could happen in the other sectors: that is, you make a demand for more women, and they bring in women who aren't necessarily feminist or interested in the kinds of issues that you say you want to discuss, and you encourage the women to paint and do their own thing, and not to be engaged with the politics or polemics outside the institution, and lo and behold, then you give institutions the perfect opportunity to dismiss feminism because here they have women doing something that fits in with the tradition. I'm only asking you to consider the dialectic of this, but not to be prescriptive in any final sense at all.

## Modernism and postmodernism

*Mary Kelly:* One night at some event in New York, Peter Wollen and I decided we'd become postmodernist, strategically speaking, that we had to acknowledge it and think of some way that we would be able to take this on, polemically. So it's not that I feel you can justify or theorize the links in terms of art, but you clearly can, at another level, in terms of economic and social relations. There is a case to be made. I just think that I was pulled more into talking about that strategically, in a way that isn't very consistent with what I said in 'Re-Viewing Modernist Criticism'.[15]

*Griselda Pollock:* There are so may different terminologies in use. If you believe in political change, then you have to admit that modernism is the enlightenment project. I'm still caught up in that belief, including the women's movement – that's what I mean by saying I'm a modernist.

But that is an assumption about why I remain convinced of the necessity for certain kinds of political struggle and commitments. But that is not to say I don't recognize that I live in a post-modernist universe, which has put those things into question as one of the defining elements of it. For example, you're a Marxist – in the name of Marxism, several thousand Chinese students were gunned down in the most revolting way, two weeks ago. If that isn't exactly what that process is saying, what has it delivered us? Has it delivered us freedom? Dignity?

*Mary Kelly:* No, but what it's pointing out is that just as there are different feminisms, there are different socialisms. In China, the Communists of the initial revolution didn't even execute the emperor. They rehabilitated him. And now, you have an inflection (to use your words) of this ideology such that it allowed them to give the death sentence to two students, just recently.

*Griselda Pollock:* That's true enough. I remember Gayatri Spivak being interviewed about this, and what she said comforted me greatly, because she said that the fact that Marxism is no longer something that one necessarily believes has the scientific faith to deliver what it promised does not mean you abandon it, you make it provisional, and you retain a certain skepticism towards any of its claims. So the very notion of feminist intervention such as we're talking about, shows that we remain within the ambience of modernism, in the Habermasian sense (as the project of modernity) and we retain that in the presence of all the things that have made us skeptical about the claims of the Enlightenment – that rationality produces progress, or whatever.

On the other hand, if you take it in the cultural sense of 'Modernism', there is also embedded in it the sense that art has some relationship to an understanding of the social world – that it is a cognitive enterprise, and produces some kind of knowledge. That is 'Modernist' and against that one would see the most extreme versions of postmodernisms saying, 'you can't say anything; it's all been said before, and it's all relatively pointless because it's all part of an endless circuit and exchange of signifiers meaning nothing and ultimately you're captured in it'. I resist that. I know that to be a profound insight into the nature of the signifying universe in which I live, but I retain my skepticism towards accepting it. Anybody who operates within some belief in the political possibilities of change or the cultural domain as a site of producing knowledge and understanding, seems to me, inevitably, to have to recognize that we are modernists living in a postmodernist universe. Therefore, we have a skeptical, critical, reflective view of the claims that we make.

Now feminism, as we've been talking about it, explicitly presents itself as a calculated, optimistic intervention, fully aware of the incredible depths and complexities of the structures that we're struggling to comprehend – and by comprehending them to devise some means of displacing and, ultimately, overthrowing – so we don't have simple beliefs in the notions of what would effect political change, out there in the real world. We have to go out and struggle. We have to have sophisticated beliefs that perhaps by intervening in 'the forest of signs' we're contributing to constructing chains of signification. So what you're really asking me to do is to participate in that, which is to say, 'what are the sites where certain voices and certain statements and certain battles should be engaged?' I think that's a very important point to come out. Where should we be making these interventions? We've got two kinds of models in play. One is that which is specifically local – a sense of place, a sense of community, a sense of understanding the immediate coordinates in which we can operate – and one which is aware that we all have some responsibility to the centres of the global system, because it's very easy, in the postmodern era, just to feel so appalled by this.

## Audiences and communities

*Sara Diamond:* I'd like to shift the discussion to feminist practice engaged with current popular culture and that kind of critique (or dismissal of it) and approach that from a different direction, which has argued within feminist cultural practices for trying to redefine a sense of audience, partially in class terms, in terms of race, and those issues of representation. I'd like to open up that area in terms of the nexus of discourses that you are describing.

What I was trying to understand is how one can connect that to the attempt by feminist artists to reach out to different audiences and construct an audience that's outside of the art world (because of the critiques of the art audience being essentially a petit bourgeois or bourgeois audience) and therefore, engaging with both practices of mass culture and popular culture.

This has been particularly true for film making and video practice. I am wondering how one develops a critical language to deal with that, because some of feminist film criticism has been engaged within a linguistic and structuralist/post-structuralist discourse which has to do with the nature of the film as a text and its readings. How does one bring in the dimension of understanding the audience and how one communicates to an audience that is outside of the art film, or the art practice audience, because I think that has been an important area of intervention, and how do we understand that practice in the late 80s and where it's going? And I'm wondering partially in terms of Britain because I was recently in England for a video exhibition and I was struck by the dramatic division between people – three camps – people who work with Channel 4, having a theoretical practice but the potential for a broader audience; people who work in the community with video and film using realist practice or documentary realism; and then people who were interested in high art (I use that term advisably here), and it was different from what has happened in Canada in terms of video art.

*Mary Kelly:* I think every practice emanates from the decision about audience, on two levels, psychically speaking, the question of desire and how it transgresses the consumption model and, secondly, audience in the very specific sense of a social, political or other constituted group. This comes up in my teaching very often. It's like, what's a good agitational work because I think we've lost the sense of the importance of 'agitational'. In the best sense, an agitational work is aimed for a specific moment and community. It adopts certain procedures in the work. I've seen some really interesting things done like this. Canada's produced some of the best, like John Greyson's tape on AIDS. There are many examples to give of the different genres here, and that's a point that it was good to bring out, actually, it's not just in terms of the critical, curatorial preservation of these, but actually in the techniques of making them and preserving the kind of traditions and techniques involved in that kind of work too. That's important.

*Griselda Pollock:* I think you can take it in a number of ways. One sort of argument is that we have targeted communities, and there is no way that we can talk about art for a non-art world audience, because what art is is that which is constituted by precisely the nature of the interactions and exchanges that take place. It's not art just because it's a piece of video. It's not art because it's art. It's art because it circulates and is used in a certain way, in a certain space around which certain things are conceived of it and represented for it. So at one logical level, there is no art for non-art audiences.

But there is a way to extend the nature of that art audience, and that involves quite radical and interesting ranges of interventions. What are the places, what are the ways in which you can provide people with a number of different handles on or ways into certain practising institutions? You have to ascertain, first of all, who would be interested – whom might it be useful for? With whom could I have an interesting conversation? Then you have to think quite specifically about how to do that.

Now the trouble is that most people in the art community are not in any way aware of the massive literature and bodies of knowledge that exist precisely to teach people how to break down notions of the community into specific groups with whom you wish to have decent and respectful dialogue. In a sense, I think these are quite legitimate techniques that people ought to be thinking about in relation to certain activities. Some practices have done this, in a variety of ways, and you can make work which has to function in a number of different sites and will do so differently. I don't think it should be confused with generalities about the communities in the art world. These categories have to go.

## References

1. This discussion was the last of five consecutive evenings of a seminar with Griselda Pollock entitled 'Different Perspectives: Perspectives on Difference' held at the Vancouver Art Gallery from June 12–16, 1989. It coincided with the first week of the Summer Intensive in the Visual Arts at Simon Fraser University which was led that year by Mary Kelly. Both seminar groups were present for this dialogue, and it was transcribed by Judith Mastai.
2. *Art and Language* is a Conceptual Art group formed in Britain in the sixties; members include Terry Atkinson and Michael Baldwin.
3. The previous evening, Griselda Pollock had given a public lecture at

Robson Square Auditorium entitled 'Feminism, Painting and History'.

4. This is a reference to an article which Pollock had assigned as pre-reading for the seminar and which was discussed the first evening – Julia Kristeva's 'Women's time' from Toril Moi (ed.) *The Kristeva Reader*. (1986). New York, Columbia University Press.

5. These debates have been chronicled in two books: Francis Frascina (ed.), *Pollock and After: The Critical Debate*. (1985). London, Harper & Row, and Buchloch, Benjamin H.D., Guilbaut S. and Solkin D. (eds), *Modernism and Modernity* (1983). The Vancouver Conference Papers, Halifax, Press of Nova Scotia College of Art and Design.

6. This term 'botching' and the definition used here by Pollock of 'disaffirmative practices' are discussed in an essay by the British artist, Terry Atkinson, in a catalogue of his work, *Mute I*. (1988). Copenhagen, Galleri Prag. See footnote 10.

7. Roberts, John. 'Painting and sexual difference', *Parachute*, **55**, July–September, 1989, 25–31.

8. Pollock's book is *Vision and Difference: Femininity, Feminism and the Histories of Art*. (1988). London and New York, Routledge.

9. *Forest of Signs*. (1988). Museum of Contemporary Art, Los Angeles.

10. Terry Atkinson has defined 'disaffirmative practices' in a catalogue essay entitled 'Disaffirmation and negation', *Mute I*. (1988). Galleri Prag, Copenhagen, pp 8–9. He based his definition on an author's note by T.J. Clark in 'Clement Greenberg's theory of art' in *Pollock and After*, op. cit., 55. In this footnote, Clark lists 'practices of negation' as 'some form of decisive innovation, in method or materials or imagery, whereby a previously established set of skills or frame of reference – skills and references which up till then had been taken as essential to art-making of any seriousness – are deliberately avoided or travestied, in such a way as to imply that only by such incompetence or obscurity will genuine picturing get done.'

Atkinson comments as follows: 'This assertion of Clark's is not, either, unique to him. It matches, at different points and perhaps in different ways, a number of other protagonists in the debate on the character of what modernist practice is, and, perhaps more contentiously, what it ought to be. There are two which I think bear, with Clark's, particularly upon my own views of practice. One is Adorno's explicit, if constricted, call for a disaffirmative practice (specifically, Adorno says, in a world trailing in the destructive and demonic wake of events such as Auschwitz and Hiroshima). The second is *Art and Language's* recurrent call for absolute critical suspicion as the proper basis, and only basis, for practice today. *Art and Language's* call is twinned with a warning, against the specious and dangerous calls for a monotheoretical critical edifice.

Put bluntly, the contradiction of making a disaffirmative practice is this: that in undertaking the act of making a work, say a painting, then the practice is itself affirmed, and vis à vis Adorno, at least one part of the world, and a part with some grand cultural investments in the construction of the framework which produced Auschwitz and Hiroshima, is also affirmed.'

11. Rose, Jacqueline. 'The man who mistook his wife for a hat or a wife is like an umbrella: fantasies of the modern and postmodern,' in A. Ross (ed.) *Universal Abandon? The Politics of Postmodernism.* (1988). Minneapolis, University of Minnesota Press.

12. *Difference: On Representation and Sexuality.* (1984). New Museum of Contemporary Art, New York.

13. *Beyond the Purloined Image.*(1983). Riverside Studio, London.

14. Richard, Nelly. 'Art in Chile since 1973', in *Third Text*, Winter, 1987/8, 2.

15. Kelly, Mary. 'Re-viewing modernist criticism', *Screen*, 1981, 2/3, 41–62. Reprinted in Brian Wallis (ed.) *Art After Modernism.* (1984). New York, New Museum of Contemporary Art, Goodine.

# Index